THE CHEAP BASTARD'S® GUIDE TO

Chicago

We would love to hear from you concerning your experiences with this guide and how you feel it could be improved and kept up to date. Please send your comments and suggestions to:

editorial@GlobePequot.com

Thanks for your input, and happy travels!

CHEAP BASTARD'S® SERIES

THE CHEAP BASTARD'S® GUIDE TO

Chicago

Secrets of Living the Good Life—**For Free!**

Second Edition

Nadia **Oehlsen**

gpp® travel

Guilford, Connecticut
An imprint of Globe Pequot Press

The prices, rates, and hours listed in this guidebook were confirmed at press time. We recommend, however, that you call establishments to obtain current information before finalizing your plans.

ISSN: 1932-3514
ISBN: 978-0-7627-5023-8

Printed in the United States of America

10 9 8 7 6 5 4 3 2 1

For Mom and Dad, who were thrifty before it was cool.

CONTENTS

SECTION 2: Living in Chicago

SECTION 3: Exploring Chicago

INTRODUCTION:

LAND **OF** THE **FREE**

Life is really simple, but we insist on making it complicated.
—CONFUCIUS

It all started with a reverse burglary.

Just out of college, I was helping renovate a big old house into a shelter for homeless families, and word got out that we needed furniture and household goods. Generous donors quickly filled the place with an eclectic mix of furniture, lamps, dishes, linens, toys, food, and just about everything a group of thirty could possibly need. We even set up an attic storage space with some clothing and extra goods to give as parting gifts to guests as they moved out of our shelter and back into their own homes.

Once we were filled to the rafters with all the worldly possessions we could possibly fit, we provided generous callers with names and numbers of other local groups that could use similar donations. Most people thanked us and said they'd call around. But a few called back and kept begging us to take their stuff after we'd explained that we still had no room for it. They argued that the other places had turned them down too, that their gifts were very nice, that we'd be lucky to have them, and that we were profoundly rude to so ungratefully turn them away.

The morning after one such call, in which a woman had extolled the fine features of her 1970s orange-green-and-brown-plaid sofa, complete with faux walnut colonial accents, we found a behemoth couch matching her very description on our front lawn. We suspected that the antiburglar's aggressive largess had little to do with some insatiable urge to make sure our guests could lounge in stylish comfort. She just didn't want to pay to get rid of her large-item refuse, as the municipal code called it. After all, our Central Illinois city had just dramatically increased the fees to haul waste to its overflowing dumps.

Whatever the motives, mostly generous, of countless future donors, the couch and subsequent tsunamis of durable goods, clothing, toiletries, food, games, toys, office supplies, mementos, curios, and knickknacks that washed through our home, much of which we needed and appreciated, much of which we didn't, taught me one thing: There's too much stuff in the world, or at least there's too much stuff in my corner of it.

A couple of years later, I moved to Chicago and fell in with a wacky group of folks who found it amusing to see who among them could spend less than anyone else while legally getting the most bang for their nonexistent bucks. They were classic cheap bastards, proud of it, and a bit jealously competitive of anyone who seemed to outperform their cheapness.

They introduced me to a strange parallel Chicago universe whose citizens wore fetching scavenged fashion and decked their homes in lovely used decor without leveraging their credit to do so. People traveled for free on pretty used bicycles all over the city, where they viewed fine art, heard fine music and poetry, drank fine wine, and ate stinky cheese, all for free. They ushered to see plays for free. They educated themselves and their kids for free or in exchange for volunteering. They bartered. They beautified their neighborhoods by planting flowers and vegetables in public garden spaces. Most struggled now and then to make ends meet but generally maintained nice homes with rents and mortgages that matched their incomes.

The sun, the moon, the golden sands and gentle waves of mighty Lake Michigan were theirs every weekend, all for free. They worked less overtime and donated more free time than did their counterparts I knew in the expensive Chicago universe. They smiled and laughed more. They exchanged knowing glances with other cheap bastards.

Oddly, drawing from the bounty of this alternate Chicago universe only seemed to enhance its resources rather than diminish them. Inspired by the cheap-bastard life they discovered, more people shared more free or cheap stuff, services, entertainment, and thrifty tips. The free resources continued to grow, and most still do today, even during tough economic times.

I'll never live up to the standards of the cheapest of my cheap-bastard senseis, but, thanks to their inspiration, I've reached a level of cheap bastardom of which I'm quite proud. It's a nice life, really, and there are good reasons for trying to live it.

A few years ago, our collective consumer spending outpaced earnings in the United States, representing a negative national consumer savings rate for the first time since the Great Depression. It didn't take a genius to guess that such debt-driven spending would eventually hit the fan. It's sad now to see so many people suffering from layoffs, charge-offs, foreclosures, shrunken investment portfolios, and general economic malaise.

At least big economic slowdowns produce one beneficial side effect. In previous recessions, the U.S. Environmental Protection Agency has noted improved air quality, thanks to fewer people driving to work and fewer factories churning out and delivering consumer goods. The Earth could use a little lessening of our consumption. For years the United States, though comprising less than 5 percent of the world's population, consumed 30 percent of its resources and produced 25 percent of its waste and greenhouse gasses.

Let's hope we emerge from this recession a little wiser. We all need to cut back on the resources we suck from the Earth and the stink we expel back into it. And many of us still need to learn how to spend less than we earn and—here's an idea—start saving a little money like our boring elders once did.

The good news is that living more simply doesn't have to mean having less fun or becoming less generous to yourself or others, especially in a great city like Chicago. Sure, you've got to toss a bit of money into the local economy to keep it going. But with a little creativity, you can dress, feed, transport, exercise, heal, educate, and entertain yourself well for free or a lot closer to free in its alternate universe of bountiful cheapness.

Look around Chicago's alleys, and you'll see treasures placed neatly next to Dumpsters with notes that say "free to a good home." Compliment people on their outfits, and they may proudly recommend the thrift stores where they bought them.

If you're a visitor just passing through or a new arrival hoping to put down roots, you'll find Chicago natives who want to show you around, show off their city, and make sure you have a good, cheap time. And this book is designed to show you around Chicago's realm of the free and ridiculously cheap.

Whatever your needs or interests, Chicago offers a wealth of free-to-ridiculously-cheap ways to meet most of them. Whether you're dirt poor, filthy rich, or somewhere in between, whether you want to have more fun while spending as little as humanly possible or just be able to direct a bit more of your cash toward better causes; whether you live here or are just passing through, I hope this book will help you enjoy all that Chicago offers its nobly cheap bastards.

SECTION 1:
Entertainment in Chicago

THEATER:
FREE SHOW

*"If you really want to help the American theater,
don't be an actress, dahling. Be an audience."*
—TALLULAH BANKHEAD

Chicago's a world-class theater town, with famous stages paced by celebrity master thespians and grassroots performance co-ops whose members invent new forms of dramatic expression. The city's also busy with top-notch, all-volunteer productions where kids amaze audiences with their prodigious talents and adults without head shots show off some high-quality hobby acting. We've even got a little Broadway going on here, complete with long lines, jaded critics, and excited tourists. Whatever your tendencies toward the dramatic, you can find many shows that are completely free, free to volunteer ushers, or at least half price to those in the know. So find your seat, turn off your cell phone, and enjoy the show.

THEATERS **SEEKING** USHERS

Very few of the people who tear tickets, hand out programs, or show people to their seats in medium-to-small Chicago live theaters are paid to do so. Most are volunteer ushers who get to see the performances for free. Usually they just have to arrive an hour or so early, get a little orientation lecture, help get everyone seated for performances, and then sit down to enjoy the show. They may have to direct folks to concession areas and bathrooms during intermissions. How theaters find and schedule their volunteers, and what they require of them, varies by company. For popular shows you may need to reserve your performance several weeks in advance. Other times you can call a week or a few days before a show and find a grateful house manager happy to sign you up. Most theaters will try to accommodate two people who want to ush together. After performances, ushers usually help clean up, but that rarely involves much more than a few minutes of picking up discarded programs. As a bonus, you'll meet like-minded theater fans and get a hearty thanks from the house manager.

While many theaters use only ushers from an organization called The Saints (see page 9), many organize their own (at no cost to you), and some use a combination. If you're a Saints member, you'll generally call the Saints coordinator for the theater you want to attend, as listed in the members' monthly newsletter. If you're not a Saint (but still a nice person, I'm sure), start by checking the Web site or calling the box office of the theater you're interested in attending. They'll route you to their own volunteer coordinator, a voice mail box or e-mail address, or their personal Saints coordinator. Don't be deterred if a theater has the Saints coordinate all of its ushers but you're not a Saints member and don't want to pay to be one. For some venues the Saints fill ushering gigs with nonmembers too. For others they use Saints members almost exclusively but will make occasional exceptions when they're short-handed. The number and type of ushers (Saints, non-Saints, or a combination) are listed by each theater.

About Face Theatre
Center on Halsted,
3656 North Halsted Street (at Waveland Avenue)
(773) 784–8565
www.aboutfacetheatre.com
Ushers per performance: 2 to 4 Saints

This theater company works within and beyond the gay, lesbian, bisexual, and transgender community to create and present plays about gender and sexual identity. Performances take place in different venues. The company also includes a youth theater with plays by young folks from fourteen to twenty years old.

American Theater Company
1909 West Byron Street (at North Wolcott Avenue)
(773) 409–4125
www.atcweb.org
Ushers per performance: 2 Saints

American Theater Company produces plays about the American experience, with stories from decades past and today. The company welcomes volunteers for ushering and other short-term assignments.

Apollo Theater
2540 North Lincoln Avenue (at West Lill Avenue)
(773) 935–6100
www.apollochicago.com
info@apollochicago.com
Ushers per performance: 2 Saints

The venue that hosted *The Vagina Monologues* and *Menopause the Musical* keeps the place booked with pop-theater hits. Apollo generally won't book you much earlier than the week you want to usher.

A Reasonable Facsimile Theatre Company

(773) 418–4475
www.arftco.com
Ushers per performance: 1; organizes own usher

This company puts on performances in a variety of venues. The company asks ushers to wear their company T-shirt over their own clothes, which can be casual as long as they're "decent." Though the theater can use only one usher per show, it will sell a half-price ticket to your guest.

Athenaeum Theatre

2936 North Southport Avenue (at West Oakdale Avenue)
(773) 935–6860
www.athenaeumtheatre.com
Ushers per performance: varies by show; Saints only

This venue, which has served a number of recreational, educational, and spiritual roles since 1911, hosts productions by guest theater and performance companies.

Briar Street Theatre

3133 North Halsted Street (at Briar Place)
(773) 348–4000
www.blueman.com
Ushers per performance: 4; organizes own ushers

Blue Man Group's Chicago troupe took over Briar Street Theatre a long time ago, and this critically acclaimed sensation shows no sign of moving out. Ushers show up an hour early, hand out programs, and help the house staff clean up after the show. Don't worry: Cleaning up involves hoisting armfuls of paper into trash cans but stops before you have to mop up the colorful fluids spewn during the show.

Chicago Shakespeare Theater

800 East Grand Avenue (on Navy Pier)
(312) 595–5659
www.chicagoshakes.com
Ushers per performance: 11 to 12 Saints and non-Saints

Would an usher by any other name still see the show for free? Sure! The theater's ushering hotline announces which shows have booked all the ushers they need and which still need volunteers. The theater uses ushers for all shows, even kids' matinees during the day. The Saints also coordinate ushers for them.

Chopin Theatre
1543 West Division Street (at North Milwaukee Avenue)
(773) 278–1500
www.chopintheatre.com
Ushers per performance: varies by production; Saints only

This venue has hosted thousands of plays, films, and other events from visiting companies and performers over the years. It also has produced more than 110 of its own works, most of which spring from Eastern European and Polish roots.

City Lit Theater Company
1020 West Bryn Mawr Avenue (inside Edgewater Presbyterian Church, wheelchair accessible, between North Kenmore Avenue and North Sheridan Road)
(773) 293–3682
www.citylit.org
Ushers per performance: 2 Saints

This theater's work is based on literature and plays from famous playwrights such as Edward Albee to local Chicago playwrights. The theater's mission is to "spark literary imagination." Some works have also sparked the occasional controversy.

Dress the Part

Spiffy black slacks and a crisp white shirt are the traditional costume that many theaters require of their volunteer ushers. Others ask ushers to wear all black or just ask that you dress up a bit. Be sure to ask what to wear when you make reservations for your ushering gig. Not all theaters have dress codes, but those that do take them seriously and may not let you ush if your attire isn't up to snuff.

Court Theatre

5535 South Ellis Avenue (between East 55th Street and East 56th Street)
(773) 753–4472
www.courttheatre.org
Ushers per performance: 4 to 7 Saints

This theater company produces classic works of such venerable playwrights as Chekhov, Wilson, Williams, and Shakespeare.

eta Creative Arts Foundation

7558 South South Chicago Avenue (near South Kimbark Avenue)
(773) 752–3955
www.etacreativearts.org

This South Shore institution has been preserving and promoting "the African American aesthetic" in Chicago for nearly forty years. To that end, the eta hosts theater, music, and dance performances, an art gallery and studio, and classes for adults and children. Most charge a fee, but the center welcomes long-term volunteers for ushering, clerical help, and other tasks. Eta offers free author readings and book signings the third Thursday of most months, starting at 6:00 p.m.

Goodman Theatre

170 North Dearborn Street (between West Randolph Street and West Lake Street)
Ushering hotline: (312) 443–3808
www.goodmantheatre.org
ushering@goodmantheatre.org
Ushers per performance: 6 to 12 Saints and non-Saints

Each season the Goodman rounds up some of the country's best talent to perform its new and classic works. It needs some of the city's best ushers to see them for free. Start by leaving a message with the theater's ushering voice or e-mail systems. Provide your name, phone number, dates you're available to usher, and the number of others in your group who would like to usher with you. The Goodman can accommodate up to four theatergoers in one party. A volunteer coordinator will let you know if they can use you for any of those dates. Goodman prefers to use ushers who sign up for several shows over the entire season, but it always has holes to fill. Once you're registered as an usher, you'll receive a welcome packet and additional mailings that let you know what's coming up.

Greenhouse Theater Center

2257 North Lincoln Avenue (between West Belden Avenue and West Webster Avenue)
(773) 404–7336
www.greenhousetheater.org
Ushers per performance: 4 Saints per main stage, 2 Saints per studio performance

This theater space, formerly occupied by the Victory Gardens Theater, now hosts classic and new plays by a variety of Chicago theater companies.

Lifeline Theatre

6912 North Glenwood Avenue (at West Farwell Avenue)
(773) 761–4477
www.lifelinetheatre.com
Ushers per performance: 2 Saints

This theater in a former electric company substation puts on plays for adults, kids more than two years old, and families. Past performances have included *Pride and Prejudice, A Wrinkle in Time,* and *Cat's Cradle.*

Links Hall

3435 North Sheffield Avenue (at North Clark Street and West Newport Avenue)
(773) 281–0824
www.linkshall.org
info@linkshall.org
Ushers per performance: Varies by performance; organizes own ushers

This free-spirited venue rents its space to a lot of fine (and often cash-strapped) performers, spoken-word events, and small theater companies. Links welcomes volunteers for ushering, office work, bulk mailing pizza parties, cleaning, and general office work and lets those volunteers see performances for free.

Lookingglass Theatre Company

821 North Michigan Avenue (inside Chicago Water Works at East Pearson Street)
Box office: (312) 337–0665
www.lookingglasstheatre.org
Ushers per performance: 5 to 6, mostly Saints

Meet the Saints

The Saints (P.O. Box 170164, Chicago, IL, 60617–0164; (773) 529–5510; www.saintschicago.org) is a nonprofit group that rounds up ushers and other volunteers for several theater, dance, and music companies and venues in Chicago. That allows performing arts folks to concentrate on producing great work rather than worrying about trying to find good, free help. Becoming a member of The Saints will set you back $65 per year. That's as much as a single ticket to many big-time plays here, so don't sign up just to see a play or two. But it's not a bad deal if you usher to see a lot of plays throughout the year, and the money raised goes toward scholarships for young thespians and grants to help struggling companies keep the lights on and their spaces up to code.

Once you sign up, you'll receive monthly paper or e-mail copies of the group's newsletter, *Spotlight,* which highlights an extensive list of upcoming events for which Saints can usher. You'll get additional announcements and alerts almost daily of shows that need ushers ASAP, and you can call the group's twenty-four-hour hotline to hear about events needing help. When you find shows you want to see, call or e-mail their Saints coordinators, give them a couple of dates that work for you, and they'll see which of those dates work for them. Coordinators usually will accommodate two ushers who want to work together, but they generally don't like to set up larger groups of acquaintances. That's because when one usher cancels, they all cancel, leaving the coordinator shorthanded.

Make sure you understand and do everything the Saints ask of you. Show up when they ask you to show up, follow instructions, and don't mess with their dress codes. If you prove yourself unreliable, the house manager or Saints coordinator may turn you away, boot you out of the syndicate, and you'll never ush in this town again. These are powerful people you're dealing with here, but they're good folks who work hard to support cash-strapped Chicago theaters.

The Catch Annual $65 memberships run from June 1 through May 31, and they're not prorated if you join late in that fiscal year. So get your money's worth and join in early June to get the most ushing for your buck.

Lookingglass has settled its off-Loop company into this historic, castlelike Loop building. Architects designed the space to change with the needs of different performances. Call the box office or check the theater's Web site for contact information of its current Saints coordinator. Scheduling begins about six weeks before previews of new plays.

The Neo-Futurists / The Neo-Futurarium
5153 North Ashland Avenue (between West Foster Avenue and West Winona Street)
Show hotline: (773) 275–5255
www.neofuturists.org
volunteer@neofuturists.org
Ushers per performance: uses long-term volunteers for a variety of tasks, not as onetime usher

Located above a funeral home, the Neo-Futurarium is home of the Neo-Futurist ensemble, whose members write and perform plays based, for the most part, on their own life experiences and ideas. They're best-known for the wildly popular, long-running Friday through Sunday show, *Too Much Light Makes the Baby Go Blind*. It's a collection of thirty plays that actors attempt to perform in an hour or less. The company also produces four prime-time productions each year, which generally run Thursday through Saturday at 8:00 p.m. All previews and Thursday night performances are pay what you can (it's up to you whether that's big bucks or a hug). You can also become a long-term volunteer and see plays for free.

Pegasus Players Theatre
O'Rourke Center for the Performing Arts, Truman College
1145 West Wilson Avenue (between North Magnolia Avenue and North Broadway Street)
(773) 878–9761
www.pegasusplayers.org
Ushers per performance: 2 to 4 Saints

You can usher through the Saints for this company or pay what you can at most Friday performances. If you're with a social service agency and would like to bring a group of your clients or guests for free, call extension 17 at the box office to speak with the outreach coordinator.

Raven Theatre

6157 North Clark Street (between West Granville Avenue and West Hood Avenue)
(773) 338–2177
www.raventheatre.com
Ushers per performance: 2 Saints

This theater company presents classic and new plays that explore American life, from Mamet, Williams, and Miller to playwrights you haven't heard of yet. Raven also presents children's theater.

Redmoon Theater

1438 West Kinzie Street (enter at 1463 West Hubbard Street)
(312) 850–8440
www.redmoon.org
information@redmoon.org
Ushers per performance: 2 to 40 Saints and non-Saints

Redmoon Theater produces fanciful contraptions, artwork, music, dance, and plots, then ties them all together into their famous "spectacles." They take place indoors, often at Redmoon Central, or in outdoor public spaces that can draw crowds as big as 2,000 people. Thus the wide range of ushers needed.

Steppenwolf Theatre Company

1650 North Halsted Street (between West North Avenue and West Willow Street)
House manager's office: (312) 932–2445
www.steppenwolf.org
Ushers per performance: 2 to 12 Saints and non-Saints

This venerable staple of Chicago theater began as a company in a church basement and since then has included ensemble members Gary Sinise, Laurie Metcalf, Joan Allen, and John Malkovich. Call as early as possible to book an ushering opportunity for any show you want to see. Steppenwolf books slots quickly, but it's worth calling even on the day of a performance in case they need some last-minute help.

Strawdog Theatre Company

3829 North Broadway Street (between West Grace Street and West Sheridan Road)
(773) 528–9696
www.strawdog.org
Ushers per performance: 1 to 2 Saints or non-Saints

This small theater puts on new interpretations of classics and new work all its own.

Theatre Building Chicago

1225 West Belmont Avenue (west of North Racine Avenue)
(773) 327–5252
www.theatrebuildingchicago.org
Ushers per performance: 2 Saints only

This venue hosts the performances of guest theater companies, and the Saints organize the ushers for all events.

TimeLine Theatre Company

615 West Wellington Avenue (between North Broadway Street and North Clark Street)
(773) 281–8463
www.timelinetheatre.com
Ushers per performance: 1 to 2 Saints

TimeLine presents plays inspired by history on topics that are still relevant today.

Victory Gardens Theater

2433 North Lincoln Avenue (in Biograph between West Montana Street and West Fullerton Avenue)(773) 871–3000
www.victorygardens.org
Ushers per performance: 4 Saints

In addition to providing ushering opportunities through the Saints, the theater also offers free performance viewings through open rehearsals.

CHEAP **SEATS**

Goldstar Events
www.goldstar.com

This California-based purveyor of discount performance tickets serves the
Chicago area too. Get yourself on the Goldstar Events mailing list by entering a bit of your personal information (to be sold to marketers, no doubt),
and they'll send you notices of discount tickets to local performances, many
of which are half-price. Some theaters offer tickets to free previews of performances through Goldstar too.

Hot Tix
www.hottix.org
72 East Randolph Street (across the street from the Chicago Cultural Center
between North Wabash Avenue and North Garland Court)
Chicago Water Works Visitor Center, 163 East Pearson Street (east of North
Michigan Avenue, south of Water Tower Place)

The League of Chicago Theatres runs these ticket centers to move half-price
tickets for same-day and next-day shows at Chicago-area theaters (including
many of those listed in this chapter), dance companies, and other performance venues. Hot Tix publishes the day's available tickets on its Web site.
For those performances, you can use a credit card to purchase tickets online
and then pick them up at the performance venue's will call window. Be pre-
pared to show the card you used to purchase the tickets along with a photo

Rush Tickets
Many theaters and other live performance venues offer students, and
sometimes teachers and senior citizens, significant discounts for tickets purchased right before shows open. If you fit the bill, contact the
box office hosting the show you'd like to see to discuss their terms.
If you're buying tickets right before the show anyway, ask at the box
office when you arrive, and be ready to show your current student ID
or other proof of age or status.

ID. You can also stop by one of the Hot Tix locations listed above to buy tickets to performances, including those not listed on the Web site.

SUGGESTED **DONATION**

Chicago Dramatists
1105 West Chicago Avenue (at North Milwaukee Avenue)
(312) 633–0630
www.chicagodramatists.org
The Catch $5 suggested donation.

Chicago Dramatists helps playwrights hone their craft and polish their scripts. You can help by attending the organization's "Saturday Series," which are staged readings and discussions of plays being developed.

The Neo-Futurists / The Neo-Futurarium
5153 North Ashland Avenue (between West Foster Avenue and West Winona Street)
Show hotline: (773) 275–5255
www.neofuturists.org volunteer@neofuturists.org

You can pay what you can for all previews and Thursday 8:00 p.m. performances by this ensemble, which creates and performs plays based on the life experiences and ideas of its members. Or you can become a long-term volunteer and see its plays for free.

Pegasus Players Theatre
O'Rourke Center for the Performing Arts, Truman College
1145 West Wilson Avenue (between North Magnolia Avenue and North Broadway Street)
(773) 878–9761
www.pegasusplayers.org

Pay what you can at most Friday performances. If you're with a social service agency and would like to bring a group of your clients or guests for free, call extension 17 at the box office to speak with the outreach coordinator.

Scrap Mettle Soul

4750 North Sheridan Road, suite 375
(773) 275–3999
www.scrapmettlesoul.org

This neighborhood theatrical effort uses volunteer actors performing the works of volunteers writing stories and plays about their own lives. Many plays are about life in the eclectic Uptown neighborhood of Chicago. Plays have included actors from four to ninety-two years old, from many countries, and from homeless to wealthy. The organization produces a play or two per year in various Uptown venues. All plays include suggested donations, and Scrap Mettle Soul welcomes volunteers to help with tasks before opening day.

Theater Oobleck

(moves from venue to venue)
(773) 347–1041
www.theateroobleck.com

The actors of this collective theater write their own plays and work without directors. The result is fresh, experimental theater with a staunch policy of "$12 suggested donation, more if you've got it, free if you're broke." Well, bless your souls, Theater Oobleck.

JUST **PLAIN** FREE **THEATER**

Alliance Francaise

810 North Dearborn Street (between West Chestnut Street and West Chicago Avenue)
(312) 337–1070
www.afchicago.com

Chicago's epitome of Frenchness has been known to host the occasional free play, usually in French.

Chicago Cultural Center

78 East Washington Street (at North Michigan Avenue)
Wheelchair access at 77 East Randolph Street
(312) 744–6630 / TTY: (312) 744-2947
www.chicagoculturalcenter.org

What better venue in which to enjoy free live theater than "The People's Palace"? The Chicago Cultural Center is buzzing with plenty of free culture, including plays, dance, music, lectures, literary programs, history, and art.

Chicago Public Library

(312) 747–4300
www.chipublib.org

Yep, your hardworking public library hosts free theater, too. To see what's happening at the Harold Washington or your local branch, check the library's monthly calendar, available online or in paper form, or watch local theater listings.

Hungry Brain

2319 West Belmont Avenue (at North Oakley Avenue)
(773) 935–2118

Every February this bar hosts GroundUp Theatre's annual Letters/X, a comical cabaret performance of actual letters to ex-, soon-to-be-ex-, and unrequited loves.

The Newberry Library

60 West Walton Street (between North Clark Street and North Dearborn Street)
(312) 943–9090
www.newberry.org

This private library hosts a lot of great cultural events, including such free theater as abbreviated versions of Shakespeare plays.

Victory Gardens Theater

2433 North Lincoln Avenue (in Biograph between West Montana Street and West Fullerton Avenue)
(773) 871–3000
www.victorygardens.org

The theater offers free performance viewings through open rehearsals.

SPOKEN WORD:
FREE SPEECH

"There's no money in poetry, but then there's no poetry in money, either."
—ROBERT GRAVES

Talk is cheap, and so are recitations of some of the finest words committed to print, notebook, and cocktail napkin. Whether you crave poetry, short stories, novels, or nonfiction diatribes for children or adults, Chicago's got a coffeehouse, library, bookstore, bar, gallery, or lecture hall with the out-loud lit to scratch your itch. Meet famous authors, those who should be, and a few who shouldn't quit their day jobs. Don't use poverty as your excuse for not attending, buster! Most of the listings here are all scot-free. (In fact, one is even organized by a guy named Scott Free.) Besides, poverty only enhances the poetic experience. As with most event listings in this book, venues and circumstances change—

like death poet's bar
bulldozed for new loft condos
sad bastard's new verse

—(okay, I won't quit my day job either) so call or check Web sites to confirm schedules before you venture out.

MOSTLY **POETRY**

Black Rock
3614 North Damen Avenue (at Addison Street)
(773) 348–4044
www.recroomers.com

"The Reconstruction Room" at the Black Rock bar in the North Center neighborhood pretty much covers your live entertainment needs the first Wednesday of each month at 8:00 p.m. Ya got yer poets, musicians, actors, and other performance-artist types who claim common goals: to "take risks" and "challenge the dominant power structure." United States currency being a key component of that aforementioned power structure, the recroomers don't want you sullying up the joint with yours. Okay, maybe a donation would be nice, if you've got a little extra. Register at 7:30 p.m. if you want to share your talent.

The Slam That Started Them All

Sure, $6 is an outlandish sum of money by the high standards set for this book, but the "Uptown Poetry Slam" is worth the occasional splurge. The original, now widely copied poetry slam is held in the historic Green Mill jazz bar every Sunday from 7:00 to 10:00 p.m. The well-attended open mike features readings by special guests followed by hard-core competition among some of the country's greatest and up-and-coming poetry slam competitors. You'll find the Green Mill at 4802 North Broadway Street (at West Lawrence Avenue); (773) 878–5552. Slam founder and organizer Marc Kelly Smith dishes the details at www.slampapi.com. Shows are recorded for later broadcast on XM Radio 163 and Sirius 117.

The Café

5115 North Lincoln Avenue (between West Winona Street and West Carmen Avenue)
Charlie Newman, poetry organizer: (312) 386–1656

The Catch Admission is pocket change of $2 and whatever else you want to add when they pass the Crown Royal bag for donations.

Every Tuesday from 8:00 to 10:00 p.m., join kindred spirits at this bar and restaurant for their poetry open mike. Presenters share three poems of their own or those of others for no more than five minutes per poet. Well-known (in the poetry world, anyway) local poets usually read the last twenty minutes each week.

Coffee Chicago

5256 North Broadway Street (between West Berwyn Avenue and West Foster Avenue)
(773) 784–1305

The Catch Suggested donation of $3, but it's $2 if you get up and read.

The poetry open mike in this coffee cafe is every Friday at 7:30 p.m.

eta Creative Arts Foundation

7558 South South Chicago Avenue (near South Kimbark Avenue)
(773) 752–3955
www.etacreativearts.org

This South Shore institution has been preserving and promoting "the African American aesthetic" in Chicago for nearly forty years. It offers free author readings and book signings the third Thursday of most months starting at 6:00 p.m. The eta also hosts theater, music, and dance performances, an art gallery and studio, and classes for adults and children. Most charge a fee, but volunteer ushers can see performances for free. The center welcomes long-term volunteers for ushering, clerical help, and other tasks.

Hotti Biscotti

3545 West Fullerton Avenue (at North Drake Avenue)
(773) 292–6877

This Logan Square bar presents open-mike poetry the second Thursday of each month starting at around 8:00 p.m.

Jak's Tap

901 West Jackson Boulevard (at South Peoria Street)
(312) 666–1700
www.jakstap.com

The Waiting 4 the Bus poetry series brings a poetry open mike to the West Loop the first and third Mondays of most months from 7:30 to 10:00 p.m. A donation is requested.

Mercury Cafe

1505 West Chicago Avenue (at North Armour Street)
(312) 455–9924
www.chimercurycafe.com

Vito Carli hosts an open mike and featured poets the second and fourth Fridays of most months from 7:00 to 9:00 p.m.

Myopic Books

1564 North Milwaukee Avenue (southeast of the intersection of North Milwaukee Avenue with North Damen Avenue and West North Avenue)
(773) 862–4882
www.myopicbookstore.com

This chummy Wicker Park bookstore runs poetry readings and talks by accomplished poets. They start at 7:00 p.m. every other Sunday.

St. Paul's Cultural Center

2215 West North Avenue (between North Albany Avenue and North Whipple Street)
Host Charlie Newman: (312) 386–1656

The First Friday Poetry Series in this former church offers four featured poets in exchange for free admission, cheap beer, wine, and soft drinks. Performances start at 7:30 p.m. the first Friday of the month. A small donation is requested.

Trace

3714 North Clark Street (north of West Waveland Avenue)
(773) 477–3400
www.tracechicago.com

The Catch Suggested donation is $3, but collection is pretty laid-back.

The PolyRhythmic Arts Collective hosts an open mike in this tavern every Tuesday at 10:00 p.m. It's about three-quarters poetry and a quarter stand-up comedy and acoustic music. Only adults age twenty-one and older are admitted.

Global Warming

In case July's not hot enough for you, come add some more hot air or hear it being made at The Newberry Library's annual Bughouse Square Debates. Speakers with important local, national, and international issues to share stand on soapboxes to tell the world. Judges encourage heckling of soapbox speakers, who all vie for the big prize, the great Dil Pickle, or at least an honorable-mention Dil Pickle pin. The Bughouse Square Debates are in Washington Square Park across from The Newberry Library at 60 West Walton Street (at North Dearborn Street); (312) 255–3510, www.newberry.org.

Tweet Let's Eat
5024 North Sheridan Road (between West Argyle Street and West Carmen Avenue; enter through Big Chicks)
(773) 728–5511

"Homolatte" includes the poetry, music, and other cafe-culture talents of gay, lesbian, bisexual, and transgender performers. The event commences the first and third Tuesday most months, and it gets extra Cheap Bastard brownie points for being emceed by a local poet and musician named Scott Free.

Weeds
1555 North Dayton Street (at West Weed Street)
(312) 943–7815

The venerable open mike at this hip tavern has been going on for more than twenty years. Readings are sort of supposed to start around 9:30 p.m. but usually don't get under way until about 10:30 p.m. Hey, some poetry shouldn't be held to a schedule. To sign up to read, show up about a half hour earlier than you think the event will start. Or whenever you feel like it.

A Week of Stories
Every year around March, Columbia College presents Story Week, a festival of free literary events held at the college, at the Harold Washington Library, and at bars, cafes, and other venues around the city. Past storytelling greats have included Studs Terkel, Dorothy Allison, Richard Price, and Stuart Dybek. For more information, contact Columbia College's Fiction Writing Department at (312) 344–7611, or check local listings as the event approaches.

STORY **TIMES** FOR **GROWN-UPS**

Chicago Public Library
(312) 747–4300
www.chipublib.org

The Chicago Public Library hosts weekly story hours at the Harold Washington Library, Sulzer and Woodson Regional Libraries, and many of the neighborhood branches. To find out what's going on near you or across the city, stop by your local branch, call the library's main number, check its comprehensive Web site, or pick up a calendar at your local branch.

The Whistler
2421 North Milwaukee Avenue
(773) 227–3530
www.whistlerchicago.com

Jason Behrends hosts the Orange Alert Reading Series at Whistler the third Sunday of each month, starting at 5:00 p.m.

AUTHOR **APPEARANCES** AND **BOOK** DISCUSSIONS

57th Street Books
1301 East 57th Street (at South Kimbark Avenue)
(773) 684–1300
http://semcoop.booksense.com

You won't hear Danielle Steel reading romances here. This smart shop basks in the University of Chicago's amazing mind powers, and it hosts the serious authors to prove it.

Barbara's Bookstore

www.barbarasbookstore.com
1218 South Halsted Street (at West Roosevelt Road); (312) 413–2665
111 North State Street (on lower level of Macy's at East Washington Street);
(312) 781–3033
1100 Lake Street, Oak Park (at North Marion Street); (708) 848–9140

This small, mostly local chain hosts authors reading a variety of fiction and nonfiction work.

Barnes & Noble Booksellers

1441 West Webster Avenue (at North Clifton Avenue)
(773) 871–3610
www.barnesandnoble.com

Barnes & Noble beckons you to hear authors read so you'll buy their books. Check for upcoming events on their Web site.

The Book Cellar

4736–38 North Lincoln Avenue (between West Lawrence Avenue and West Leland Avenue)
(773) 293–2665
www.bookcellarinc.com

This bookstore, wine bar, and cafe with cozy couches offers half-price wine during book club discussions. It also hosts acoustic music and, of course, author readings and discussions. Local authors are featured the third Wednesday of each month at 7:00 p.m.

Books-a-Million

114 South Clark Street (between West Monroe Street and West Adams Street)
(312) 857–0613
www.booksamillion.com

This South Loop bookstore hosts many author appearances starting at noon on weekdays, perfect timing for downtown office workers to fit in a little literary lunch break.

Literary Ambitions

Chicago inspires reading, what with having five months of hibernation-inducing winter and another five months of decent beach-reading weather. (Yes, the other two months we watch TV like everybody else.) And we've got an active community of local literati to help make reading a communal experience. Here are a few of my favorites, devoted to organizing and promoting readings of poetry and prose in a variety of venues. Check out their Web sites for upcoming events, interviews, reviews, and blogs about books.

Bookslut Reading Series

www.bookslut.com

This Chicago literary Web site hosts three or four local and visiting authors reading and discussing their works at each event. Readings take place in venues such as bars, cafes, and the Museum of Contemporary Art. Check the Web site for upcoming events. They're free, but you're asked to chip in to help the authors cover their travel expenses.

The Guild Literary Complex

(877) 394-5061

www.guildcomplex.org

The Guild sponsors a variety of spoken-word events around town, including Palabra Pura, a monthly bilingual reading by Chicano and Latino wordsmiths.

Literago

www.literago.com

This Web site includes news, opinion, and heads up about local literary events, including spoken word events, author signings, and lectures.

Borders Books & Music

www.bordersstores.com
150 North State Street (at Randolph Street); (312) 606–0750
755 West North Avenue (east of North Halsted Street); (312) 266–8060
830 North Michigan Avenue (at East Pearson Street); (312) 573–0564
1539 East 53rd Street (between South Lake Park Avenue and South Harper
Avenue); (773) 752–8663
2210 West 95th Street (at South Leavitt Street); (773) 445–5471
2817 North Clark Street (north of West Diversey Parkway); (773) 935–3909
4718 North Broadway Avenue (at West Leland Avenue); (773) 334–7338
6103 North Lincoln Avenue (at North Jersey Avenue); (773) 267–4822

National and local authors alike read their best passages aloud hoping you'll
like what you hear and line up to buy a signed copy. See announcements at
the store near you or check upcoming events listed on the national Borders
Web site.

Chicago Public Libraries

(312) 747–4300
www.chipublib.org

Not to keep harping about the library, but it hosts some literary giants reading
their works, too, usually at its main Harold Washington Library location downtown and at some of the larger branches. Best of all, you won't feel the least
bit guilty about slinking out without buying a book. It's a library, after all.

Gerber/Hart Library

1127 West Granville Avenue (between North Winthrop Avenue and North
Broadway Street)
(773) 381–8030
www.gerberhart.org

This private library hosts regular book discussion groups and lectures related
to gay, lesbian, bisexual, and transgendered themes. Pass-the-hat donations
are welcome.

Instituto Cervantes Chicago

31 West Ohio Street (between North State Street and North Dearborn Street)
(312) 335–1996
http://chicago.cervantes.es

This institute for the study and promotion of Spanish in European and American dialects hosts free readings and book presentations throughout the year.

International House

1414 East 59th Street (between South Blackstone Avenue and South Dorchester Avenue)
(773) 753-2274
http://ihouse.uchicago.edu

This cosmopolitan residence and cultural center on the University of Chicago campus hosts a variety of events, including performances, lectures, and discussions with visiting authors, many of which are free.

Newberry Library

60 West Walton Street (between North Dearborn Street and North Clark Street)
(312) 943-9090
www.newberry.org

The Newberry hosts readings, author visits, lectures, and storytelling throughout the year. Most events are free.

Powell's Bookstores

2850 North Lincoln Avenue (between West George Street and West Diversey Parkway)
(773) 248-1444
www.powellschicago.com

This local outpost of the venerable used-book chain boasts more than a million books, and it hosts author visits and readings by students of the School of the Art Institute's writing program.

Quimby's

1854 West North Avenue (between North Honore Street and North Wolcott Avenue)
(773) 342-0910
www.quimbys.com

Quimby's is a new and used books and zines store regularly visited by the likes of Dave Eggers and members of the McSweeney's literary family. It keeps a busy schedule of author readings, lectures, potlucks, and more.

Revolution Books

1103 North Ashland Avenue (at West Thomas Street)
(773) 489-0930
http://chicagorevolutionbooks.blogspot.com

The revolution may not be televised, but it will be blogged about. This bookstore operated by the Revolutionary Communist Party offers a bounty of noncapitalist reading materials, fashions, and knickknacks at bargain prices. They let some non-RCP progressive authors (Michael Moore, Noam Chomsky, Toni Morrison) mix with the communist manifestos on their shelves. The store also hosts free lectures, book discussions, and overthrow planning sessions.

Roosevelt University Auditorium
430 South Michigan Avenue (at East Congress Parkway)

The Roosevelt Reading Series gives famous authors, semi-famous authors, and Roosevelt Creative Writing Program students a forum in which to read their fiction and nonfiction work. Refreshments are served. For information on upcoming readings, usually held weekdays starting at 5:00 p.m., contact creativewriting@roosevelt.edu

Seminary Co-op Bookstore
5757 South University Avenue (between East 57th Street and East 58th Street)
(773) 752–4381
http://semcoop.booksense.com

This affiliate of 57th Street Books books great minds to mull their literary and nonfiction works of genius.

Women & Children First Bookstore
5233 North Clark Street (at West Farragut Avenue)
(773) 769–9299
www.womenandchildrenfirst.com

It's okay, guys. You're welcome here, too, and you won't be the only male at most readings, though you'll be outnumbered by XX chromosomes. The store hosts an active lineup of mostly female authors reading their books. It also hosts ongoing book discussion groups.

MUSIC:
OF FREE I SING

*"Anywhere in the world you hear a Chicago blues-
man play, it's a Chicago sound born and bred."*
—*RALPH METCALFE*

Whether you prefer blues, country, classical, hip-hop, or rock, Chicago's hardworking musicians take requests for free live music all week long. The town that helped incubate blues, jazz, and house music keeps the beat with no-cover performances in cafes, bars, concert halls, parks, and libraries, and on street corners and el platforms. Some bars that offer no-cover music recover their costs for hiring bands by requiring purchases of a minimum number of high-priced drinks, so check prices as you plan your evening outing. But most places are pretty laid-back about purchases and don't mind if you nurse a single cranberry juice for most of the evening. And there are plenty of concerts under the stars or in churches and libraries that require nothing but your kind attention.

BARS, CLUBS, AND RESTAURANTS

Abbey Pub
3420 West Grace Street (between North Kimball Avenue and North Elston Avenue)
(773) 478–4408
www.abbeypub.com

The Abbey charges to see most of its bands but regularly offers no-cover music in its pub area. Check out the open mike every Tuesday night and Irish jam sessions every Sunday.

B.L.U.E.S.
2519 North Halsted Street (at West Lill Avenue)
(773) 528–1012
www.chicagobluesbar.com

This blues staple of the North Side thanks residents and employees living and working in the surrounding zip codes of 60614, 60657, 60613, and 60610 with free admission on Tuesday night.

Buddy Guy's Legends

754 South Wabash Avenue (between East Balbo Drive and East 8th Street)
(312) 427–0333
www.buddyguys.com

Would Buddy let you down? The legend's venue charges $10 and up for its primetime shows but gives us lunchtime free blues on Tuesday from noon to 2:30 or 3:00 p.m. Tell your boss Buddy defines that as a proper lunch hour. Buddy has been threatening for years to move the venue to a new building, but at Cheap Bastard press time, no new address has been announced.

California Clipper

1002 North California Avenue (at West Augusta Boulevard)
(773) 384–2547
www.californiaclipper.com

Chicago's only bar with grape soda on tap, the Clipper also offers no-cover bands on Friday and Saturday starting around 10:00 p.m. Styles range from jazz and country to rockabilly and blues.

Chicago Brauhaus

4732 North Lincoln Avenue (between West Leland Avenue and West Lawrence Avenue)
(773) 784–4444
www.chicagobrauhaus.com

The hardest-working trio in Chicago accompanies your bier purchase almost every night the place is open (closed Tuesday) with German ballads and polka classics and American tunes (especially Elvis) sung in German and English. They accompany themselves with a synthesizer, guitar, and often drums and other instruments as older fans cut up the dance floor and younger ones cut the knockwurst.

Chief O'Neill's Pub & Restaurant

3471 North Elston Street (at North Albany Avenue)
(773) 583–3066
www.chiefoneillspub.com

This authentic Irish pub and restaurant founded and staffed by Irish just off the boat, and frequented by Irish just off the boat and Irish just in their dreams, offers some of the city's best sessions of traditional Irish music every Tuesday and Sunday, for no cover.

Cobra Lounge

235 North Ashland Avenue (at West Fulton Street)
(312) 226–6300

The rock at this "rough-yet-polished" West Loop joint is always free.

Coq d'Or

140 East Walton Place (in the Drake Hotel at North Michigan Avenue)
(312) 932–4623
www.thedrakehotel.com/hotel/coq.html

The Drake Hotel always feels like a James Bond movie set to me. Not saying whether that's good or bad. Just is. The hotel's chic piano bar and restaurant charges no cover for its sultry jazz piano and vocalist shows each Tuesday from 7:30 to 11:30 p.m. and each Thursday through Saturday from 8:30 p.m. to 12:30 a.m. Drinks are as pricey as you'd expect at the Drake.

Cuatro

2030 South Wabash Avenue (between East Cullerton Street and East 21st Street)
(312) 842–8856
www.cuatro-chicago.com

This bar, restaurant, and dance club accompanies its Sunday brunch with the no-cover Brazilian jazz of Bossa Tres.

Davenport's Piano Bar and Cabaret

1383 North Milwaukee (southeast of North Wolcott Avenue)
(773) 278–1830
www.davenportspianobar.com

This venue offers plenty of free shows in its Cabaret Room Thursday and Friday nights starting around 8:00 p.m. Stay (if you dare) for free karaoke starting at 10:30 p.m. on Fridays. Check out the free music in the Piano Bar most nights ($2 on Fridays and Saturdays). On Mondays, George Howe hosts open-mike performances in a variety of styles from 7:30 to 11:30 p.m.

Delilah's

2771 North Lincoln Avenue (southeast of West Diversey Parkway and North Racine Avenue)
(773) 472–2771
www.delilahschicago.com

Delilah keeps her patrons amused with no-cover music and free movies, art exhibitions, pinball, and pool. She keeps the drink specials cheap too.

Duke's Bar
6920 North Glenwood Avenue (between West Morse Avenue and West Farwell Avenue)
(773) 764–2826

This small Roger's Park bar keeps the drinks cheap, the juke box twangy, and the live country, blues, and bluegrass music free. Friendly regulars (including pooches) are all ages, with the median age decreasing a bit late at night.

Empty Bottle
1035 North Western Avenue (at West Cortez Street)
(773) 276–3600
www.emptybottle.com

This busy little rock club charges a cover most nights of the week but gives you a free taste of an ever-changing selection of bands every Monday starting at 9:30 p.m. And on Fridays at 5:30 p.m., the Hoyle Brothers will help you drown a workweek of sorrow with their free country honky-tonk.

Gallery Cabaret
2020 North Oakley Avenue (at West McLean Avenue)
(773) 489–5471
www.gallerycabaret.com

The Bucktown bar that helped give Smashing Pumpkins, Liz Phair, and Urge Overkill their starts wouldn't dream of charging a cover any night of the week. They're just glad you're there to drink their cheap beer or fancy brews and hear who's up next. Music includes rock, jazz, blues, and folk.

The Grafton Pub and Grill
4530 North Lincoln Avenue (between West Sunnyside Avenue and West Wilson Avenue)
(773) 271–9000
www.thegrafton.com

This friendly Irish pub and restaurant hosts no-cover traditional Irish and American folk music.

Green Dolphin Street
2200 North Ashland Avenue (at West Webster Avenue)
(773) 395–0066
www.jazzitup.com

This swelligantly swank (and pricey) restaurant and music club will set you back anywhere from $7 to $20 for full-price shows, but the venue offers free Latin jazz with the Jose Valdez Trio Tuesdays from 8:00 to 11:00 p.m. Dress up a little, cheap bastard. The place doesn't allow hats or athletic wear.

The Green Mill
4802 North Broadway Avenue (at West Lawrence Avenue)
(773) 878–5552
www.greenmilljazz.com

The Green Mill is as old as Uptown, having opened in 1907. Al Capone's mob buddies ran the place in the 1920s, and it still sports a restored 1920s decor. If you're an insomniac, come bask in its historic jazzy splendor any Monday through Thursday after 1:00 a.m.; stop by Friday night (Saturday morning— sorry, I'm a stickler for accuracy) for drop-in jam sessions with the Green Mill Quartet from 1:30 to 4:00 a.m.; or in the wee hours of Sunday from 2:00 to 5:00 a.m. for the After Hours Jazz Party with Sabertooth.

The Heartland Café
7000 North Glenwood Avenue (at West Lunt Avenue)
(773) 465–8005
www.heartlandcafe.com

This bastion of Midwest leftiness hosts a variety of quality music acts with cheap ($5) covers. But the freebie that gets it listed here is a recital every Sunday starting at 7:00 p.m. by students of The Guitar Friend Studio.

Hideout
1354 West Wabansia Avenue (1 block east of Elston Avenue and 2 blocks north of North Avenue)
(773) 227–4433
www.hideoutchicago.com

Unless you work at the Chicago Sanitation Headquarters, this delightfully scruffy little bar is tricky to find, but it's worth finding. The unpretentious club packs in an impressive blend of live pop, rock, country, blues, hip-hop, and spoken-word performances, along with the cheap bastards who love them. Devil in a Woodpile plays Tuesdays starting at 9:30 p.m. for the suggested donation of $5.

Horseshoe
4115 North Lincoln Avenue (between West Belle Plaine Avenue and West Warner Avenue)
(773) 248–1366

This Texas roadhouse on Chicago's North Side pairs cold (cheap) beer, Texas barbecue, and really cheap bar food specials with live country, bluegrass, and country rock music. Shows Thursday through Saturday are $5, but music any other night is free. Check out the roadhouse's MySpace page for details and schedules. Regulars include the likes of Long Gone Lonesome Boys and June Carter Clash and the Tex Pistols.

Hotti Biscotti
3545 West Fullerton Avenue (at North Drake Avenue)
(773) 292–6877

This bar rolls out the free live music Tuesdays through Saturdays starting at 9-ish or 10-ish p.m. Wednesdays are open-mike music, and the second Thursday of each month is open-mike poetry starting around 8:00 p.m.

The Kinetic Playground
1113 West Lawrence Avenue (between North Racine Avenue and North Winthrop Avenue)
(773) 769–5483
www.thekineticplayground.com

If you've blown your wad on a pricey concert at the Aragon Ballroom but want to challenge your eardrums for a few more hours, bring your ticket stub across the street to the Kinetic Playground bar for free admission. And check their Web site for occasional no-cover music too.

Lee's Unleaded Blues
7401 South South Chicago Avenue (at East 74th Street)
(773) 493–3477

This is the kind of true Chicago neighborhood blues joint that draws local musicians to sit in with that night's band. There's no cover, but tables go

fast, so show up early. There's an expected minimum purchase of two affordably priced drinks. The crowd includes college students, retirees, and all ages
in between. Dress ranges from jeans and T-shirts to clubbing finery. Open
Friday, Saturday, and Sunday from 8:00.

Martyrs'

3855 North Lincoln Avenue (between West Berenice Avenue and West Byron
Street)
(773) 404-9494
www.martyrslive.com

Martyrs' books great acts throughout the week, but the only ongoing free
gig is the Big C Jamboree the first Thursday of every month starting at 9:30
p.m. The open mike draws rockabilly, western swing, jump blues, and vintage rock musicians.

Morseland

1218 West Morse Avenue (between North Sheridan Road and North Lakewood
Avenue)
(773) 764-8900
www.morseland.com

This Rogers Park restaurant, bar, and music stage offers up no-cover jazz on
Sundays and Mondays, electronica on Wednesdays, and hip-hop and funk on
Thursdays. On other nights, cover charges generally stay an affordable $5.
Country and rock make appearances too.

The Mutiny

2428 North Western Avenue (between West Fullerton Avenue and West Montana Street)
(773) 486-7774
http://themutiny.bravepages.com/

The quintessential dive music bar, The Mutiny rocks the borderland between
Logan Square and Bucktown most nights of the week with free rock, punk,
hardcore, and, on Tuesdays from 5:00 to 8:00 p.m., karaoke. Wooooo!!

Peninsula Hotel

108 East Superior Street (at North Michigan Avenue)
(312) 337-2888
www.peninsula.com

No, you probably shouldn't take out that line of credit against your home's equity to stay a weekend at the Peninsula. But you should stop by The Lobby, a swelligant tearoom and bar on the fifth floor, for no-cover jazz by a variety of performers on Friday nights and by the Stephanie Browning Quartet on Saturday nights. The music starts at 8:30 p.m.

Poitin Stil
1502 West Jarvis Avenue (at North Greenview Avenue)
(773) 338-3285

It's pronounced "poo-chine still" and means moonshine in Gaelic. The owner is originally from Galway, Ireland, and her father and grandfather used to make the stuff. She sells imported pints and domestic drafts to accompany the occasional classic rock band or Sunday Irish jam session. The gigs average about twice a month and are free.

Red Line Tap
7006 North Glenwood Avenue (at West Lunt Avenue)
(773) 274-5463
www.heartlandcafe.com

Run by the Heartland Cafe folks, this over-21 bar offers free bluegrass on Tuesday starting at 9:00 or 10:00 p.m., and a variety of rotating bands, from metal to jazz, on "Wasted Wednesdays" starting at 9:00 p.m. As the name implies, the booze is extra cheap that night. Perform in the free open mike on Thursday night starting at 9:00 p.m. (sign-up starts at 8:00 p.m.), and you'll even get a free drink.

The Whistler
2421 North Milwaukee Avenue
(773) 227-3530
www.whistlerchicago.com

The Whistler never charges a cover for its wide variety of live music, DJ spins, and spoken-word events. But you have to be twenty-one to enter.

SCHOOLS, **CHURCHES,** AND **CULTURAL** CENTERS

Chicago Cultural Center
78 East Washington Street (at North Michigan Avenue)
Wheelchair access at 77 East Randolph Street
(312) 744–6630 / TTY: (312) 744–2947
www.chicagoculturalcenter.org

The Palace of the People keeps the people entertained with free concerts, dance performances, and other cultural programming year-round. Some events will cost you, but most are free.

Chicago Water Works Visitor Center
163 East Pearson Street (across from Water Tower Place east of North Michigan Avenue)
(312) 744–8783
www.choosechicago.com

This gallery and performance space welcomes tourists and townies with free music, theater, art, and other cultural events throughout the year.

Concert Hall, DePaul University
800 West Belden Avenue (at North Halsted Street)
http://music.depaul.edu/events

See free faculty and student recitals at this beautiful Lincoln Park campus facility.

Fourth Presbyterian Church
126 East Chestnut Street (between North Ernst Court and North Michigan Avenue)
(312) 787–4570
www.fourthchurch.org

If you need a little sonic stress relief during your Friday lunch hour, Presbyterians are here to help. Fourth Presbyterian Church's Noonday Concerts are a free, year-round series of forty-five-minute classical music performances that begin most Fridays at 12:10 p.m. Check the church's Web site for other free concerts scheduled throughout the year.

Instituto Cervantes Chicago
31 West Ohio Street (between North State Street and North Dearborn Street)
(312) 335–1996
http://chicago.cervantes.es

This institute for the study and promotion of Spanish in European and American dialects hosts free concerts of a variety of musical styles, including classical, flamenco, and folk.

Irish American Heritage Center
4626 North Knox Avenue (at West Wilson Avenue)
(773) 282–7035
www.irishamhc.com

This Northwest Side cultural institution presents free, live Irish music in its pub room on Friday and Saturday night starting at 9:00 p.m., and it hosts other concerts in its library.

JazzCity Concert Series
Various City of Chicago parks
(312) 427–1676
www.jazzinstituteofchicago.org

The Jazz Institute gives Chicago a wealth of free jazz educational and entertainment programs throughout the year. JazzCity is a series of free jazz concerts held in Chicago Park District parks. They're a free way for the whole family to see some of Chicago's jazz masters.

Latino Cultural Center
University of Illinois at Chicago
803 South Halsted Street, Lecture Center B2 (enter campus through 750 South Halsted Street)
(312) 996–3095
www.uic.edu/depts/lcc

This center for students hosts free evenings of La Peña, which means live music and dance in an intimate setting, the third Thursday of each month beginning at 7:00 p.m. The center hosts free films and poetry and variety shows the other Thursday nights.

Newberry Library

60 West Walton Street (between North Dearborn Street and North Clark Street)
(312) 943–9090
www.newberry.org

This fabulous private library offers the public a host of free concerts, particularly classical.

Northeastern Illinois University

Fine Arts Center Recital Hall
3701 West Bryn Mawr Avenue (on campus)
(773) 442–4636
www.neiu.edu

Faculty and students perform free concerts here throughout the year. Check local newspapers and the school's Web site for upcoming performances.

The Old Town School of Folk Music

www.oldtownschool.org
4544 North Lincoln Avenue (between West Wilson Avenue and West Sunnyside Avenue)
909 West Armitage Avenue (between North Fremont Street and North Russell Street)
(773) 728–6000

Volunteer for the Old Town School to earn points toward free performances and classes. One point equals $4. The number of points earned varies per task, but ushering the average concert will snag you three points.

PianoForte Chicago

1312 South Michigan Avenue (in Columbia College's Sherwood Conservatory)
(312) 291–0291
www.wfmt.com

The PianoForte Salon Series at Columbia College Chicago tapes in front of a live audience forty-three Fridays each year, starting at 12:15 p.m., to broadcast on WFMT (98.7 FM). Despite its name and beginnings in a local piano shop, the show includes a variety of classical instruments and voices.

Renaissance Society

5811 South Ellis Avenue (between East 57th Street and East 59th Street)
(773) 702–8670
www.renaissancesociety.org

This art museum on the University of Chicago campus hosts occasional music events too. Most events are free.

River East Art Center

435 East Illinois Street (between North McClurg Court and North Lake Shore Drive)
(312) 321–1001
www.rivereastartcenter.com

The former North Pier Terminal Building is now a center for visual and performing arts, including occasional free music.

Saint James Cathedral

65 East Huron Street (use doors at North Wabash Avenue)
(312) 787–7360
www.saintjamescathedral.org

Let's all give a shout out to those classy Episcopalians for throwing more high-culture events open to the masses. You rock, Church of England! St. James Cathedral's Rush Hour Concerts are half-hour chamber music performances that begin at 5:45 p.m. every Tuesday from June through August. Show up early, at 5:15 p.m., for free hors d'oeuvres and wine! The concerts are popular, often drawing more than 300 people, many of whom contribute to the "freewill tip basket" near the door, grateful for a little Brahms before facing their commutes.

South Shore Cultural Center

7059 South South Shore Drive (between East 70th Place and East 71st Street)
(773) 256–0149
www.chicagoparkdistrict.com

Most events and classes at this center seem pretty pricey to me, but some concerts are free.

The University of Chicago Folklore Society
1212 East 59th Street (at South Woodlawn Avenue)
(773) 702–9793
www.uofcfolk.org
info@uofcfolk.org

The annual University of Chicago Folk Festival runs for a three-day winter weekend. Volunteers can see concerts for free. And anyone can join free daytime workshops in traditional folk-musical styles and dances from around the world. Check the society's Web site and local newspaper listings as the month approaches.

University of Chicago Ida Noyes Hall
1212 East 59th Street (at South Woodlawn Avenue)

The concert space in this U of C building hosts many free musical and other performance events for nonstudents as well as scholars. It's a lovely campus to visit, too.

THE **GREAT** OUTDOORS

DOWNTOWN FESTIVALS

The Catch Attend a few festivals and you'll have "City of Chicago Mayor's Office of Special Events, Richard M. Daley, mayor" repeating in your brain until March.

From the Petrillo Music Shell to Millennium Park to smaller temporary stages, Grant Park hosts free live music festivals throughout the summer and into the early fall. Starting with the Chicago Blues Festival around Memorial Day, the Mayor's Office of Special Events rolls through the summer months with the Gospel Music Festival, Country Music Festival, Taste of Chicago (which charges for the food but not for the music), Viva! Chicago Latin Music Festival, Jazz Festival, and Celtic Fest.

Chicago SummerDance

Spirit of Music Garden, Grant Park
601 South Michigan Avenue (between East Harrison Street and East Balbo Drive)
SummerDance hotline: (312) 742–4007
www.chicagosummerdance.org

Even if you'd rather sit on your groove thing than shake it, SummerDance's live bands make for fine free concerts. And the amazing dance moves of your fellow Chicagoans are fun to watch too. For eleven weeks every summer, SummerDance runs Thursday through Saturday evening from 6:00 to 9:30 and on Sunday from 4:00 to 7:00 p.m., weather permitting. The first hour of each evening is occupied by a free lesson in whatever dance styles will complement the music that night. The rest of the time, live bands cover just about every danceable style of the globe.

Chicago SummerDance in the Parks

Chicago SummerDance at Navy Pier
SummerDance hotline: (312) 742-4007
www.chicagosummerdance.org

If you're in the mood for summer music but don't want to drag yourself to South Michigan Avenue, you're in luck. SummerDance has expanded to additional events at Navy Pier (600 East Grand Avenue at North Lake Shore Drive) and several neighborhood parks, including:
Athletic Field Park, 3546 West Addison Street (at North Drake Avenue)
Humboldt Park, 1440 North Sacramento Avenue (between West North Avenue, West Division Street, North California Avenue and North Kedzie Avenue)
Jackson Park 63rd Street Beach, 6300 Sourh Lake Shore Drive

Free Streets

Every summer and fall, street festivals fill Chicago neighborhoods with fun, fried food, and live music. Many street-festival gatekeepers charge what some organizers will try to convince you are mandatory admission fees. But by city ordinance, street fairs can charge only suggested donations. After all, they're taking place on the streets you've already paid for. Politely donate what you think is best (even if that's nothing), and go on in. Hey, any excuse for a party!

Washington Park, 5531 South Martin Luther King Drive (at East Garfield Boulevard).

Check the Web site or hotline for event dates and times.

Grant Park Music Festival
(312) 742-7638
www.grantparkmusicfestival.com

This "festival" is actually a series of about thirty-five free outdoor concerts by the Grant Park Orchestra and Grant Park Chorus every mid-June through mid-August. They're performed in the Jay Pritzker Pavilion (see next entry) on the east side of Millennium Park most Wednesday and Friday evenings starting at 6:30 p.m. and Saturday evenings starting at 7:30 p.m. Times vary with other festival and event schedules, so check before you go. Donors sit in seats near the stage, but general seating areas and lawn space for picnic blankets or lawn chairs are free. The orchestra and chorus occasionally perform there on Sundays, too, and they present nearly sixty more concerts in neighborhood parks around the city from July through mid-August. If you're looking for afternoon entertainment, check the orchestra and chorus rehearsal schedule. They generally run from 11:00 a.m. to 1:30 p.m. and from 2:30 or 3:00 p.m. to 5:00 p.m. many Tuesdays through Fridays during the performance season.

Jay Pritzker Pavilion in Millennium Park
100 North Michigan Avenue (at East Washington Street)
(312) 742-1168
www.millenniumpark.org

This 4,000-seat venue with lawn space for an additional 7,000 could host the Second Coming of Jesus in grand acoustic and architectural style, should the Lord choose to pop up in Chicago for his encore. Meanwhile, the City of Chicago will continue to work out its redemption for the bazillions of dollars over budget it spent on the park by offering free concerts and festivals in a variety of musical styles throughout the year. Check local listings and the park's Web site for upcoming events.

Under the Picasso
Daley Civic Center
50 West Washington Street (at South Racine Avenue)

Most weekdays, the City of Chicago entertains its hardworking Downtown workers and tourists with free cultural programming starting at noon, held indoors or outdoors depending on the weather. Catch a grab bag of high-school choirs, ethnic dancers, and professional musicians. Beats eating lunch at your desk.

MUSIC **AND** BOOK **STORES**

Borders Books & Music
www.bordersstores.com
150 North State Street (at Randolph Street); (312) 606–0750
755 West North Avenue (east of North Halsted Street); (312) 266–8060
1539 East 53rd Street (between South Lake Park Avenue and South Harper Avenue); (773) 752–8663
2210 West 95th Street (at South Leavitt Street); (773) 445–5471
2817 North Clark Street (north of West Diversey Parkway); (773) 935–3909
4718 North Broadway Avenue (at West Leland Avenue); (773) 334–7338
6103 North Lincoln Avenue (at North Jersey Avenue); (773) 267–4822

Borders hosts in-store performances by musicians, usually whose CDs they sell. Ask at your local Borders store, or go to the national Borders Web site and enter the zip code of the store near you to check what's coming up.

Commuter Music

I often see a woman decked in traditional Chinese garb play haunting melodies on an erhu, a Chinese cello-type of instrument, at the Jackson stop of the Red Line train. Other times, at other stops, you'll find jazz musicians good enough for any club. And then there are the upturned bucket drummers, the synthesizer player songwriter, the karaoke contest leader, the sax player, and the league of acoustic guitar and harmonica folks who make my commutes more interesting. They all hope for your tips, which is up to you. Most congregate around the busiest Downtown el stops with the best acoustics. You'll also find decent acts aboveground, competing with doomsday preachers near the most touristy shopping and festival areas, especially Water Tower Place (at Pearson Street and Michigan Avenue).

Myopic Books

1564 North Milwaukee Avenue (southeast of the intersection of North Milwaukee Avenue with North Damen Avenue and West North Avenue)
(773) 862–4882
www.myopicbookstore.com

Besides the three stories of books, Myopic expands Wicker Park minds with
free music and spoken-word events. On Experimental Music Mondays, beginning at 7:30 p.m. musicians perform on various traditional and nontradi-
tional instruments, such as guitar, trombone, violin, and laptop computer.

FILM:
CHEAP SEATS

"The cheaper the movie, the more creative the experience."
—ALFRED MOLINA

I once had a pal who liked to "double dip" at movie theaters, paying once and then sneaking into second or third shows without paying again, even at the neighborhood mom-and-pop cinema that charged only $2 to $4 per show and struggled to keep the place up to code and the development wolves from the door. Have a little class, cheap bastards. If you don't like The Man's prices, don't watch his movies on his turf. There are plenty of places to legally see great films in Chicago. Sure, you may not get surround sound, but you'll see locally produced work, and a bunch of new, old, cutting-edge, quirky, and classic gems in libraries, bars, cafes, lecture halls, and parks.

MOVIES **UNDER** THE **STARS**

Chicago Outdoor Film Festival
Butler Field, in Grant Park (at Lake Shore Drive and Monroe Street)
www.explorechicago.org

For seven weeks every summer, see such classics as *Guess Who's Coming to Dinner, Mr. Smith Goes to Washington,* and Hitchcock's *The Birds* (all the creepier outside where they can get you!). Movies begin at sunset on a 50-foot-by-34-foot screen, backed by a fabulous view of the Chicago skyline. Bring your blanket or lawn chair, and leave the alcohol and dogs at home (not permitted). Nearby public transit and bike trails make it easy to leave the car at home or near an el stop that has better parking than Downtown.

Busting Blockbuster
Several branches of the Chicago Public Library have large collections of DVDs and videos that you can borrow for free. Just return them on time, or you'll face late fees that rival the commercial ventures. To check the collection for the locations and availability of your favorites, go to www.chipublib.org.

Movies in the Parks
Chicago Park District Parks
(312) 742–PLAY
www.chicagoparkdistrict.com

During the summer the park district shows free movies in various parks throughout the city. They're heavy on the kid-pleasing family-movie genre; if junior loses focus anyway, the play lot is nearby.

MOVIES **UNDER** THE **CEILING**

Alliance Francaise
810 North Dearborn Street (at West Chicago Avenue)
(312) 337–1070
www.afchicago.com

This cultural vortex of all things French hosts free French-language films throughout the year, culminating with the annual Festival de la Francophonie in March.

Chicago Filmmakers
5243 North Clark Street (at West Farragut Avenue)
(773) 293–1447
www.chicagofilmmakers.org

This organization, which offers classes, equipment rental, and other support for local filmmakers, also shows a lot of movies. They're usually $8 for the general public ($4 for members). But once in a while, they show free movies in any of several formats (digital, Super 8, 16mm), particularly on open movie nights, when people can bring in their own work, found footage, and other fun stuff to share.

Chicago Public Library
(312) 747–4300
www.chipublib.org

Chicago Public Library hosts films at many of its branches, and the Harold Washington main library has films on-site to watch. To see what's happening at the Harold Washington or your local branch, check the library's monthly calendar, available online or in paper form, or watch local theater listings.

Delilah's
2771 North Lincoln Avenue (southeast of West Diversey Parkway and North Racine Avenue)
(773) 472–2771
www.delilahschicago.com

Delilah's hardworking hosts show free videos and DVDs such as Steve McQueen movies and punk videos. There's plenty of no-cover music, pinball, pool, and art, too, all of which you can wash down with cool, cheap drinks.

DuSable Museum of African American History
740 East 56th Place (in Washington Park west of South Cottage Avenue)
(773) 947–0600
www.dusablemuseum.org

The Children's Penny Cinema, held Tuesday, Wednesday, and Thursday at 10:30 a.m., costs only a penny per person, and the museum shows occasional free dramas for the grown-up set too.

Gerber/Hart Library
1127 West Granville Avenue (west of North Winthrop Avenue)
(773) 381–8030
www.gerberhart.org

This small library archives documents and books important to the past and present of lesbian, gay, bisexual, and transgender people in the Midwest, and it holds public events, including occasional movie screenings on a television monitor. They usually pass the hat for pay-what-you-can donations.

Goethe-Institut Chicago
150 North Michigan Avenue (at East Randolph Street), suite 200
(312) 263–0472
http://www.goethe.de/ins/us/chi/

This center for the learning and enjoyment of German language and culture hosts a generous schedule of free events, including German-language films for adults and kids.

Hotti Biscotti

3545 West Fullerton Avenue (at North Drake Avenue)
(773) 292-6877

This el-cheapo cafe, bar, and performance space regularly shows movies via video projection.

Instituto Cervantes Chicago

31 West Ohio Street (between North State Street and North Dearborn Street)
(312) 335-1996
http://chicago.cervantes.es

This institute for the study and promotion of Spanish in European and American dialects hosts free film and video screenings throughout the year.

Latino Cultural Center

University of Illinois at Chicago
803 South Halsted Street, Lecture Center B2 (enter campus through 750 South Halsted Street)
(312) 996-3095
www.uic.edu/depts/lcc

This center for students hosts free movie nights with free refreshments the first Thursday of each month beginning at 7:00 p.m. The center hosts free music, poetry, and variety shows on the other Thursday nights.

Mess Hall

6932 North Glenwood Avenue (at West Morse Avenue)
(773) 465-4033
www.messhall.org

The Mess Hall is a cultural center, gallery, potluck party, performance venue, lecture space, sewing parlor, spoken-word cafe, clothing exchange, and meeting place for the confluence of all ideas lefty. Its members screen videos too.

The Motel Bar

600 West Chicago Avenue (at North Larrabee Street)
(312) 822-2900
www.themotelbar.com

This celebration of motel bar kitsch hosts weekly free fun, including Bingo the first and third Mondays of the most months from 7:00 to 9:00 p.m., trivia games the second and fourth Tuesdays starting at 8:00 p.m., and Monday night movies from June through September starting around sundown.

Museum of Contemporary Photography
Columbia College
600 South Michigan Avenue (at East Harrison Street)
(312) 663–5554
www.mocp.org

This institution shows photographic images from Chicago and the rest of the world, both still images and moving pictures.

The Neo-Futurists / The Neo-Futurarium
5153 North Ashland Avenue (between West Foster Avenue and West Winona Street)
Show hotline: (773) 275–5255
www.neofuturists.org
volunteer@neofuturists.org

Some movies are so bad they must be recited rather than seen. Members of the Neo-Futurist troupe perform staged readings of some of the worst films of the twentieth century during their annual Summer Film Festival. They're on Thursday nights, which happen to be pay-what-you-can nights.

Oriental Institute of Chicago
1155 East 58th Street (at South University Avenue)
(773) 702–9514
http://oi.uchicago.edu/OI/default.html

If you like watching PBS documentaries about the ancient Middle East but feel like you should get off your couch and out into the world more often, get out to the Oriental Institute's free film screenings Sundays, usually around 2:00 p.m. (check the museum's event calendar for shows and times). Movies range from documentaries about ancient Nubian potters to Cleopatra's close-up in the Cecil B. DeMille classic.

Spertus Institute Asher Library
610 South Michigan Avenue (at East Harrison Street)
(312) 322–1700
www.spertus.edu

The library at this school and museum of Judaica holds an extensive collection of films by, for, and about Jews. From comedies by Woody Allen and early vaudeville performers to documentaries about the Holocaust and the founding of modern Israel, you can find and view it here.

University of Chicago Doc Films

1212 East 59th Street (between South Woodlawn Avenue and South Kimbark Avenue)
(773) 702–8575
http://docfilms.uchicago.edu

This long-running club at the University of Chicago has been showing cheap movies, documentary and drama, high culture and low, since about the time the first sustained nuclear reaction occurred on campus. If you're so cheap you don't even want to cough up a measly $3 for Doc Films Sunday matinees ($4 at other times), well, good for you. You can become a weekly volunteer for an academic quarter and receive two passes for you and your cheap dates to see all of the movies shown that quarter for free. You must attend a new volunteer meeting and then take on duties, such as fireguard, ticket seller, projectionist, or apprentice projectionist.

University of Chicago Film Studies Center

Cobb Hall 306
5811 South Ellis Avenue (between East 57th Street and East 59th Street)
(773) 702–8596
http://filmstudiescenter.uchicago.edu

If you crave thoughtful discussions with screenings of gems such as rare films from the silent era or hard-to-find contemporary movies from around the world, this is the perfect venue. Screenings are often part of lectures and symposia with U of C and visiting scholars. Most events are free.

The Five Buck Club

Kerasotes Theatres offers a discount card that gives holders $5 admission to movies that have been in their theaters for at least a couple of weeks. Provide your name, contact information, and birth date in a form on the Five Buck Club Web site (www.fivebuckclub.com) and you're in. They'll send you a Five Buck Club Card and weekly e-mails listing discount (to you) films at participating theaters.

TV AND RADIO TAPINGS:
PUBLIC ACCESS

"Television! Teacher, mother, secret lover."
—HOMER SIMPSON

Chicago doesn't have as many television and radio shows in need of live audiences as do the fame-centric cities of New York and L.A. But our little town has a few stalwarts of international and local broadcast television, including the famous, the infamous, and the obscure but fun. Chicago is also the epicenter of some cutting-edge public radio shows and public tapings of a classic old Christian melodrama.

TV

Check, Please!
www.wttw.com

If you'd like to play guest restaurant reviewer on the show that won Obama the White House (OK, maybe it wasn't his review of Dixie Kitchen that propelled him to the national spotlight), fill out an application form on WTTW's Web site. The producers will only consider restaurants they haven't reviewed in the past, so check the show's archives. If you're chosen, you and two other guests will visit each other's favorite dining spots and then show up for a few hours on a weekday to be taped dishing about your experiences with host Alpana Singh.

Chic-A-Go-Go
taped at Chicago Access Network Studios
322 South Green Street (1 block west of Halsted Street)
www.roctober.com/chicagogo/taping.html

Garfield Goose died long ago, and when the last Bozo retired, no one could fill his clown shoes. But the *Chic-A-Go-Go* dance show has been going strong since 1996. Kids and adults of all ages and kinetic talents (or lack thereof) are welcome to dance to the live music on the show, broadcast on Chicago Cable Access. Check the Web site for information or send an e-mail message to Ratso, the show's spunky puppet co-host, at ratso@roctober.com, to sign up for announcements about upcoming monthly tapings. No reservations are needed, goofy costumes are encouraged, and you can invite as many friends as you'd like.

The Jerry Springer Show
454 North Columbus Drive (between East Illinois Street and East North
Wacker Street), second floor
Chicago, IL 60611
(312) 321–5365
www.jerryspringertv.com

If you insist on rotting your brain, at least you can do so for free. This
king of all chair-throwing, profanity-bleeping, sleazy American talk shows
is filmed right here in Chicago. To get tickets, write to the address, call the
telephone number listed here, or send an e-mail message through the Web
site.

Judge Mathis
(866) 362–8447
www.judgemathistv.warnerbros.com/tickets

Here's proof once again that justice can be unintentionally, tragically hilarious. If you're at least eighteen years old, call the show or fill out a form
online to reserve your spot in the audience.

The Oprah Winfrey Show
Harpo Studios
110 North Carpenter Street (at West Washington Boulevard)
(312) 591–9222
www.oprah.com

The queen of the self-help talk show and its offshoot empire of women's
media still graces Chicago after all these years. And she often gives out free
loot to lucky audience members, too. Taping schedules vary from week to
week from August through November and from January through May. There
are no weekend tapings. Tickets are free but not easy to get. Occasionally,
last-minute reservations are available via e-mail through the Web site. But
you can usually get a reservation only by calling the phone number listed
here. Keep trying if all lines are busy, as you're one of minions hoping Oprah
will save your soul, put you in gawking distance of some other celebrity,
or at least give you a nifty parting gift. Once you've reached an Audience
Department member, he or she will determine whether you're worthy of a
reservation. You may reserve up to four seats for a taping. Reservations to

particular shows are not guaranteed, but if your show is canceled or needs a specialized audience, the Audience Department will notify you and try to reschedule you for another show. Once you're in, remember to bring a photo ID to prove you're at least eighteen years of age.

RADIO

Live from the Heartland
Heartland Café
7000 North Glenwood Avenue (at West Lunt Avenue)
(773) 465–8005
www.heartlandcafe.com

Like to ponder bioregional organic farming with a room full of like-minded folks as you eat your free-range omelet from, oh, say 9:00 to 10:00 a.m. on a given Saturday morning? Bring your perky Saturday morning self to the Heartland Cafe restaurant for its weekly live radio show, *Live from the Heartland,* on WLUW 88.7 FM, and watch its host interview local politicians, organizers, teachers, artists, environmentalists, and others in a decidedly left-end-of-the-dial experience. Yeah, it would be nice if you ordered a cup of coffee or something, but they won't oppress you by forcing a purchase. Plan ahead, and you can tell your friends to listen at home for you yelling the traditional "Woo!" during audience applause.

PianoForte Chicago
1312 South Michigan Avenue (in Columbia College's Sherwood Conservatory)
(312) 291–0291
www.wfmt.com

The PianoForte Salon Series at Columbia College Chicago tapes in front of a live audience forty-three Fridays each year starting at 12:15 p.m. to broadcast live on WFMT (98.7 FM). Despite its name and beginnings in a local piano shop, the show includes a variety of classical instruments and voices.

Radio Arte
1401 West 18th Street (at South Loomis Street)
(312) 455–9455
www.wrte.org
training@radioarte.org

The National Museum of Mexican Art runs an educational youth radio station that broadcasts in Spanish and English to the Pilsen and Little Village neighborhoods from WRTE 90.5 FM and to the rest of the world via its Web site. Check the station's Web site for live events at the station and museum. The station also offers a free one-year training program in radio broadcasting to young people ages fourteen through twenty-four. Students learn to research, interview, and write for radio news stories, and they learn digital production and other modern radio technical skills. Registration starts in December and classes begin in March each year.

Third Coast International Audio Festival Listening Room
(events at various locations)
www.thirdcoastfestival.org
(via WBEZ Radio, Chicago's National Public Radio Affiliate, 91.5 FM)

The Third Coast International Audio Festival collects some of the world's best audio documentaries, personal stories, and sound experiments for its annual competition. It then presents them via its Web site, via the weekly WBEZ 91.5 FM radio program *Re:sound,* a two-hour annual broadcast, and via a series of public events in Chicago called the Listening Room. Most of the public-listening events are ridiculously cheap; occasionally they're free. To find out when and where the next one is scheduled, go to the Web address listed above. To reserve your seat, send an e-mail message to info@ thirdcoastfestival.org.

Unshackled!
1458 South Canal Street (at 14th Place)
(312) 492–9410
www.unshackled.org

Since 1950 the Pacific Garden Mission has been churning out these radio melodramas (broadcast locally on WMBI, 90.1 FM) about lives changed by Jesus Christ. And they've changed the format little since then. Old-fashioned

Wait! What About "Wait Wait"?

Yes, Wait Wait . . . Don't Tell Me! the hit National Public Radio news quiz funny heard on Chicago Public Radio, WBEZ 91.5 FM, is recorded before a live audience at the Chase Bank Auditorium right here in Chicago. Tapings last from 7:30 to 9:30 p.m. many Thursday nights throughout the year. Chicago Public Radio uses volunteer ushers for the show and other special radio events, such as very occasional tapings before live Chicago audiences of its other big hit, This American Life. But don't call the station asking to reserve your volunteer ushering post to see a show for free. These spots go to the station's most dedicated volunteers. If you'd like to become one of them, go to WBEZ's Web site at www.chicago publicradio.org. There you'll find information about volunteering for pledge drives and other events. If you prove yourself worthy, you'll get to volunteer for a live show and see it for free, but probably only after you've done your share of 5:00 a.m. pledge-drive shifts. If not, you can just pony up for the ticket price ($21.99 for Wait Wait), which helps support Chicago Public Radio too. For more information about any Chicago Public Radio show, check out its Web site at www.chicagopublicradio.org.

soap opera organ music still accompanies the stories of modern vices being exchanged for inner peace. Tapings take place before a live audience that is separated by soundproof glass from the actors, organist, and sound-effects technicians. The weekly Saturday tapings start at 4:30 p.m. The organizers ask that you arrive early and welcome you to stay late for a full day of activities. A tour of the Pacific Garden Mission, including dorms for formerly homeless residents, a clinic, classrooms, and dining facilities, starts at 3:00 p.m. Free dinner and fellowship with staff and "mission converts" starts in the dining room at 5:30 p.m. At 6:30 p.m. a praise and testimony service includes group singing, special music, and testimonies of people whose stories may serve as good fodder for future *Unshackled!* episodes. Reservations are recommended, especially for groups of eight or more.

Vocalo

89.5 FM
848 West Grand Avenue (on Navy Pier)
(312) 893–2956
www.vocalo.org

I list the Web site for Vocalo first because this new-media venture of Chicago Public Radio set out to be more of a Web site with a radio station than a radio station with a Web site. From 7:00 a.m. to 7:00 p.m. Monday through Friday, Vocalo hosts present topical, musical, conversational, quizzical content streaming on Vocalo's Web site and broadcast in Chicago and Northwest Indiana at 89.5 on your FM dial. The rest of the time, the station's vast library is set to a computerized shuffle, which generates quite the eclectic mix. Vocalo encourages the masses to contribute their own original content to its Web site. Not sure how to do that? Attend one of Vocalo's Open Studio Nights the first Tuesday of every month at 6:00 p.m. Producers will be available to help you hone your new media craft.

COMEDY:
CHEAP JOKES

*"This morning, shortly after eleven o'clock,
comedy struck this little house in Dibbley—
sudden, violent comedy."*
—MONTY PYTHON

The city that brought the world Second City and the Blues Brothers is on a mission from God to make you laugh. You can spend big bucks for your yucks, or you can laugh all the way to the bank by sticking to free shows throughout the week. The gigs feature stand-up comics honing their chops, sketch and improv troupes in training programs, and funny people with all sorts of day jobs they don't want to quit. Their comedy ranges from hilarious to painful, but at least when it's painful, you're not paying for the torture. Venues range from smoky bars just for grown-ups to cultural centers and lecture halls fine for the whole family.

Angelo's Taverna
1612 North Sedgwick Street (at West North Avenue)
(312) 397–1900
www.angelostaverna.com

This Old Town bar hosts open mike, stand-up, and sketch comedy on Tuesdays at 10:00 p.m.

Diversey River Bowl
2211 West Diversey Avenue (at West Logan Boulevard)
(773) 227–5800
www.drbowl.com

The world's rockin-est bowling alley brings you open-mike stand-up comedy on Mondays starting at 8:00 p.m.

Globe Pub
1934 West Irving Park Road (between North Damen Avenue and North Wolcott Avenue)
(773) 871–3757
www.theglobepub.com

Cristiano Ronaldo and a duck walk into a bar... To hear the punch line, stop by this World's Best Soccer Bar for its open mike every Monday except the first Monday of the month. The show starts at 9:00 p.m.

Hog Head McDunna's
1505 West Fullerton Avenue (at North Greenview Avenue)
(773) 929–0944
http://mcdunnas.com

With a name like Hog Head, you learn early to be funny, for self-defense. Some of the amateurs at this open mike are just that. Others most definitely are not. It's held Wednesday starting at 9:30 p.m.

iO Theater
3541 North Clark Street (at West Eddy Street)
(773) 880–0199
http://chicago.ioimprov.com

Every Wednesday at 8:00 p.m., this improv theater gives Chicago a taste of free sketch comedy, hoping we'll come back for more. The show is held in the Cabaret Theater.

Jake Melnick's Corner
41 East Superior Street (at North Wabash Avenue)
(312) 266–0400

Sign up at 9:00 p.m. on Tuesdays to join Jake's open mike. Or show up at 10:00 p.m. just to laugh.

O'Shaughnessy's Pub
4557 North Ravenswood Avenue
(773) 944–9896
www.healthyorhearty.com

This Irish bar serves up open-mike comedy on Mondays starting at 9:30 p.m., free trivia games on Tuesdays at 8:00 p.m., and traditional Irish music on Wednesdays starting at 8:00 p.m. The place has free Wi-Fi too.

Phyllis' Musical Inn
1800 West Division Street
(773) 486–9862

Join the Phyllistine's open mike on Tuesdays from 7:30 to 9:30 p.m. Show up at 7:00 p.m. if you want to join in the act, which is mostly comedy with a bit of music.

Pressure Comedy Café
6318 North Clark Street (at West Highland Avenue)
(773) 743–7665
www.pressurebilliards.com

This no-pressure billiards joint hosts occasional no-cover bands and, on Fridays, features stand-up and improv comedy starting at 8:30 p.m.

Schubas Tavern
3159 North Southport Avenue
(773) 525–2508
www.schubas.com

Your Sunday Best open mike runs Sundays starting at 9:00 p.m. You must be twenty-one to enter.

Second City
1616 North Wells Street (at West North Avenue)
Second City e.t.c.
1608 North Wells Street (at West North Avenue)
(312) 337–3992
www.secondcity.com

The institution started with some University of Chicago smart alecks and has been sending great sketch comics on to *Saturday Night Live* and other forms of fame and fortune ever since. It offers free improv sets after the last regular performances on its main stage and its e.t.c. second stage every night except Friday.

Town Hall Pub
3340 North Halsted Street (at West Buckingham Place)
(773) 472–4405
www.myspace.com/townhallpub

Stand-up and improv comedy are part of a mix of live entertainment here on Sundays at 8:30 p.m. Mondays mellow out with an acoustic music open mike at 10:30 p.m.

U.S. Beer Company
1801 North Clybourn Avenue (at West Willow Street)
(773) 871–7799
www.usbeercompany.com

Check out the calendar of events for special events.

DANCE:
FREE EXPRESSION

*"Dance first. Think later.
It's the natural order."*
—SAMUEL BECKETT

Sure, we may be one of the chubbiest cities in the United States, but we're remarkably agile dancers. You can watch your fellow Chicagoans groove on free dance floors, in a broad range of styles, all over the city, all year-round. And if you'd like to learn the moves to join them, talented teachers offer free lessons too. Chicago also hosts several world-class hometown and visiting professional dance companies that perform amazing and beautiful feats with their bodies. They dance at architectural marvels designed just for dance, humble grade-school auditoriums, and even el platforms.

DOING **AND** WATCHING

Chicago Cultural Center
78 East Washington Street (at North Michigan Avenue)
Wheelchair access at 77 East Randolph Street
(312) 744–6630 / TTY: (312) 744–2947
www.chicagoculturalcenter.org

The Chicago Cultural Center's diverse activities, many of which are free, include dance classes and performances to watch and join.

Chicago SummerDance
Spirit of Music Garden, Grant Park
601 South Michigan Avenue (between East Harrison Street and East Balbo Drive)
SummerDance hotline: (312) 742–4007
www.chicagosummerdance.org

SummerDance shakes Chicago's collective booty for eleven weeks every summer with a free outdoor dance and music festival. Weather permitting, the hoedown goes down on a big outdoor dance floor every Thursday through Saturday evening from 6:00 to 9:30 p.m. and on Sunday from 4:00 to 7:00 p.m. The first hour of each evening is occupied by a free lesson in whatever dance styles will complement the music that night. The rest of the time, neophytes and pros, kids and adults, groove to live music du jour by local and visiting bands. Latin, ballroom, Latin ballroom, salsa, big band, big band salsa, Cajun, zydeco, R&B, soul, funk, jazz, swing, country, African, Latvian, Irish, and square dancing are just part of the world-beat mix.

Chicago SummerDance in the Parks

Chicago SummerDance at Navy Pier
SummerDance hotline: (312) 742-4007
www.chicagosummerdance.org

If you're in the mood for summer music but don't want to drag yourself to South Michigan Avenue, you're in luck. SummerDance has expanded to additional events at Navy Pier (600 East Grand Avenue at North Lake Shore Drive) and several neighborhood parks, including:
Athletic Field Park, 3546 West Addison Street (at North Drake Avenue)
Humboldt Park, 1440 North Sacramento Avenue (between West North Avenue, West Division Street, North California Avenue and North Kedzie Avenue)
Jackson Park 63rd Street Beach, 6300 Sourh Lake Shore Drive
Washington Park, 5531 South Martin Luther King Drive (at East Garfield Boulevard)
Check the Web site or hotline for event dates and times.

JUST **WATCHING**

Chicago Public Library

(312) 747–4300
www.chipublib.org

The library shakes it, too, providing free dance performances by the likes of Thodos Dance Chicago and Hubbard Street Dance 2. Some will cost you, but most are free. To see what's happening at the Harold Washington or your local branch, check the library's monthly calendar, available online or in paper form, or watch local newspaper listings.

Harold Washington Library Cindy Pritzker Auditorium
400 South Michigan Avenue (Plymouth Court entrance at Congress Parkway)
(312) 747–4300
www.chipublib.org

The Chicago Public Library is about a lot more than books. Harold Washington Library's theater space regularly hosts plays, lectures, concerts, and dance performances by local and traveling companies.

Harris Theater for Music and Dance
205 East Randolph Drive (in Millennium Park between North Michigan Avenue and North Columbus Drive)
(312) 334–7777
www.harristheaterchicago.org

This huge new venue in Millennium Park hosts such dance companies as Hubbard Street Dance Chicago, the Mexican Dance Ensemble, River North Chicago Dance Company, and other hometown and visiting companies. The Saints (see page 9) coordinate ushers for some performances.

Links Hall
3435 North Sheffield Avenue (at North Clark Street and West Newport Avenue)
(773) 281–0824
www.linkshall.org
info@linkshall.org

This venue rents its space to a lot of fine performers and companies, including dancers. It welcomes volunteers for ushering, office work, bulk-mailing pizza parties, cleaning, and general office work, and it lets those volunteers see performances for free.

SO **YOU** WANT **TO** BE **A** DANCER?
WORK-STUDY PROGRAMS

Chicago Human Rhythm Project
2936 North Southport Avenue (at West Oakdale Avenue)
(773) 281–1825
www.chicagotap.org

The Chicago Human Rhythm Project school of tap and other percussive dance offers ten to fifteen full scholarships each year, valued at more than $15,000.

Lou Conte Dance Studio
of Hubbard Street Dance Chicago
1147 West Jackson Boulevard (312) 850–9766
www.hubbardstreetdance.com

The Catch Work-study students exchange ten hours per week of front-desk work in exchange for unlimited classes. Space is very limited.

The dance school of Chicago's venerable Hubbard Street Dance company offers basic through advanced dance classes in its Lou Conte Dance Studio. Scholarships and work-study arrangements are available.

The Old Town School of Folk Music
www.oldtownschool.org
4544 North Lincoln Avenue (between West Wilson Avenue and West Sunnyside Avenue)
909 West Armitage Avenue (between North Fremont Street and North Russell Street)
(773) 728–6000

Volunteer for the Old Town School to earn points toward free performances and classes. One point equals $4. They may ask for help with a variety of tasks. Ushering the average concert earns three points.

FOOD:
ON THE HOUSE

"I warn you, Jedediah, you're not going to like it in Chicago. The wind comes howling in off the lake, and gosh knows if they ever heard of lobster Newburg."
—ORSON WELLES IN *CITIZEN KANE*

Chicago's a big eating town. With so many ethnicities represented here and more arriving every day, you can consume the cuisines of almost every corner of the world. From a filling selection of gourmet grocery-store samples, to yer basic bar wings and "sossages" (that's Chicagoan for sausages, my new-to-town friend), you can eat your way around much of the city for free. So put on your expandable eatin' pants and bring your appetite out on the town for a great, cheap taste of Chicago. And if you'd rather grow than buy your food, Chicago has a growing community of urban farmers who want to help you learn to do just that. See the end of this chapter as well as the gardening chapter, beginning on page 229.

HAPPY **HOURS** AND **BUFFETS**

I know what you're thinking: There are only so many free buffalo wings and pizza slices a person can eat. Yes, this chapter includes plenty of those happy hour staples, but only yummy ones. And it includes a variety of other foods served from weekend brunch through the wee hours of weeknights. Some establishments toss in some entertainment to make the happy hour crowd even happier. Most explicitly or implicitly require you to buy at least one drink, but your server usually doesn't mind if you order something cheap. Whatever beverage you buy, don't be too greedy. One bar owner says she spent $500 on a weekly spread only to see some jerks sneak in their own drinks and eat so much that latecomers missed out. And always remember to tip generously. Your bartenders, cooks, and servers need to pay their bills too. While the establishments included here have well-established free-food traditions, things change, so call before you show up with an empty stomach.

DOWNTOWN

Brasserie Jo
59 West Hubbard Street (between North Dearborn Street and North Clark Street)
(312) 595–0800
www.brasseriejo.com

Oh, this ain't just pizza, my friend. These are tart flambé, little Alsatian thin-crust aperitifs topped with fatty French goodness like bacon and bacon-fat-sautéed onions. Servers pass them around the bar area on trays starting at 5:00 p.m. every Tuesday.

NORTH SIDE

Big Chicks
5024 North Sheridan Road (between West Argyle Street and West Carmen Avenue)
(773) 728–5511
www.bigchicks.com

Being a big chick myself, I've always loved this straight-friendly but mostly gay and lesbian neighborhood bar with free pool and darts. So do a lot of other people, and the place gets crowded on weekends. The free Sunday-afternoon buffets feel like dinner with a happy family. Buffets are full meals, including salads of fancy mixed greens, Italian beef sandwiches with giardinara, pasta salad, and desserts such as raspberry brownies or apple crumble. You're sort of expected to buy a $2.50 vodka lemonade or other drink, but no one really seems to care if you don't. They usually set out the spread sometime between 3:00 and 4:00 p.m.

Boston Blackies
120 South Riverside Plaza (at West Monroe Street)
(312) 382–0700
www.bostonblackies.com

Lose your highly paid job in the Financial District? Come bail yourself out of hunger at this most generous bar and restaurant near the river. A skilled carver will pile the meat as high as a modestly sized dinner roll can handle. Of course, you should toss a little of your misdirected TARP funds in the carver's tip jar. The place is usually noisy and crowded, but a back room and outdoor seating during warm weather provide space to chat with coworkers.

Celtic Crown
4301 North Western Avenue (at West Cullom Avenue)
(773) 588–1110
www.celticcrownpub.com

This hearty British Isles fun zone offers free wings on Tuesday from 4:00 to 7:00 p.m. and Friday from 3:00 to 6:00 p.m., accompanied by good-size pitchers of beer for $3. Stay for free Bingo on Fridays starting at 7:00 p.m., karaoke Saturday at 10:00 p.m., and trivia Wednesday at 7:00 p.m. The $2 burgers on Monday are worth a trip, too.

Chicago Sports Bar and Grill
223 West Jackson Boulevard (at South Franklin Street)
(312) 427–2856

Nothing cheers up a drink-to-the-downsized outing like free food, and this unassuming sports bar in the basement of 223 West Jackson has plenty. Fare such as quesadillas, fried macaroni and cheese, and raw vegetable sticks should please a wide variety of coworker tastes. The drinks are cheap, and the music and conversation are usually quiet enough to allow real conversations—unless the karaoke flares up.

Clybar
2417 North Clybourn Avenue (at North Marshfield Avenue)
(773) 388–1877
www.clybar.com

This chummy little lounge serves pizza from 5:00 to 8:00 p.m. on Friday. Free TV too.

Frank's
2503 North Clark Street (at West St. James Place)
(773) 549–2700

This neighborhood bar is often crowded, but that's because people love it. Your friendly hosts put out free buffets for many big sporting events, such as Bears games, the Super Bowl, and March Madness basketball. And they celebrate holidays with such free fare as corned beef and cabbage on St. Patrick's Day and Cajun food on Fat Tuesday.

The Full Shilling Public House
3724 North Clark Street (between West Waveland Avenue and West Grace Street)
(773) 248–3330
www.fullshillingpub.com

This Irish pub a foul ball's distance from Wrigley Field offers wings most Fridays from 5:00 to 7:00 p.m. When the Cubs play at home, buy a beer and they'll toss in a free hot dog, starting one hour before and ending one hour after the game.

McGee's Tavern & Grille
950 West Webster Avenue (between North Sheffield Avenue and North Bissell Street)
(773) 549–8200
www.mcgeestavern.com

Madness ensues every Friday at midnight in this DePaul University bar when the staff brings out free pizza. Check out euchre tournaments on Mondays and live music on Thursdays with no cover before 7:00 p.m.

Sedgwick's Bar & Grill
1935 North Sedgwick Street (between West Armitage Avenue and West Wisconsin Street)
(312) 337–7900
www.sedgwickschicago.com

Soccer and rugby fans rejoice! Sedgwick's broadcasts European soccer and international rugby games in this sporty paradise. It also shows a lot of American sports, especially Iowa football and Duke basketball. To ward off the chance of European jet lag, Sedgwick's sets out a buffet on Friday starting around 11:00 p.m. and on Saturday starting around midnight. Fare includes such appetizers as pizza, wings, quesadillas, meatballs, and macaroni and cheese.

Will's Northwoods Inn
3030 North Racine Avenue (at West Nelson Street)
(773) 528–4400
www.willsnorthwoodsinn.com

Calling all Cheeseheads! Step into this bar and grill and you'll think you're in the deep woods of Wisconsin. This "official" University of Wisconsin alumni bar shows Wisconsin Badgers and Green Bay Packers football games. Free buffets during games include cheese curds, beer-soaked brats (of course), hot dogs, hamburgers, and other tailgate staples, often accompanied by raffles at halftimes. In late September or early October, Leinenkugel's Brewing Company sponsors Musky Fest, a one-day street festival with live bands, food, and fun to celebrate all things Wisconsin.

WEST SIDE

The California Clipper
1002 North California Avenue (at West Augusta Boulevard)
(773) 384–2547
www.californiaclipper.com

This delightfully frumpy fun bar hosts a number of free events throughout the week, but for now, let's focus on the pizza. The Clipper's Bingo nights include prizes and free pizza most Mondays starting around 9:30 p.m.

Cleos
1935 West Chicago Avenue (at North Winchester Avenue)
(312) 243–5600
www.cleoschicago.com

Just when late night hipsters at this bar and restaurant realize they've got the Saturday-night munchies from a night of DJ-spun music, Cleos is there to help. The staff sets out a buffet of appetizers, such as potato skins, hand-made pizzas, and quesadillas, from 11:00 p.m. to 1:00 a.m.

A Week of Fine Dining

If you're like me, you splurge for a meal at a high-end restaurant once or twice a year, if that. Or, if you're like me, you order appetizers at said fancy joint rather than a main course or multiple courses. (Hey, I still tip the server well, and so should you!) Now, once a year, you have the chance to enjoy a full lunch or dinner at some of Chicago's fanciest food joints for what you'd normally pay for a single entree. Look for Chicago Restaurant Week, in late February, just when we need late-winter comfort food the most. In the second year of the annual event, about 130 Chicago-area restaurants offered $22 prix-fixe three-course lunches, $32 prix-fixed three-course dinners (excluding beverages, tax, and gratuity), or both. The Chicago Convention & Tourism Bureau organizes Restaurant Week and offers information about the event, including links to participating restaurants, at http://www.choosechicago.com/EATITUP/Pages/default2.aspx. Some restaurants extend the deals beyond the official week.

The Map Room
1949 North Hoyne Avenue (at West Armitage Avenue)
(773) 252–7636
www.maproom.com

The Catch A two-drink minimum is strictly enforced on Tuesday's International Nights. When you enter, you're given a ticket that the bartender stamps when you order a drink. Once it has been stamped twice, you're welcome to a free plate of food.

Nothing sets my heart a flutter quite like the phrase "complimentary meats and cheeses." That's what you'll find on Monday nights here, and the free food keeps coming as the week rolls on. On weekends at around 12:30 p.m., stop by for free barbecue, coleslaw, and potato salad, accompanied by $5 Bloody Marys, Virgin Marys, or mimosas. Hearty first helpings of food, but seconds politely turned away. There's a great international beer selection too. On Tuesday's International Nights, chefs from local restaurants provide free servings of their home countries' cuisines. The bar's travel theme, including a decor of maps, flags, and back issues of *National Geographic* and *Condé Nast,* make it the perfect hangout for travel addicts and those who love them.

Brain Food
Jane Addams Hull House Museum
800 South Halsted Street (between West Harrison Street and West Roosevelt Road)
(312) 413–5353
www.uic.edu/jaddams/hull
Hours: Tuesday through Friday, 10:00 a.m. to 4:00 p.m.; Sunday, noon to 4:00 p.m. Closed Mondays, Saturdays, and during holidays and many semester breaks when the University of Illinois is closed.

This remaining building of the original Hull House complex celebrates Jane Addams's pioneering work in creating community-based programs and political pressure to address a host of social ills, such as crushing poverty, xenophobia, and child labor. Addams and her colleagues founded the Hull House settlement house in 1889, and she lived and worked in its complex of buildings until her death in 1935. Hull House's Re-Thinking Soup lecture series, every Tuesday from noon to 1:30 p.m. covers topics related to the politics of food and includes free soup. Donations are welcome.

FREE **SAMPLES:** A **SAMPLING**

Blommer Chocolate Store
600 West Kinzie Street (at North Jefferson Street)
(312) 492–1336
www.blommerstore.com

You'll smell the Blommer Chocolate Factory long before you see it. The facility wafts choc-o-rific fumes into the surrounding neighborhood year-round. Inside the store, at the northwest corner of the building, you'll find delights such as chocolate-dipped pretzel sticks, peanut butter cups, chocolate tattoo kits, lots of varieties of dark, milk, and white chocolate, and lots and lots of samples.

Bronzeville Community Market
Cottage Grove Avenue and 44th Street
http://www.qcdc.org

Vendors at this new farmers' market occasionally offer free samples of their locally grown and fair-trade products, but food is only part of the free fun. Catch free live music by local musicians. The first year's market included a wellness area that featured a chiropractor and health screenings by a local medical facility. The market runs Saturdays from June through October. Check the Web site of the Quad Communities Development Corporation (above), which organizes the market, for updates and news of the market.

Fox & Obel
401 East Illinois Street (at North McClurg Court)
(312) 410–7301
www.fox-obel.com

This delectable gourmet grocery has everything a food and drink connoisseur could ask for, including free samples of fine cheeses, breads, meats, and produce throughout the store. Wash it down in the wine and spirits department every Thursday and Friday evening from 5:00 to 8:00 p.m. and Saturday afternoon from 2:00 to 5:00 p.m. Winemakers and producers are on hand to explain the special characteristics of various vintages.

How to Eat a Pushcart Tamale

Chicago's Mexican and Guatemalan tamale vendors have asked me to relay this public service announcement to all Chicagoans who tried tamales once but thought they didn't like them because they were "too tough and stringy to chew": You don't eat the corn husk, honey. It serves as a biodegradable wrapper for steamed-to-perfection masa dough and whatever meat, chile, or cheese surprises are tucked inside. Tamale vendors have popped into some of my favorite no-cover music bars right at the point in the evening when cheap bastard patrons realize their hankerings for some steaming hot, muy sabrosa cuisine. You'll also find vendors with carts of tamales, elotes (steamed sweet corn on a stick), mangoes, and other south-of-the-border delicacies on street corners, in parks, and outside thrift stores in neighborhoods that have large enough populations of thrifty connoisseurs to fund a business. For a dollar an item (less if you buy half a dozen tamales), you've got a fast-food meal better than anything you'll find at Taco Bell.

Most tamale and elote vendors are unlicensed by the city health department. But by following the common-sense rule of avoiding pushcart mayonnaise (go with Parmesan on the corn instead, and hot chili powder if you're feeling sassy), I've enjoyed many a street-corner meal for years now with nary a digestive complaint.

Godiva Chocolatier Boutiques

www.godiva.com
10 South LaSalle Street (at West Madison Street); (312) 855–1588
Water Tower Place, 845 North Michigan Avenue (between East Pearson Street and East Chestnut Street); (312) 280–1133

The boutique stores of gourmet chocolate diva Godiva Chocolatier regularly offer free samples to weekend shoppers. Check out their Web site to see what sample promotions are coming up.

Green Grocer

1402 West Grand Avenue (at North Noble Street)
(312) 624–9508
www.greengrocerchicago.com

If you prefer food with a low carbon footprint, stop by this shop to sample organic delectables, most of which come from midwestern farmers and food producers. Check the store's Web site for information about free food-related classes, lectures, and other events.

Trader Joe's

www.traderjoes.com
40 East Ontario Street (between North Rush Street and North Wabash Avenue); (312) 951–6369
1840 North Clybourn Avenue (between West Wisconsin Street and West Willow Street), second floor; (312) 274–9733
3745 North Lincoln Avenue (between West Grace Street and West Waveland Avenue); (773) 248–4920

Joe's attended sample stations give sampling at these stores the distinct feeling of one's days as a cheap little bastard, when one wondered how

Urban Chickens (and Bees)

A growing number of Chicagoans are relearning the old practice of keeping chickens in their backyards. Some, particularly in some Chicago Hispanic communities, have been keeping chickens for years. Unfortunately, there have been a few—ahem—ruffled feathers between urban chicken activists and some baffled city aldermen. Count me in the camp of those who argue that Chicago has no ordinance saying you can't keep chickens in your backyard and never should. Just don't keep a rooster. Then we've got issues, and I've got rooster soup, dear neighbor. Want to learn how to keep pets that contribute to the household with free eggs? Check out these local organizations, Web sites, and blogs:

Angelic Organics Learning Center; 6400 South Kimbark Avenue (inside church at East 64th Street); (773) 288–5462; www.csalearning center.org. Midwest organic grower Angelic Organics provides classes and helps organize community gardens and other initiatives for better urban food from this center in Woodlawn. Classes include all aspects of urban farming, from growing vegetables in gardens and on rooftops to keeping chickens and bees. Most classes cost around $30, but you can earn back your learning costs in free food.

BackyardChickens.com and www.urbanchickens.net: Both of these sites provide how-to tips and news from chicken-dwelling cities around North America.

Chicago Food Policy Advisory Council; 2215 West North Avenue; (773) 486–6005; www.chicagofoodpolicy.org

many little cups of freebies one could consume before the sample maven cocked an eyebrow or Mom dragged one away. Sunday sample noshes include such items as fettuccine Alfredo or sausage slices, washed down by swigs of organic juices or spritzers.

Whole Foods Market

www.wholefoodsmarket.com

30 West Huron Street (between North Dearborn Street and North State Street); (312) 932–9600

1000 West North Avenue (at North Sheffield Avenue); (312) 587–0648

1101 South Canal Street (between West Taylor Street and West Roosevelt Road); (312) 435–4600

3300 North Ashland Avenue (at West School Street); (773) 244–4200

3640 North Halsted Street (at West Addison Street); (773) 472–0400

6020 North Cicero Avenue (at West Peterson Avenue); (773) 205–1100

Whole Foods Market is a great stop for organic and gourmet treats on any given weekend afternoon. Samples are located at departments throughout the store, including meats and seafood, cheeses and crackers, hummus and pita, baked desserts, and fresh fruit. Upon request, Whole Foods will place items you purchase in free blue recycling bags at checkout. They're printed with information about how to use them for Chicago's official blue bag recycling program.

WINE TASTINGS:
CHEAP DRUNK

"I'm going to St. Petersburg, Florida, tomorrow. Let the worthy citizens of Chicago get their liquor the best they can. I'm sick of the job. It's a thankless one and full of grief."
—AL CAPONE

There's a heckuva lot of free wine flowing in Chicago. You'll find the fruit of the vine at opening receptions for art galleries (see the Art Galleries chapter) and, of course, at wine and liquor stores. Some even throw in free nibbles to cleanse the palate between sips. The point is to make events and venues more welcoming, guests more relaxed, art more beautiful, and, yes, patrons more likely to buy. Don't just brush off the store staff or wine distributors' representatives if they try to explain the special characteristics of the sample you're trying. Not all, but many, are knowledgeable folks who know their stuff and can provide you with a bit of free smarts to take home, whether or not you decide to buy a bottle to go with it.

Artisan Cellar

222 Merchandise Mart Plaza (inside Merchandise Mart at 350 North Orleans Street), main floor, suite 116
(312) 527–5810

This little store of big wines, cheeses, and other gourmet treats offers free tastings of wine, usually paired with cheese and crackers, on Friday from about 4:00 to 6:00 p.m. A wine representative pours samples and explains their salable qualities, but there's no pressure to buy.

Binny's Beverage Depot

www.binnys.com
213 West Grand Avenue (at North Wells Street); (312) 332–0012
1531 East 53rd Street (in Hyde Park Bank building west of South Lake Park Avenue); (773) 324–5000
3000 North Clark Street (at West Wellington Avenue); (773) 935–9400

This Chicagoland institution offers free tastings sometimes, though not with the regularity of its competitors.

Fine Wine Brokers

4621 North Lincoln Avenue (at West Eastwood Avenue)
(773) 989–8166
www.fwbchicago.com

This fine Lincoln Square shop hosts free tastings every Saturday from 1:00 to 4:00 p.m.

Fox & Obel

401 East Illinois Street (at North McClurg Court)
(312) 410–7301
www.fox-obel.com

This gourmet food store hosts free wine tastings on Saturday from 2:00 to 5:00 p.m. Representatives of wine companies pour samples and explain their finer qualities, but there's no pressure to buy. The store also sets out free little yummies in other departments.

In Fine Spirits

5418 North Clark Street (between West Rascher Avenue and West Balmoral Avenue)
(773) 506–9463
www.infinespirits.com

This wineshop and school offers free wine tastings two Saturdays per month from 3:00 to 6:00 p.m.

Just Grapes

560 West Washington Boulevard (at North Clinton Street)
(312) 627–9463
www.justgrapes.net

This West Loop wineshop, educational center, and tasting bar offers free tastes Saturdays from 2:00 to 4:00 p.m.

Pastoral

53 East Lake Street (between North Garland Court and North Wabash Avenue); (312) 658–1250
2945 North Broadway (near West Wellington Avenue); (773) 472–4781
www.pastoralartisan.com

Watch the Web site of these wine, cheese, and gourmet-sundry shops for free wine-tasting events.

Randolph Wine Cellars

1415 West Randolph Street (at North Ogden Avenue)
(312) 942–1212
www.tlcwine.com

This wineshop, school, and tasting room has thousands of wines, many of which are affordable even for cheap bastards. The free themed tastings are on Saturday between noon and 6:00 p.m.

Sam's Wine & Spirits

1720 North Marcey Street (west of North Clybourn Avenue, between West Wisconsin Street and West Willow Street)
(312) 664–4394
www.samswine.com

You'll find free samples at Sam's on most Thursdays and Fridays from 4:00 to 7:00 p.m. and most Saturdays and Sundays from 1:00 to 4:00 p.m. If you get a free preferred-customer card, once a month you can attend a special wine tasting with experts on hand to explain those tastes.

Taste Food & Wine

[li1506 West Jarvis Avenue (at North Greenview Avenue)
(773) 761–3663
www.tastefoodandwine.com

This Rogers Park purveyor sells gourmet meats, cheeses, snacks, condiments, sweets, and wines. Come sample free tastes of the wine on Mondays and Fridays from 6:00 to 7:30 p.m.

Todd's Wine

1616 North Damen Avenue (north of West North Avenue)
(773) 489–0373
www.toddswine.com

On weekends, at no specific times, this Wicker Park/Bucktown shop shares some of its finest wine samples with patrons.

Wine Discount Center

1826 North Elston Avenue (south of West Cortland Street)
(773) 489–3454
www.winediscountcenter.com

Every Saturday from noon to 4:00 p.m. the shop uncorks some of its favorites to share for free.

HAIR, BEAUTY, AND MASSAGE:
FREESTYLE

*"I'm tired of all this nonsense about beauty
being only skin-deep. That's deep enough.
What do you want, an adorable pancreas?"*
—JEAN KERR

Even cheap bastards can afford to stay well-groomed and nicely kneaded in Chicago. For the cost of a tip to half of the usual cost, you can help supervised budding stylists perfect their snipping skills and student massage therapists practice their muscle-rubbing techniques. Once you're relaxed and well-groomed, you can get a free makeover at department-store cosmetics counters. Some stores will even send you home with free samples. Voila! You're ready for your close-up, Mr. DeMille. Or, more importantly, your cheap date.

HAIR **SALON** MODELS

Many of Chicago's finest salons run training programs for beauticians wanting to make it into the beauty big time. That's where you come in. Year-round, students of salon training centers need models on which to practice hair-styling techniques. Don't worry, they've graduated from beauty school but require more training for their new salon's high standards. Think of it as a stylist's master's degree program. Trainees are closely supervised by the salons' stylist-teachers. Some haircuts, colorings, and other treatments are completely free, and sometimes there's a charge for treatment products. Students frequently post ads seeking models (you) on such free web sites and in such free publications as craigslist (http://chicago.craigslist.org/), the Chicago Reader (www.chicagoreader.com), and SalonApprentice.com (www.salonapprentice.com). Most salons will accept female or male models but require models to accept a style much different from their current do. Expect your appointment to last an hour or two as trainer and trainee stop occasionally to discuss the lessons your hair is teaching. Here are some high-end Chicago salons that regularly offer cuts from apprentices for little or no dough:

Don't Be *That* Cheap!
Sure, your free or very cheap haircut is helping a beautician in training fulfill requirements for a certificate or new job, but trainees need to eat too. If you can afford a little extra, be a nice cheap bastard and give the beauty-school scholar a nice tip.

Art + Science Salon
1552 North Milwaukee Avenue (at North Damen Avenue); (773) 227–4247; www.artandsciencesalon.com

C Salon
621 West Jackson Boulevard (between South Jefferson Street and North Desplaines Street); (312) 876–2660; www.csalon.net

Fringe Hair Salon
1437 North Milwaukee Avenue (at West Evergreen Avenue); (773) 862–1000; www.fringechicago.com

Gro Salon
2119 North Damen (at West Charleston Street); (773) 772–1153; www .grosalon.com

Johnathan Breitung Salon & Luxury Spa
3226 North Lincoln Avenue (at North Ashland Avenue); (773) 348–1800; www.johnathanbreitungsalon.com

Red 7 Salon
210 West Kinzie Street (at North Wells Street); (312) 644–RED7 (7337); www .red7salon.com

Salon Maxine
712 North Rush Street (at East Superior Street); (312) 751–1511; www .maxinesalon.com

Salon SOCA
1400 West Webster Avenue (at North Southport Avenue); (773) 244–0999; www.salonchicago.com

Sine Qua Non Salon
2766 North Lincoln Avenue (at North Racine Avenue); (773) 871–2280; http://sinequanonsalons.com

Studio 110 Salon
110 East Delaware Place (at North Michigan Avenue); (312) 337–6411; www .studio110salon.com

The Salon at Ulta

114 South State Street (at East Monroe Street); (312) 279–5081; http://stores.ulta.com/StateStreet

Tirra Salon and Spa

375 West Erie Street (West of North Orleans Street); (312) 951–8255; www.tirrasalon.com

BEAUTY **SCHOOLS**

At some point in their educational careers, beauty-school students must graduate from those freakish mannequin heads to the hair of real human beings. If you're willing to risk a small chance of a hairstyle mishap (and sign a release form to that effect), you can save some of your style budget while helping a student get the experience and class credit he or she needs to move toward certification. Students are supervised and eager to do a good job on your hair. As with professional stylists, the better you explain what style you want, the better chance you'll get something close to it.

The Catch All four schools charge fees for services performed by students.

Aveda Institute Chicago

2828 North Clark Street (north of West Diversey Parkway)
(773) 883–1560
www.avedainstitutechicago.com

Women, men, and children age six or older can enjoy Aveda's aromatherapeutic vibes at this school for expensive natural beauty. Bang or beard trims are $5. Cuts start at $14 during the week and $16 on Friday and Saturday. Colorings start at $25, and a stress-relieving scalp and neck massage with Aveda products is $10.

Cameo Beauty Academy

9714 South Cicero Avenue (at West 94th Street), Oak Lawn
(708) 636–4660
www.cameobeautyacademy.com

The Catch *They charge fees for services performed by students.*

In case you don't know how to wash your own hair, a student here will wash it for you for a buck. Rates go up from there. Haircuts start at $6.50, and colorings start at $20.00. Manicures start at $5.00. If you want to ask for a senior student you like, that will cost you another dollar.

Pivot Point Student Clinic
www.pivot-point.com
3901 West Irving Park Road (at North Springfield Avenue); (773) 463–3121
1560 Sherman Avenue (between Grove Street and Davis Street), 200a Annex, Evanston; (847) 905–5300

Pivot Point's student clinics try to emulate the complete spa experience with basic cuts at $7.50 for adults and $6.00 for kids, $9.00 manicures, $40.00 perms, and an array of waxing, buffing, wrapping, parafinning, and balancing treatments just like the big kids offer. A "Day of Beauty" package deal costs $50 for a color, cut, style, facial, manicure, and pedicure. Or you can go all out (for a cheap bastard) with the "Ultimate Indulgence" for $85. It gets you a body wrap; body relaxation treatment; and facial, lip, eye, and elbow treatment.

Tricoci University of Beauty
5321 North Harlem Avenue (at West Summerdale Avenue)
(773) 467–1900
www.triciouniversity.com

Hair, beauty, and spa treatments at this Norwood Park campus range from $3 for a bang trim to $45 for a foil color wrap.

FREE SAMPLES

Sephora
www.sephora.com
Northbridge Mall, 520 North Michigan Avenue (at East Grand Avenue), suite 129; (312) 494–9598

Hours: Monday through Saturday, 10:00 a.m. to 8:00 p.m.; Sunday, 11:00 a.m. to 6:00 p.m.
Water Tower Place, 845 North Michigan Avenue (between East Chestnut Street and East Pearson Street); (312) 335–9391
Hours: Monday through Friday, 10:00 a.m. to 9:00 p.m.; Saturday, 10:00 a.m. to 8:00 p.m.; Sunday, noon to 6:00 p.m.

With an overwhelming array of products by Sephora and other cosmetic lines, chances are this store has your perfect shade. This local outpost of the international beauty superstore chain offers free makeup consultation and application and free samples. That way, you can see how products work on your skin overnight or a couple of applications before laying out a bundle. Walk-ins or appointments are welcome.

Department Store Beauty Secrets

If you feel like you never really learned how to correctly apply concealer or always go home with the wrong shade of lipstick, stop by a makeup counter in a finer department store for a free makeover and beauty advice. Which counter to choose? For starters, if you like the makeup of the cosmetologists working there, it's more likely you'll like the way they apply it on you. It doesn't hurt to do a little research ahead of time on the best brands for your skin type and best prices for your budget on the off-chance you want to buy something. Here are some stately old Downtown stores that host several makeup line counters:

Bloomingdale's, 900 North Michigan Avenue (at East Delaware Place); (312) 440–4460

Macy's

111 North State Street (between East Randolph Street and East Washington Street); (312) 781–1000

Water Tower Place, 835 North Michigan Avenue (between East Chestnut Street and East Pearson Street); (312) 335–7700

Saks Fifth Avenue, Chicago Place Mall, 700 North Michigan Avenue (at East Huron Street); (312) 944–6500

MASSAGE **AND** MORE

Cortiva Professional and Student Massage Clinic
18 North Wabash Avenue (at East Madison Street)
(312) 753–7990
www.cortiva.com/locations/csmt/clinic/

The student clinic of the Cortiva Institute—Chicago (formerly the Chicago School of Massage Therapy) gives students a variety of aching muscles on which to practice. In return, those muscles pay $40 per one-hour, full-body, Swedish massage, about half what they'd pay a certified pro in Chicago.

Midwest College of Oriental Medicine
909 West Montrose Avenue, suite 201 (at North Hazel Street)
(773) 975–1295
www.acupuncture.edu/midwest

The Catch Patients pay for herbs.

The college's walk-in clinic offers free acupuncture treatments and advice about healing Chinese herbs. If the idea of students poking you with needles and suggesting you consume unfamiliar plants makes you a little nervous, relax. The college is accredited to provide bachelor of science and master of science degrees in nutrition and oriental medicine, the students are overseen by instructors, and the clinic has a physician on staff. If you show up without a referral from a doctor, the clinic's physician will give you a free intake screening.

The New School for Massage, Bodywork & Healing
800 North Wells Street (at West Chicago Avenue), suite 300
(312) 654–0900
www.newschoolmassage.com

Student therapeutic massages at this Old Town campus and clinic cost $35 for 55 minutes.

Pacific College of Oriental Medicine

3646 North Broadway (a block north of West Addison Street), second floor
(773) 477–4822
www.pacificcollege.edu

Treatments by interns and licensed professionals include acupuncture, massage, and herbal consultations and range from $8 with a first-month intern to $35 with an experienced intern.

Soma Institute

55 East Jackson Boulevard (at South Wabash Avenue)
(312) 939–2723
www.soma.edu

Students in the Student Teaching Clinic of this national school of clinical massage therapy provide a full, one-hour massage for $20.

REAL ESTATE:
THIS LAND IS YOUR LAND

*"Home is not where you live but where
they understand you."*
—CHRISTIAN MORGANSTERN

Chicago's housing and hotel markets aren't quite as expensive as those in big cities on the right and left coasts. But finding a truly affordable Chicago home to rent or own, or even a cheap bed for a quick visit, can be a challenge, even in a "down" market. The best way to find affordable housing is to avoid neighborhoods that real estate ads dub "hot." Like most trendy items, they'll generally cost you more. There are some decent housing prices here in off-the-radar communities that host essential businesses, parks and other life-enhancing amenities and are quick commutes from the action of more "fashionable" neighborhoods. Chicago is also home to families seeking live-in helpers and hostels for those just passing through. And for residents, public and private agencies offer classes, loans, and advice about buying your first home, fixing it up, and maintaining it. Let's check out your options for everything from a quick visit to putting down roots.

HOSTEL **HOSPITALITY**

Hostels have long been a staple of the world-trekking young backpacker set, but they're not just for twenty-somethings. Elders and families with kids (check age requirements) also enjoy great travel values at hostels around the world, and Chicago is no exception. Many hostels offer private rooms that can cost nearly as much as budget motel rooms, but their real value is shared dorm rooms, especially for solo travelers who don't have someone to split room costs. Most dorm accommodations cost at least half what an economy motel room in the same neighborhood would cost. Almost all hostels provide lockable lockers or safes for storing valuables and shared kitchen spaces, where guests can store and cook their own food. Some even throw in free coffee and tea or simple meals to make visitors feel at home. Free food or not, hostels are great places to meet friendly fellow travelers and get knowledgeable tourist advice too.

Arlington House International Hostel
616 West Arlington Place (1 block north of Fullerton Avenue near Clark Street)
(773) 929–5380 or (800) 467–8355
www.arlingtonhouse.com

Rates: Bed in dorm room (separate for male and female) is $33 ($35 summer) per night including tax for members of Rucksacker, AAIH, IYHF, and ISIC hostel networks; private room with no bathroom is $68; private room with semi-bathroom (toilet and sink but no shower) is $70; private room with complete bathroom including shower is $83. Private room rates are for up to two people. Add $15 extra per third or fourth person.

This hostel in upscale Lincoln Park is designed more for the young party crowd than for families with kids or travelers who want quiet digs. Alcohol is allowed, and so is smoking in designated rooms. Use their community computer for free Internet access or pay $4 for up to three days of wireless Internet access. There's a coin-operated laundry on-site, small security lockers, twenty-four-hour check-in, and no imposed quiet hours or curfew. Guests get over their Lincoln Park hangovers with free coffee in the community kitchen.

Chicago International Hostel
6318 North Winthrop Avenue (north of West Rosemont Avenue)
(773) 262–1011
www.hostelworld.com
info@hostelinchicago.com
Rates: Bed in dorm room (separate for male and female) is $25 with tax included. Private rooms are $40 to $81 with tax included, based on the number of beds.

This comfortable international hostel is a few blocks from the lake, near Loyola University, on the far North Side of Chicago. You must be at least sixteen years old to stay here, and no alcohol is permitted. There's no curfew, so check in anytime and come and go as you like. Bedding and towels are provided, along with lockers for storing valuables and free Wi-Fi Internet access. The shared kitchen beckons with free coffee every morning.

Hostelling International Chicago
24 East Congress Parkway (west of South Wabash Avenue)
(312) 360–0300
www.hichicago.org
Rates: A bunk bed in a dorm room is $32 to $38 plus tax per night ($3 less per night if you have a membership with Hostelling International: www .hihostels.com).

This hostelling hub of international education, culture, and fun offers guests free daily outings to local sites. Guests include everyone from families with kids, to single backpackers, to retirees enjoying their budget-travel golden years. You can come and go anytime day or night, 365 days a year, but the well-enforced quiet hours are from 11:00 p.m. to 7:00 a.m. Alcohol and Chicagoland residents (anyone living at a 606xx zip code) are not allowed.

> ## Gimme Shelter!
>
> If you're really down on your luck, please don't be too proud to accept a little kindness from strangers. Call the City of Chicago's free general services and information line, which is 311. An operator will help you find emergency shelter, food, medical or mental health care, and other services from government and private groups. If you can't get to a shelter on your own, ask for help with transportation too.

FOR **RENT**

You shouldn't need to pay a broker's fee to find a decent, affordable apartment in the Chicago area. Many free newspaper and online services list hundreds of apartments you can search by price, location, and amenities. Free services can help you find compatible people seeking roommates to share the rent and other household expenses. Agents of property-management companies will drive you around to see several apartments that meet your requirements for price, location, and amenities, but landlords pay for such services, not prospective tenants.

Most landlords expect a security deposit equal to a month's rent (sometimes two) in addition to the first month's rent before you move in. They should keep the security deposit in an escrow account that will earn interest while you occupy the apartment. If something in the apartment is damaged, missing, or unreasonably messy when you move out, the landlord may deduct part or all of the security deposit to fix the place up before mailing you a check for whatever's left. If the place is intact when you move out, the landlord must refund your security deposit plus the interest within forty-five days or face paying you extra. Many landlords and tenants on casual terms just use the security deposit (before interest) for the last month's rent.

Keeping Tabs on Utilities

The Citizens Utility Board is in your corner, fighting the Powers That Be against rate increases of natural gas, electricity. and other essential services for Chicago-area citizens. CUB also offers tips for greening up your utility use and online assessment tools for lowering your local and mobile-phone service fees. Check it out at www.citizens utilityboard.org.

To start searching for apartments and roommates, check these Web sites with extensive free, searchable listings.

Chicago Reader: This free weekly paper is distributed throughout the city on Thursday. Housing ads are also online at www.chicagoreader.com.

craigslist for Chicago: http://chicago.craigslist.org.

Free Voice Mail—No Home Required

Chicago Community Voice Mail, a local service of a national organization, provides a limited number of homeless people with personal telephone numbers linked to free private voice mail boxes. That way, prospective employers, landlords, and loved ones can reach you and need not know you're homeless. The service is arranged through more than sixty local social service agencies. To find out more, contact Inspiration Corporation at (773) 878–0981 or www.inspiration corporation.org/programs/voicemail.html, or stop by their offices at 4554 North Broadway (1/2 block east of Red Line el stop at Wilson Avenue). Inspiration Corporation provides a host of other services too, such as job training and help finding housing.

CITY **HELP** FOR **RENTERS** AND **OWNERS**

The city offers a plethora of programs to help renters and prospective home owners find apartments, condos, and houses they can better afford. It helps qualifying home owners and landlords keep their buildings in tip-top shape,

Home Economics Class

The City of Chicago offers a full schedule of free classes for renters, homeowners, homebuyers, and landlords. Check out your options at http://egov.cityofchicago.org (click the "Home & Property" link). You'll also find classes and tips offered by not-for-profit and private entities listed here:

Chicago Center for Green Technology, 445 North Sacramento Boulevard; (312) 746–9192; www.chicagoofchicago.org/Environment/GreenTech. You can learn a lot about eco-friendly living just by touring Chicago Center for Green Technology's building and grounds. The center also offers a variety of free classes and tips on its Web site related to greening up your home and garden.

Living Room Realty, 1530 West Superior Street (between Ashland Avenue and Armour Street); (312) 226–3020; www.livingroomrealty.com. This team of eco-certified real estate brokers hosts a variety of free lectures in their West Town gallery space and office. Topics range from property taxes to insulation to biophilic home and garden design.

Neighborhood Housing Services of Chicago, 1279 North Milwaukee Avenue, fifth floor, (773) 329–4010, www.nhschicago.org. Want to avoid winding up on the news explaining how you got the wrong mortgage for the wrong house and the wrong time? Neighborhood Housing Services has seen and heard plenty of tales of woe as part of their foreclosure prevention programs. If you're having trouble, give them a call. They also offer free classes for prospective home buyers, from budgeting and polishing up your credit to sealing the deal on the right house or condo. When you're ready to buy, Neighborhood Lending Services can help you through the process, even arranging "gap loans" with participating lenders.

seniors retrofit their homes for better accessibility, folks falling behind on mortgage payments to catch up, property owners facing skyrocketing taxes to find relief, and people with enough money learn how to save energy or renovate their bungalows. Don't assume you earn too much to qualify for rental or ownership programs. The median income requirements to qualify for some programs are surprisingly high. To find out more, contact the Chicago Department of Community Development at (312) 742–8400 / TTY: (312) 742–1564. Or go to http://egov.cityofchicago.org and click the "Home & Property" link to find the programs that best fit your needs. Chicago firefighters, police officers, and public-school teachers can also get breaks on listing prices and mortgages that will help them fulfill that pesky city-address requirement.

SITCOM **SIDEKICKS**

You, too, can live in an expensive Chicago-area home completely free while living out the plots of countless American sitcoms. Find a live-in job, become "the help," and have fun as the know-it-all butler who delivers witty one-liners, the nanny who gives the kids loving advice about how to deal with first crushes and bullies at their private grade schools, or the personal assistant who helps maintain the boss's tenuous grip on sanity while hilarity ensues. Or be the personal chef who helps your employer lose weight, for which she puts you on her talk show to declare you a dietary guru and promote your new cookbook.

Of course, real-life domestic employment is usually nothing like the TV version, but the free live-in part is real. The most common live-in job, especially for women, is as a nanny, but the busy affluent will pay for people to help with a variety of tasks, from deep daily cleaning and constant chauffeuring to keeping sleepy pets company and being caretakers for otherwise empty estates. Payment varies but ranges from free use of the house for caretakers and pet sitters to $250 to $800 net per week for child care. It all depends on your talents and background and the family's willingness and ability to pay. Some even throw in benefits for full-time staff. All should allow reasonable time off throughout the week as well as vacation time. Whatever live-in job you pursue, you'll have to undergo extensive background checks and sometimes additional child care or first-aid training. Screen potential employers as carefully as they screen you. Make sure all parties involved understand which tasks and times are your responsibilities and which are not, and don't settle for situations that seem overly demanding or dysfunctional.

An easy way to find families who need live-in staff is through placement agencies. Most will expect at least a one-year commitment from you, and the reputable ones will not charge you a fee for their job-matching services; those recruitment fees should be paid by the families. Here are a few local and national placement agencies to get you started.

A+ Domestic Agency, Inc., (773) 957–0500; www.looking4nanny.com. Local agency that places nannies and housekeepers.

Chicago Nannies Inc., (773) 720–5505; www.chicago nanniesinc.com. Local agency that places nannies only.

GoNannies.com, (866) 876–2973 or (972) 539–9909; www.gonannies.com. National agency that places nannies, governesses, housekeepers, chefs and cooks, elder caretakers, and personal assistants.

Robert Hanselman Domestic Agency, www.planetdomestics.com. National firm lists varieties of domestic jobs, information, and a chat room for domestic professionals to talk about the biz.

If you'd like to study part-time in the United States or just want to visit Chicago for the summer and would enjoy caring for kids in exchange for room, board, and a stipend, apply to be an au pair. It's a worldwide tradition that provides cross-cultural exchange between temporary nannies and families needing child care for a summer or longer. Your second language and foreign-to-us culture make you more attractive to families who want their kids to learn about the world outside the United States. Au pairs are usually female college-age students, but if you're a guy, I encourage you to try to break this discriminatory barrier and apply too. The pay is usually less than what long-term nannies earn, as the position is considered more an educational experience and travel opportunity for au pairs than a long-term career. The upside is that au pair agencies will help you arrange the appropriate temporary immigration status if you're not a U.S. citizen, and many will pay for or share your flight and other travel expenses. Here are a few national agencies that place au pairs with Chicago families.

GreatAupair, (775) 215-5770; www.greataupair.com. National agency that welcomes young men and women as au pairs.

Au Pair USA, www.aupairusa.org; (800) 287-2477 or (212) 924-0446.

Cultural Care Summer Au Pair, www.culturalcare.com; (800) 333-6056.

CHILDREN AND TEENS:
OLLI OLLI OXEN FREE

"The easiest way for your children to learn about money is for you not to have any."
—KATHERINE WHITEHORN

Chicago offers a wealth of free resources and fun for kids, both young Chicagoans and tourists. Sure, keeping the brood happy, healthy, housed, educated, and amused is always a challenge. But city, state, and private resources can help low-income parents meet kids' basic needs. And Chicago hosts a wealth of fun and enriching activities that are free for all kids and their families. Bring the bunch to free storytelling sessions, concerts, movies, museums, gardens, and zoos. Enroll them in free classes, after-school programs, and youth clubs. Take them to the park, pool, beach, gym, and libraries. The next thing you know, they'll be all grown up with fond memories of a happy, cheap-bastard Chicago childhood.

GOOD **START**

La Leche League
www.lllusa.org

It costs a suggested donation of $40 to join a local La Leche chapter, but think of all the money you'll save feeding your little sucker with milk you make with—get this—your very own body. Sounds crazy, I know, but it can be done. These educational and support groups promote breast feeding, teach new mothers how to do it right, and offer advice on any issues that might come up. They'll show you how to work one of those newfangled breast pumps, too, so Dad won't miss out on his turns at 3:00 a.m. feedings. Groups meet throughout Chicago. See the Web address for names and telephone numbers of group leaders.

Women, Infants, and Children Nutrition Program (WIC)
Toll-free information and clinic finder: (800) 323–4769 (Voice and TTY)
(Illinois information): www.dhs.state.il.us/page.aspx?item=30513
(Federal information): www.fns.usda.gov/wic

Lower-income pregnant or nursing mothers and children from infants through five years old can get the supplemental nutrition they need through the federal Women, Infants, and Children nutrition program. (Fathers and

Cheap Diapers

For cheapness, cloth diapers win the disposable versus cloth debate, bottoms down. A few dozen deluxe pinless-closure nappies, which can be washed and reused through several babies' pre-potty years, cost only a little more than a few dozen disposable diapers that can be used only once. You can find them at most stores that sell baby clothing and supplies. If you're worried about the health effects of cloth, consider this: According to the University of Chicago Comer Children's Hospital, cloth diapers pose no greater risk of diaper rash than do disposables. Parents tend to change cloth diapers more often than they change disposables, which is a good thing. And cloth-diaper kids tend to potty train sooner because they know when they're wet.

If you decide to go the cloth route, you'll also need reusable plastic diaper covers for baby to wear over the cloth diapers, and it's good to have a diaper pail where soiled diapers can be stored stink-free in the bathroom until they're ready to toss in the washing machine with hot water and mild detergent. To clean what my dear old dad used to call "an extra poopy one," hold the diaper by one of its clean, dry ends over the toilet. Shake out the solid waste, perhaps dipping the diaper in and out of the water a few times. Place diaper in diaper pail and wash your hands. Sounds gross? It will seem a lot less so when compared with the prospect of running to the store for disposables at midnight during a snowstorm.

other legal guardians of children younger than age five can also receive WIC health screenings and food prescriptions for their children.) WIC outreach workers and nurses develop food "prescriptions" for moms and kids based on whether the woman is pregnant or breast-feeding (and therefore eating for two), the number of children younger than age five they have to feed, and health factors. Mothers use vouchers to buy WIC-eligible food items at designated grocery stores or WIC centers. WIC can also provide breast-feeding mothers with advice and breast pumps, and they'll give mothers who aren't breast-feeding vouchers for baby formula.

HEALTH **INSURANCE**

All Kids
(866) ALL-KIDS (255-5437) or TTY: (877) 204-1012
www.allkidscovered.com

The State of Illinois' All Kids insurance program provides health insurance for kids of low-income parents. It even covers middle-income families that earn too much to qualify for free medical coverage but still struggle to cover private health insurance for their children. Monthly premium costs and co-pays vary by income. For example, a family of four that earns between $42,000 and $63,000 a year pays a $40 monthly premium per child and a $10 co-pay per physician visit. All Kids covers the same services as private insurance: doctor's visits, hospital stays, prescription drugs, vision care, dental care, mental-health services, and medical devices such as eyeglasses and asthma inhalers.

Homework Hotline

Can't figure out how to work that stubborn algebra problem because you forgot a crucial step? Want someone to quiz you on the Bill of Rights? Fear not, young scholar. Volunteer University of Illinois students are standing by to help during homework prime time. The NBC5-Telemundo Homework Hotline offers help to elementary through high school students in English or Spanish. No, they won't just give the answers, kiddo, but they'll help you arrive at the answers on your own. The hotline, at (312) 645-5555, is staffed Monday through Thursday from 5:00 to 8:00 p.m.

AFTER-SCHOOL **PROGRAMS** AND **YOUTH** CLUBS

After School Matters
(312) 742–4182
www.afterschoolmatters.org

After School Matters provides Chicago public high-school students with free after-school programs that range from unstructured drop-in center fun to paid apprenticeships and unpaid "pre-apprenticeships" in arts, sports, technology, and literature. Programs are held in high schools, libraries, and park district buildings throughout Chicago. (See Appendix A for a complete list of locations.) Apprenticeship programs meet three times per week for three hours each during ten-week spring and fall sessions and an eight-week summer session. Chicago public high school attendance is required, and enrollment is required for all of the programs. Although programs are expanding capacity, space in some programs is limited, so sign up early. Here's a rundown of After School Matters areas of interest.

Gallery37: Students in this program polish their talents in visual, performance, culinary, and media arts.

Tech37: Programs offer practical experience in computer rebuilding, Website design, digital filmmaking, and producing a community talk show aired on Chicago's community television network.

Science37: This program helps teens gain and demonstrate a better understanding of scientific principles and subjects.

Sports37: Teens learn rules and training principles of a variety of sports while training to be coaches, referees, and lifeguards.

Words37: This program covers creative writing, journalism, documentary, desktop publishing, performance poetry, and comic book production.

Boys and Girls Clubs of Chicago
(312) 235–8000
www.bgcc.org

The Catch *Annual $20 registration fee allows access to any Boys and Girls Club in Chicago and elsewhere, except those based at particular schools. Most programs are free after that, except for full-day summer camps. See Appendix A for a complete list of club and child-care-center locations.*

Boys and Girls Club locations throughout Chicago (see Appendix A for a complete list) offer drop-in and ongoing fun and enrichment through programs covering academics, arts, career and job training, technology, and boys and girls sports in a fun, safe atmosphere. Program times vary by location but are generally from about 3:00 to 6:00 p.m. for kids ages six to twelve and from about 6:00 to 9:00 p.m. for youths ages thirteen to twenty.

Broadway Youth Center

3179 North Broadway Street (near Belmont Avenue)
(773) 935–3151, extension 0
www.howardbrown.org
Hours: Monday through Thursday from 1:00 to 8:00 p.m., Friday from 1:00 to 9:00 p.m. (5:00 to 9:00 p.m. the first Friday of the month), and Saturday from 1:00 to 3:00 p.m.

The Broadway Youth Center offers services for body and mind to all youth ages twenty-four and younger, including gay, lesbian, bisexual, and transgendered young people, both those with homes and those without. The drop-in center offers snacks, showers, educational, and fun activities. The center, a program of Howard Brown Health Center, offers free health education workshops, free hygiene and safer sex products for the taking, and free anonymous HIV testing and screenings for sexually transmitted diseases. Get free medical care and mental health counseling and referrals for ongoing care. See page 133. Once you've got the basics covered, check out Broadway Youth Center's arts, activism, and peer mentoring activities.

Chicago Public Schools (CPS)

Office of After School and Community School Programs (773) 553–3590
www.cpsafterschool.org

Many Chicago public schools offer free after-school recreational activities and supplemental tutoring programs for their students. Your child's CPS school should let you know what's available to its students, but if you want to check yourself, see the Web site or call the number listed above.

East Village Youth Program

3643 West Belmont Avenue (at North Monticello Avenue)
(312) 275–0440
www.evyp.org

This small, college-preparatory program on the Northwest Side of Chicago serves primarily Latino students, though other ethnicities are also represented. Students in fifth through twelfth grades attend after-school and evening programs that include mentoring, tutoring, workshops, snacks, and fun activities. Students must be motivated to attend college and receive a teacher's recommendation to be considered for the program. Those who successfully complete all program requirements receive college scholarship assistance.

FINE **ARTS,** FUN **CRAFTS**

Free Street
1419 West Blackhawk Street (in Pulaski Park between North Cleaver Street and North Noble Street)
(773) 772–7248
www.freestreet.org

Free Street runs free classes and ongoing art programs for children and teens at its Pulaski Park site and other locations throughout the city. Disciplines include writing, theater, dance, and hands-on visual art.

Museum of Contemporary Art
220 East Chicago Avenue (at North Mies Van Der Rohe Way
(312) 280–2660
www.mcachicago.org

Stop by Target Family Days every second Saturday of the month from 11:00 a.m. to 3:00 p.m. Kids can enjoy hands-on art activities, learning stations, and scavenger hunts.

Navy Pier
700 East Grand Avenue (312) 595–5436; (800) 595–5436
www.navypier.com

Bring your favorite toddlers for Toddlin' Thursdays, starting at 11:00 a.m. and 12:30 p.m. A variety of entertainers, from local performers to international celebrities like Clifford the Big Red Dog, entertain their little fans.

The People's Music School
931 West Eastwood Avenue (turn east from North Sheridan Road)
(773) 784–7032
www.peoplesmusicschool.org

Since 1976 the People's Music School has been providing children and adults free music performance and theory classes. This isn't some laid-back drop-in studio. Students or their guardians sign contracts that promise they will regularly attend scheduled classes, practice what they're assigned, volunteer eight hours per session per student (four hours in the summer), and participate in fund-raising events each semester. But the high-quality education provided by the school's professional musician faculty is worth the effort. After students attend a series of theory classes and pass a test, they may take private or group lessons in voice or any number of instruments, including piano, strings, woodwinds, brass, percussion, and guitar.

Pros Arts Studio
at Dvorak Park, 1119 West Cullerton Street (between South May Street and South Carpenter Street)
(312) 226–7767
www.prosarts.org

Pros Arts provides classes in performing and visual arts for children and youth in the Pilsen and Little Village neighborhoods.

Radio Arte
1401 West 18th Street (at South Loomis Street)
(312) 455–9455
www.wrte.org training@radioarte.org

The National Museum of Mexican Art runs an educational youth radio station that broadcasts in Spanish and English to the Pilsen and Little Village neighborhoods from WRTE 90.5 FM and to the rest of the world via its Web site. The station offers a free one-year training program in radio broadcasting to youth from ages fourteen through twenty-four. Kids learn to research, interview, and write for radio news stories, and they learn digital production and other modern radio technical skills. Registration starts in December and classes begin in March every year.

South Chicago Art Center
3217 East 91st Street (at South Burley Avenue)
(773) 731–9287
www.happyartcenter.org

A bunch of art happens throughout the week inside this colorful little building. After-school and summer art programs for kids of all ages, internships for teens, an urban farm, and programs for adults are all free.

Little Green Thumbs

Garfield Park Conservatory is helping raise a generation of gardeners with ongoing classes and programs for kids of all ages. On "Morning Glory Mondays," preschoolers plant seeds in cups, make terrariums, and take on other little greenie projects. Drop-in family hours offer more workshops and projects on weekends, and kids can color, play a pinball germination game, or dig for surprises in the soil table in the Children's Garden Discovery Area. Special events throughout the year include plant-related craft projects. The conservatory offers horticulture and arts-related events and educational programs for older youth and adults too. The conservatory is at 300 North Central Park Avenue (at West Lake Street). Call (312) 746–5100, or visit www.garfield conservatory.org for information about upcoming classes and events.

STORYTELLING

57th Street Books
1301 East 57th Street (at South Kimbark Avenue)
(773) 684–1300
http://semcoop.booksense.com

Kids hear tales of string theory and Chilean economics at this University of Chicago–area bookstore on Wednesday at 10:30 a.m. Just kidding. Staff read selections from children's books in a time slot perfect for short attention spans.

Barbara's Bookstore

at UIC, 1218 South Halsted Street (south of West Roosevelt Road)
(312) 413–2665
www.barbarasbookstore.com

This small chain hosts readings, book signings, story hours, and other free events at its stores throughout Chicago. The only regularly scheduled children's event is story hour at this store on Saturday at 11:00 a.m.

Barnes & Noble Booksellers

1441 West Webster Avenue (at North Clifton Avenue)
(773) 871–3610
www.bn.com
Picture-book story time for infants and toddlers age three and younger Monday at 10:00 a.m.; story time for infants and toddlers age three and younger Tuesday at 10:00 a.m.; story time for infants and toddlers age three and younger Thursday at 10:00 a.m.

This Barnes & Noble holds free readings, storytelling, and author events for children and adults throughout the week. B&N staff, authors, and other guests lead kids in reading, listening, singing, or playing games. Of course, your presence in their stores makes it more likely you'll buy something during those free events. But that's up to you.

Chicago Public Libraries (CPL)

www.chipublib.org

The Chicago Public Library strives to inspire a greater love of reading among kids with free readings and activities throughout the city. Check CPL's main Web site for a monthly calendar of ongoing readings and events happening throughout the city, or call (312) 747–4300. And look for events calendars and flyers when you visit your local branch. You'll find story hours, craft projects, concerts, movies, author visits, and discussion groups for youth preschool through teens.

REI

1466 North Halsted Street
(312) 951–6020
www.rei.com

This Lincoln Park outpost of the national outdoorsy co-op gets kids started off right with story time inside a big tent. It's the third Thursday of most months starting at 10:30 a.m.

Women & Children First Bookstore
5233 North Clark Street (at West Farragut Avenue)
(773) 769–9299
www.womenandchildrenfirst.com

As the name suggests, this local bookstore specializes in books for women and kids. The weekly children's story time on Wednesday at 10:30 a.m. is best for ages two through five, but parents and caregivers bring children of other ages too.

Drama Kids

Many Chicago theater companies offer free training programs or scholarships for youth who want to express themselves by writing and acting for the stage. Here are a couple.

About Face Theatre, Center on Halsted, 3656 North Halsted Street (at Waveland Avenue) (773) 784–8565; www.aboutfacetheatre.com. This company that explores issues of sexual and gender identity offers internships and training programs for lesbian, gay, bisexual, and transgendered youth (and "cool straight friends"), ages fourteen through twenty. Participants write, produce, and perform plays in venues around the city.

Victory Gardens Theater, 2433 North Lincoln Avenue (between West Belden Avenue and West Webster Avenue); (773) 328–2134; www.victory gardens.org. Students must be between the ages of thirteen and eighteen, highly motivated, and be nominated by a current or previous teacher.

EDUCATION:
YOU'VE GOT CLASS

"With our thoughts we make the world."
—BUDDHA

Chicago's a classy town, where you can fill your brain with all sorts of smarts for free, or at least much less expense than you'd expect. Most GED and beginning English-as-a-second-language classes are free, and you can even get a college degree without promising your firstborn child to pay off your student loan. From single classes to certificate programs, generous masters of their crafts are waiting to teach you whatever arts, yoga routines, investing secrets, religious practices, sports, musical styles, dances, gardening methods, or light-bulb-changing tips they've made their life's work to share. The classes in this chapter range from sample first classes to full scholarships to work-study exchanges. Many such details are spelled out in each listing, but call schools and institutions to get updated and detailed information. This chapter's listings are all geared toward adults. See the Children and Teens chapter for classes for kids. See the Gardens and Gardening chapter for classes related to growing plants (and animals) and the Real Estate chapter for classes related to house and home.

ARTS **AND** MEDIA

Chicago Dramatists
1105 West Chicago Avenue (at North Milwaukee Avenue)
(312) 633–0630
www.chicagodramatists.org

The Catch $5 suggested donation to attend readings.

Chicago Dramatists helps playwrights hone their craft and polish their scripts. The organization offers work-study arrangements for professional playwriting classes if space is available.

Chicago Filmmakers
5243 North Clark Street (at West Farragut Avenue)
(773) 293–1447
www.chicagofilmmakers.org

This organization devoted to supporting the education and development of local filmmakers runs a co-op that provides equipment rental and workshops for its members. Those who can't afford to pay rental fees can exchange their volunteer labor instead.

Hyde Park Art Center
5020 South Cornell Avenue (between East 50th Street and East 50th Place)
www.hydeparkart.org
(773) 324–5520
Hours: Monday through Thursday, 9:00 a.m. to 8:00 p.m., Friday and Saturday, 9:00 a.m. to 5:00 p.m., Sunday, noon to 5:00 p.m.

This community studio, school, and gallery offers a variety of events and classes for adults and children, some of which are free.

Neighborhood Writing Alliance
(773) 684–2742
www.jot.org

The Neighborhood Writing Alliance sponsors writing workshops in libraries, schools, and community centers all over the city. The free workshops are open to all adults. Participants are especially encouraged to write about themselves and their experiences, through poems, short stories, and nonfiction, but any subject is welcome, including politics, family and social issues, history, and space aliens. Writers can listen to others' work, read theirs aloud, and get feedback from other writers and workshop leaders. Call the phone number or check out the Web site for current workshop times and locations. Many of the compositions are published in the alliance's *Journal of Ordinary Thought,* a literary publication based on the motto "Every person is a philosopher."

Music Practice Space
Need a place to toot your horn, pluck your banjo, or oble your oboe where you won't annoy your roommates? Want to practice for your piano lessons but don't have a piano? The Harold Washington Library (400 South Michigan Avenue), the main location of the Chicago Public Library, has six music practice rooms, complete with pianos, in its Visual and Performing Arts Division on the eighth floor. Contact the Music Information Center to ask about availability. Start at www.chipublib.org or (312) 747–4300.

The Old Town School of Folk Music
www.oldtownschool.org
4544 North Lincoln Avenue (between West Wilson Avenue and West Sunny-side Avenue)
909 West Armitage Avenue (between North Fremont Street and North Bissell Street)
(773) 728–6000

The Old Town School offers scholarships to anyone who can't afford to pay, which is so nice it makes you want to help them out in exchange for your free class, doesn't it? You can volunteer in a number of ways to earn points toward free performances and classes. One point equals $4. The number earned varies per task, but ushering the average concert will snag you three points.

The People's Music School
931 West Eastwood Avenue (turn east from North Sheridan Road)
(773) 784–7032
www.peoplesmusicschool.org

The Catch There's a $15 registration fee per student, who must volunteer for fundraisers and for two hours per month.

The People's Music School opened as an oasis of free musical culture and education in Uptown in 1976, when the neighborhood was shunned as dodgy, and it continues to be a bastion of nearly free musicality now that Uptown's all the gentrification rage. Students attend theory classes, then take private or group lessons in voice or an instrument. In return, students sign contracts that promise they'll attend classes regularly, practice work assigned, volunteer two hours per month, and participate in fund-raising events each semester.

Redmoon Theater
1438 West Kinzie Street (enter at 1463 West Hubbard Street)
(312) 850–8440
www.redmoon.org
information@redmoon.org

Redmoon Theater produces fanciful contraptions, artwork, music, dance, and plots, tying them all together into their famous "spectacles." They take place indoors, often at Redmoon Central, or in outdoor public spaces that can draw crowds as large as 2,000 people. Every Redmoon spectacle welcomes volunteers to join the creation of its art. They learn to use power tools, paint, papier-mâché, and so on as they help build sets and props.

Scrap Mettle Soul
Office: 4750 North Sheridan Road, suite 375
(773) 275–3999
www.scrapmettlesoul.org

This neighborhood theatrical effort uses volunteer actors performing the works of volunteers writing stories and plays about their own lives. Many plays are about life in the eclectic Uptown neighborhood of Chicago. The public is welcome to join in writing, acting, or producing.

South Side Community Art Center
3831 South Michigan Avenue (at East Pershing Road)
(773) 373–1026
www.southsidecommunityartcenter.com
Hours: Wednesday through Friday, noon to 5:00 p.m.; Saturday, 9:00 a.m. to 5:00 p.m.; Sunday, 1:00 to 5:00 p.m. Closed Monday and Tuesday.

Since 1940, the South Side Community Art Center has hosted a variety of visual and performing arts, and its collection of fine art includes works by the likes of Charles White, Elizabeth Catlett and William Carter. In addition to gallery exhibitions, the Bronzeville gallery hosts spoken word, dance, and music events, most of which are free. Some classes also are free.

The University of Chicago Folklore Society
1212 East 59th Street (at South Woodlawn Avenue)
(773) 702–9793
www.uofcfolk.org
info@uofcfolk.org

The annual University of Chicago Folk Festival runs for a three-day weekend every February or so. It includes several free daytime workshops in such traditional folk musical styles as slide guitar, Cajun, bhangra, and traditional shape note singing. And it offers free classes in traditional dances from around the world.

Victory Gardens Theater
2257 North Lincoln Avenue (between West Belden Avenue and West Webster Avenue)
(773) 871–3000
www.victorygardens.org

Work thirty-two hours to receive half off the price of a class. Work sixty-four hours to take a class for free. The training center of Victory Gardens Theater offers classes in managing, writing, acting in, and directing productions.

TECHNICAL **HOW-TO**

Chicago Center for Green Technology
445 North Sacramento Boulevard (between West Franklin Boulevard and West Carroll Avenue)
(312) 746–9642
www.cityofchicago.org/Environment/GreenTech

The Chicago Center for Green Technology is devoted to making Chicago a more environmentally friendly city. Classes at the center are designed for everyone from professional architects and designers to home owners and renters. Learn about plant-based paints, landscaping plans that best fit the Chicago-area climate, constructing rain barrels and compost bins, and a plethora of better building designs.

The Catch Classes are free, but you may have to pay for some materials.

BODY

Bloom Yoga
4663 North Rockwell Street (between West Leland Avenue and West Eastwood Avenue)
(773) 463–9642
www.bloomyogastudio.com

Bloom offers a free introductory yoga class every first Saturday from 1:00 to 2:00 p.m. or 2:00 to 3:00 p.m. The class covers basic postures and breathing techniques for beginners.

Chicago Aikikai
3652 North Lincoln Avenue (between West Patterson Avenue and West Waveland Avenue)
(773) 935–2334
www.asu.org/Chicago

This Aikido school offers free introductory classes the first Sunday of every month from 1:00 to 2:00 p.m.

Chicago Park District
(312) 742–PLAY
www.chicagoparkdistrict.com

The Chicago Park District offers thousands of classes all over the city. Many are completely free, and those that charge small fees are cheap compared to private classes (about $4 to $5 for those classes that charge). You can search the park district's Web site by parameters such as your zip code, age range, a park name, preferred classes and programs, and special events. And you can check facility locations and hours and register online for many free and fee-based classes and events, from yoga to fencing to soccer to gymnastics.

Fleet Feet Sports
4555 North Lincoln Avenue (at West Wilson Avenue)
(773) 271–3338
www.fleetfeetchicago.com

This running and fitness apparel store offers a free yoga class every Sunday morning between 9:00 and 10:00 a.m.

Moksha Yoga
www.mokshayoga.com
700 North Carpenter Street (southwest of North Milwaukee Avenue); (312) 942-9642. Yoga class on Sunday from 3:30 to 5:00 p.m.
3334 North Clark Street (at West Buckingham Place); (773) 975-9642. Yoga on Saturday from 4:00 to 5:30 p.m.

This yoga school offers free classes and meditation sessions at two of its locations. Free classes are taught by teachers in training.

REI
1466 North Halsted Street
(312) 951-6020
www.rei.com

This Lincoln Park outpost of the national outdoorsy co-op offers a little indoor Hatha yoga the first Thursday of every month at 6:30 p.m. Bring your own mat or blanket.

Thousand Waves Martial Arts and Self-Defense Center
1220 West Belmont Avenue (between North Racine Avenue and North Lakewood Avenue)
(773) 472-7663
www.thousandwaves.org

Medical School

Many hospitals offer free classes on a variety of physical- and mental-health topics, along with free support groups for people facing serious health challenges or the stress of caring for those who do. Classes and lectures cover subjects such as the latest advancements in Alzheimer's treatments or latest controversies over stem cell research, how to eat better or stop smoking, how to care for a newborn or ailing parent, the warning signs of stroke, and basic life support. Consider it your little moment of med school, sans student loans. Many hospitals also host occasional free health screenings too.

This martial-arts program, affiliated with Thousand Waves Spa, offers free first-time classes for guests who want to try martial arts before committing money to the venture. It also offers occasional free lectures.Scholarships for ongoing training are offered to adults or children based on financial need. Limited work-study arrangements are sometimes available.

MIND

Chicago Architecture Foundation
224 South Michigan Avenue (between East Adams Street and East Jackson Boulevard)
(312) 922–3432
www.architecture.org

Teacher Training

If you have the heart and talent to teach in some of Chicago's poorest neighborhoods, a lot of people want to help you do just that, and to pay you back for your commitment. The federal government will repay part of your student loan after you've taught for a certain number of years in a public school where most of the students qualify for free school lunches. One organization will even pay while you get your master's degree. The Academy for Urban School Leadership provides a stipend of $32,000 for a yearlong residency in its teacher-training program. Residents earning their degrees teach alongside mentor teachers at AUSL-supported Chicago public schools during the day, then take evening classes to earn teacher certification and master's degrees in education. In return, AUSL residents commit to teaching for five years after graduation in under-performing CPS schools. The program is very selective but promises ongoing support for teachers in training and graduates early in their careers. To learn more, contact AUSL at 3400 North Austin Avenue; (773) 534–0129, www .ausl-chicago.org.

Libraries with Class!

You'll find hundreds of free classes and lectures at Chicago Public Library locations around the city. To see what you can learn at the Harold Washington or your local branch, ask a librarian or check the library's monthly calendar, available online or in paper form. It's at www.chipublib.org. Here's just a sampling of lectures and ongoing programs listed in a single month.

Adoption and Custody for LGBT Parents
Basic Chinese Buying and Selling a Home
Chess Club
English as a Second Language
First Aid and Safety
Financial Planning for Emergencies
Estate Planning and Advance Directives for LGBT Couples
Income Tax Return Preparation
Learning Disabilities
Lessons of the Nuremburg Trials
Library Research Basics and Research Tours
The Historic Chicago Bungalow Initiative
Money Smart
Preventing Identity Theft
Quilting Club
History of Chicago Blues

The foundation offers free lectures on architectural topics throughout the year, notably its lunchtime lecture series on Wednesday from 12:15 to 1:00 p.m. in the atrium lobby. You can bring a bag lunch.

Chicago Cultural Center

78 East Washington Street (at North Michigan Avenue)
Wheelchair access at 77 East Randolph Street
(312) 744–6630 / TTY: (312) 744–2947
www.chicagoculturalcenter.org

The Chicago Cultural Center is in several chapters of this book because it gives the city so much, including free lectures on a variety of topics.

Goethe-Institut Chicago
150 North Michigan Avenue (at East Randolph Street), suite 200
(312) 263–0472
www.goethe.de/Chicago

The Goethe-Institut Chicago hosts a number of free educational events, including performances, films, lectures, and readings.

Instituto Cervantes Chicago
31 West Ohio Street (between North State Street and North Dearborn Street)
(312) 335–1996
http://chicago.cervantes.es

This institute for the study and promotion of Spanish in European and American dialects hosts free lectures, seminars, conferences, readings, Spanish conversation groups, book presentations, and a host of other great events.

International House
1414 East 59th Street (between South Blackstone Avenue and South Dorchester Avenue)
(773) 753–2274
http://ihouse.uchicago.edu

This cosmopolitan residence and cultural center on the University of Chicago Campus hosts a variety of events, including performances, many of which are free, and free lectures and discussions by great global thinkers.

Get a Job, Get a Degree

From some of the world's most exclusive universities to quality open-enrollment colleges for the masses, Chicago offers many secondary-education opportunities. But with state and national student grant programs leaner than ever, it's tougher to get the money you need without taking out student loans that will someday need to be paid back. To reduce or eliminate your tuition costs, consider becoming an employee of a local college or university. Many schools allow staff to take classes part-time or full-time for free. You may not make much mopping the college floors or filing other students' financial aid forms, but you'll save a bunch of money as you earn your next degree. As you search for the right school, check its policies about free classes for employees.

The Basics: Reading, Writing, GEDs, Citizenship

If you or yours can't read this, need to get a high school diploma, want to learn basic English as a second language, or want to study for your U.S. citizenship exam, there are free classes and programs all over the city to fit the bill. The City of Chicago and several community colleges, community centers, and ethnic mutual-aid societies offer free instruction to all. Here's a sample of schools and organizations to get you started:

City Colleges of Chicago

Daley College, 7500 South Pulaski Road (at West 75th Place); (773) 838-7500; http://daley.ccc.edu

Harold Washington College, 30 East Lake Street (between North Wabash Avenue and North State Street); (312) 553-5600; http://hwashington.ccc.edu

Kennedy-King College, 6800 South Wentworth Avenue (between West 67th Street and West 69th Street); (312) 850-7000; http://kennedyking.ccc.edu

Malcolm X College, 1900 West Van Buren Street (between South Wood Street and South Damen Avenue); (312) 850-7000; http://malcolmx.ccc.edu

Olive-Harvey College, 10001 South Woodlawn Avenue (at East 103rd Street); (773) 291-6100; http://oliveharvey.ccc.edu

Truman College, 1145 West Wilson Avenue (at North Clifton Avenue); (773) 907-4000; http://www.trumancollege.cc/index.php

Wright College, 4300 North Narragansett Avenue (between West Montrose Avenue and West Berteau Avenue); (773) 777-7900; http://wright.ccc.edu

Erie Neighborhood House

www.eriehouse.org

1347 West Erie Street (at North Ada Street); (312) 666-3430

1701 West Superior Street (at North Paulina Street); (312) 563-5800

2510 West Cortez Street (at North Campbell Avenue); (773) 486-7161

4225 West 25th Street (at South Keeler Avenue); (773) 542-7617

Literacy Chicago

(312) 870-1100, ext. 120; www.literacychicago.org. Provides free adult education programs in reading and writing, including English language improvement.

Jane Addams Hull House Museum

800 South Halsted Street (between West Harrison Street and West Roosevelt Road)

(312) 413–5353

www.uic.edu/jaddams/hull

Hours: Tuesday through Friday, 10:00 a.m. to 4:00p.m.; Sunday, noon to 4:00 p.m. Closed Mondays, Saturdays, and during holidays and many semester breaks when the University of Illinois is closed.

This remaining building of the original Hull House complex celebrates Jane Addams's pioneering work in creating community-based programs and political pressure to address a host of social ills, such as crushing poverty, xenophobia, and child labor. Hull House also hosts a variety of educational events, dance and theater performances, and lectures. Its Re-Thinking Soup lecture series, every Tuesday from noon to 1:30 p.m. covers topics related to the politics of food and includes free soup. Donations are welcome.

Moody Bible Institute

820 North LaSalle Boulevard (at West Chestnut Street)

(800) DLM–OODY or (312) 329–4000

www.moody.edu

This interdenominational evangelical Christian college is the only four-year and graduate institution in Chicago that offers completely free tuition to all of its students. Academic degrees are double-majored with Biblical studies.

Money Smarts

Now that you've avoided spending all that money, let the experts help you figure out where to put it. Whether you want to learn which IRA is best for you or need help getting out of debt, financial experts want to show you the way to fiscal balance. Some banks and credit unions offer classes on a variety of financial basics to their members and to the broader community (try ShoreBank at www.shorebankcorp.com and the North Side Community Federal Credit Union at www.northsidecommunity fcu.org). The City of Chicago runs ongoing classes through the Chicago Public Library (www.chipublib.org), the community college system (www .ccc.edu), and other public venues. And the Chicago Federal Reserve Bank offers money management classes too. Find their resources for consumers (and savers) at www.chicagofed.org/education.

Pritzker Military Library

610 North Fairbanks Court (at Ohio Street), second floor
(312) 587–0234
www.pritzkermilitarylibrary.org

If you want to study war some more, check out a free lecture or panel discussion at the Pritzker Military Library, a local research library dedicated to the study of all things armed forces. Some events offer free food.

SPIRIT

Finding free education in religions that have long been mainstream in the United States is pretty much a no-brainer: Visit or contact a church or synagogue that interests you and find out when their weekly services and classes take place, join a friend who invites you to his or her place of worship, or read ads posted in newspapers or outside religious buildings. But checking out a religion that's less established or well-known in the United States can be trickier. Here are a few resources for just a handful of faiths that welcome inquiring souls.

Buddhist Council of the Midwest

1812 Washington Street
Evanston, Illinois
(847) 869–5806
www.buddhistcouncilmidwest.org

This organization of local Buddhist temples in Illinois, Indiana, Michigan, and Wisconsin has contact information for Buddhist temples and organizations on its Web site. They're searchable by state.

Downtown Islamic Center

231 South State Street (between East Adams Street and East Jackson Boulevard)
(312) 939–9095
www.dic-chicago.org

This center provides ongoing free classes covering the basics of Islam.

Falun Chicago
www.falunchicago.org

The Catch None, unless you're in China.

This local roundup lists Falun Dafa groups meeting in the Chicago area and how to contact them.

Institute for Islamic Information and Education
4333 North Elston Avenue (between West Montrose Avenue and West Berteau Avenue)
(773) 777–7443
www.iiie.net

The institute strives to further the cause of Islam in North America by providing information about the religion's beliefs, history, and customs. Its reading room at North Elston Avenue provides free brochures on several topics.

HEALTH AND MEDICAL:
LIVE FREE OR DIE

"Never go to a doctor whose office plants have died."
—ERMA BOMBECK

The good news is that modern medicine can cure a lot more than it used to. Of course, the bad news is that health care in the United States costs an arm and a leg. While our national health-care system is in dire need of some fiscal readjustments, several government and private programs, hospitals, clinics, and schools throughout Chicago can help ease your pain without requiring an appendage in return. Whether you have a major disease, a substance-abuse problem, or a nasty cold, you want to plan a healthy pregnancy, or you just want a checkup or advice, invest in your health with help from Chicago's dedicated medical community.

HOSPITALS **AND** CLINICS

From government-run hospitals to private clinics, you've got a lot of choices for free and sliding-scale health services here in Chicago, regardless of your ability to pay. Unfortunately, many of the larger public facilities have crowded waiting rooms, especially on weekends, and the notoriously long public clinic wait times you've heard about are true. Bring a good book, and while you wait, soothe yourself with thoughts of how much less time you'll spend paying off your sliding-scale or free care.

John H. Stroger, Jr. Hospital of Cook County
1901 West Harrison Street (at West Ogden Avenue)
(312) 864–6000 or TDD: (312) 864–0100
Twenty-four-hour emergency service every day. Outpatient service Monday through Friday from 8:30 a.m. to 5:00 p.m.; closed on Saturday and Sunday.

The Catch Waiting rooms are usually crowded.

Your tax dollars paid for this $623 million state-of-the-art facility, so if you need emergency, inpatient, or complicated outpatient care, at least you get to check out what you helped buy. The hospital provides medical services for patients who require hospitalization, or who have the most serious illnesses or injuries, regardless of their abilities to pay. Unlike the old County Hospital it replaced, Stroger boasts private and semiprivate inpatient rooms with bathrooms, telephones, and—blessing or curse—televisions.

CITY **AND** COUNTY **HEALTH** CENTERS

Chicago Department of Public Health
Main Office: 333 South State Street (between East Jackson Boulevard and East Van Buren Street), DePaul Center, room 200
Call 311 for information from anywhere inside Chicago city limits, or call (312) 747–9884 if you're outside Chicago.
www.cityofchicago.org/health

The City of Chicago runs several sliding-scale clinics, some designed to provide a range of services and treat a variety of illnesses, others specialized to serve specific health needs. See Appendix B for geographical listings of the extensive network of clinics in Chicago. Call the number listed above or go to the Department of Public Health section of the city's Web address for complete listings of city and private agencies ready to help.

Cook County Bureau of Health Services
Ambulatory & Community Health Network Bureau
Main Office: 627 South Wood (at West Harrison Street)
(312) 864–6420
www.ccbhs.org

See Appendix B for geographical listings of Cook County clinics that serve low-income residents. For additional help finding a primary-care Cook County clinic within or closest to your zip code, call the Ambulatory Clinic Finder, at (312) 864–6420. An automated system in English, Spanish, or Polish will give you options and directions.

PRIVATE **HEALTH** CENTERS

Broadway Youth Center
3179 North Broadway Street (near Belmont Avenue)
(773) 935–3151, ext. 0
www.howardbrown.org
Hours: Monday through Thursday from 1:00 to 8:00 p.m., Friday from 1:00

to 9:00 p.m. (5:00 to 9:00 p.m. the first Friday of the month), and Saturday from 1:00 to 3:00 p.m.

The Broadway Youth Center offers services for body and mind to all youth ages twenty-four and younger, including gay, lesbian, bisexual, and transgendered young people, both those with homes and those without. The drop-in center offers snacks, showers, educational, and fun activities. The center, a program of Howard Brown Health Center, offers free health education workshops, free hygiene and safer sex products for the taking, and free anonymous HIV testing and screenings for sexually transmitted diseases. Get free medical care and mental health counseling and referrals for ongoing care.

Chicago Women's Health Center
3435 North Sheffield Avenue (at North Clark Street), suite 206A
(773) 935–6126
www.chicagowomenshealthcenter.org

The all-woman health center offers gynecological and breast exams, birth-control education and samples, cervical cap fittings, emergency contraception, fertility and childbirth education, breast-feeding classes, private and group therapy services, and even sex toy parties. Caring, supportive health-care workers are overseen by an on-staff physician. Sliding-scale fees based on income can be paid right away or over time. The clinic also accepts insurance by most major providers.

Howard Brown Health Center
www.howardbrown.org

Main Health Center, 4025 North Sheridan Road (north of West Irving Park Road); (773) 388–1600
Triad Health (in Advocate Illinois Masonic Medical Center)
3000 North Halsted Street, suite 711 (at West Wellington Avenue); (773) 296–8400

The health center and clinic focus on the physical and mental-health needs of lesbian, gay, bisexual, and transgender Chicagoans, but it will serve anyone, regardless of sexual orientation. Services include primary medical care, laboratory and diagnostic work, referrals to specialists, anonymous testing for HIV, and confidential screenings for other sexually transmitted diseases. Sliding-scale fees are available if your income is low enough, and the clinic can process public aid and private insurance coverage.

Poison Control Hotline

The Illinois Poison Center is a twenty-four-hour hotline whose medical professionals offer free advice about any kind of possible poisoning emergencies from food poisoning and medication errors to household and industrial chemicals. If you wonder whether or not you should be worried about what you or yours just ingested, give them a call at (800) 222–1222. That's the same number for poison control centers in states all over the Union.

CANCER SUPPORT

Gilda's Club Chicago
537 North Wells Street (at West Grand Avenue)
(312) 464–9900
www.gildasclubchicago.org

Named after the late comedian Gilda Radner, the Chicago branch of this nationwide nonprofit provides a variety of free support services to men, women, and children living with or loving someone with cancer. A variety of support groups, lectures, and workshops provide information and support specific to various types of cancers. Yoga, tai chi, drumming, cooking, and self-hypnosis classes help provide additional stress relief and health advice. Child care provided during events at the center is also free.

Lesbian Community Care Project (LCCP)
4025 North Sheridan Road (north of West Irving Park Road), in Howard Brown Health Center (773) 561–4662
www.lccp.org

LCCP's mission is to support lesbian, bisexual, and transgendered women who are facing cancer or other serious chronic illnesses, but the center will help straight women too. The project, part of Howard Brown Health Center (see Howard Brown entry this chapter) provides referrals and advice for women seeking physicians, LGBT-specific support groups, and other services. LCCP also strives to help women avoid and detect serious health problems by offering smoking cessation support and, for women who lack health insurance, free pap smears and clinical breast exams.

Thousand Waves Spa

1212 West Belmont Avenue (between North Racine Avenue and North Lakewood Avenue)
(773) 549–0700
www.thousandwavesspa.com

This women-only spa offers up to five free full-hour massages or bio-energy treatments for women dealing with cancer and five free visits to the spa's hot tub, steam room, and sauna. Spa facilities can also be used by a female companion who accompanies a woman who has cancer to her massage treatments.

ALTERNATIVE (TO FULL-PRICE) MEDICINE

Sometimes, ancient wisdom or a good muscle kneading will cure what ails you better than anything else. Other times, it can be a nice complement to traditional medicine. But a lot of alternative therapies can be pricey too. Here are a few that are free, or at least cheaper than the average alternative cure.

Cortiva Professional and Student Massage Clinic

18 North Wabash Avenue (at East Madison Street)
(312) 753–7990
www.cortiva.com/locations/csmt/clinic/

The student clinic of the Cortiva Institute—Chicago (formerly the Chicago School of Massage Therapy) gives students a variety of aching muscles on which to practice. In return, those muscles pay $40 per one-hour, full-body, Swedish massage, about half what they'd pay a certified pro in Chicago.

Midwest College of Oriental Medicine
909 West Montrose Avenue, suite 201 (at North Hazel Street)
(773) 975–1295
www.acupuncture.edu/Midwest

The Catch *Patients pay for herbs.*

The college's walk-in clinic offers free acupuncture treatments and advice about healing Chinese herbs. If the idea of students poking you with needles and suggesting you consume unfamiliar plants makes you a little nervous, relax. The college is accredited to provide bachelor of science and master of science degrees in nutrition and oriental medicine, the students are overseen by instructors, and the clinic has a physician on-staff. If you show up without a referral from a doctor, the clinic's physician will give you a free intake screening.

The New School for Massage, Bodywork & Healing
800 North Wells Street (at West Chicago Avenue), suite 300
(312) 654–0900
www.newschoolmassage.com

Student therapeutic massages at this Old Town campus and clinic cost $35 for fifty-five minutes.

Pacific College of Oriental Medicine
3646 North Broadway (a block north of West Addison Street), second floor
(773) 477–4822
www.pacificcollege.edu

Treatments by interns and licensed professionals include acupuncture, massage, and herbal consultations and range from $8 with a first-month intern to $35 with an experienced intern.

Soma Institute
55 East Jackson Boulevard (at South Wabash Avenue)
(312) 939–2723
www.soma.edu

Students in the Student Teaching Clinic of this national school of clinical massage therapy provide a full, one-hour massage for $20.

HEALTH **INSURANCE:** FREE **TO** CHEAP

Don't assume that you earn too much to qualify for government health-insurance assistance. With prices rising, some state programs now help even middle-income families get the coverage they need. Whether you're poor as a character in a Dickens story or just somewhere in the fiscal middle, if you don't earn enough to pay for insurance for you and your family on your own, these government programs can help ease the pain.

All Kids
(866) ALL–KIDS (255–5437) or TTY: (877) 204–1012
www.allkidscovered.com

The State of Illinois' All Kids insurance program provides health insurance for kids of low-income parents. It even covers middle-income families that earn too much to qualify for free medical coverage but still struggle to cover private health insurance for their children. Monthly premium costs and co-pays vary by income. For example, a family of four that earns between $42,000 and $63,000 a year pays a $40 monthly premium per child and a $10 co-pay per physician visit. All Kids covers the same services as private insurance: doctor's visits, hospital stays, prescription drugs, vision care, dental care, mental-health services, and medical devices such as eyeglasses and asthma inhalers.

CHEAP(ER) **MEDICINE**

Illinois Rx Buying Club
Member Services: (866) 215–3462 or TTY: (866) 215–3479
www.illinoisrxbuyingclub.com

The Catch There is a $10 annual administrative fee.

Illinoisans whose income is at or below 300 percent of the federal poverty level ($32,490 for an individual) can buy drugs at a discount with this program's membership card, which is accepted at more than fifty thousand pharmacies nationwide.

WHATEVER **AILS** YOU: **CLINICAL** STUDIES

Chicago and its suburbs are home to several teaching hospitals and medical research centers. Chances are, some researcher needs volunteers willing to try the latest potential cures for your particular physical or mental-health malady, whether it's a serious illness like cancer or just an annoying condition like acne. All medicine and care are provided free of charge or at significant discounts, and some studies pay subjects for their time too.

Northwestern Memorial Hospital

251 East Huron Street (at North St. Clair Street)
(877) 926–4664
www.nmh.org/nmh/clinicaltrials/main.htm

This research and teaching hospital of Northwestern University conducts a variety of trials related to cancer, HIV and AIDS, arthritis, diabetes, and pregnancy and mental-health issues. Medical care is usually free, and sometimes subjects receive small stipends.

Pick a Study, Any Study

To find studies being conducted in Chicago or elsewhere in the United States, check out these Web sites of national study databases. They list studies by condition and the cities and states where they're being conducted, including Chicago and the surrounding region.

Center Watch lists hundreds of studies searchable by condition, city, and state, and it provides e-mail notification of those that match your criteria. Visit www.centerwatch.com.

ClinicalTrials.gov, a service of the National Institutes of Health, serves as a clearinghouse of federally and privately funded clinical studies around the country; www.clinicaltrials.gov.

AIDS Clinical Trial Information Service provides information about studies through ClinicalTrials.gov, and it also includes a toll-free number, (800) 448–0440, that includes English- and Spanish-speaking information specialists Monday through Friday from noon to 5:00 p.m. Eastern Time. Real-time online help is available at https://web contact.aspensys.com/AidsInfo/intro.jsp. Or you can send your question to ContactUs@aidsinfo.nih.gov.

National Cancer Institute Clinical Trials, another service in conjunction with the National Institutes of Health, provides brochures and fact sheets for cancer patients in addition to clinical trial listings; www.cancer.gov/clinical_trials.

National Heart, Lung & Blood Institute lists trials sponsored by the institute, including many not listed on ClinicalTrials.gov; www.nhlbi .nih.gov/studies.

Rush University Medical Center

Research and Clinical Trials Administration Office
1725 West Harrison Street, suite 439 (at South Wood Street)
(312) 942–5498
www.rush.edu
clinical_trials@rush.edu

This center conducts hundreds of clinical studies on the effectiveness and safety of new medical devices and therapies for physical and mental health. Treatment and medication or medical devices are free.

University of Chicago Hospitals

5841 South Maryland Avenue (at East 58th Street)
Medicine Clinical Trials: (773) 702–5588
Cancer Clinical Trials: (773) 834–7424
Pediatric Clinical Trials: (773) 702–2509
All Other Clinical Trials: (773) 834–8992
www.uchospitals.edu/clinical-trials

The hospital's clinical trials Web site lists several new and ongoing trials in a variety of disciplines, including dermatology, infectious diseases, and cancer.

Digestive Diseases and Liver Center: Hepatitis C trials: (312) 996–3800; Gastrointestinal clinical trials: (312) 355–4071; This center offers several continuing and new trials into preventing and treating cancer and digestive and liver disorders.

UIC Cancer Center: (312) 355–3046

University of Illinois Medical Center at Chicago: http://uillinoismed center.org

FITNESS, FUN, AND GAMES:
CHEAP THRILLS

*"The lakefront by right belongs to the people. . . .
Not a foot of its shores should be appropriated by
individuals to the exclusion of the people."*
—DANIEL H. BURNHAM, PLAN OF CHICAGO, 1909

You can spend big bucks for membership to a fitness center or recreation club in Chicago and then spend more time at work earning extra money to pay for it. Or you can take advantage of the bountiful free and cheap ways to play here, much of which you've already paid for with your share of city and county taxes. You and yours own miles of lakefront property as well as beautiful outdoor parks, forest preserves, pools, and ice rinks dotting the city and suburbs. Many of those parks include buildings that house free fitness centers, basketball courts, swimming pools, game rooms, and classes in everything from yoga to acting. Some classes cost a bit, but the prices still are much less than you would pay at private gyms or studios. You'll also find ad hoc fun in private spaces, like free board games at cafes and bars. The fun and fitness are waiting for you, so get out there and play.

PARK **IT** HERE!

Chicago Park District
(312) 742–PLAY
www.chicagoparkdistrict.com

The Chicago Park District manages more than 7,300 acres of park land, 552 parks, 33 beaches, 16 lagoons, and 10 bird and wildlife gardens. It also organizes thousands of classes, camps, and special events and programs throughout the city year-round. Work out at your nearest park district fitness center, take a Pilates class, or send your children to day camp. Many programs are completely free, and those that charge small fees are still quite cheap compared to private classes (about $4 to $5 for those classes that charge). Join a free pickup game at a basketball court or perfect your swing on a baseball field or tennis court. You can search the park district's Web site by parameters such as your zip code, age range, a park name, preferred classes and programs, and special events. You can check facility locations and hours and register online for many free and fee-based classes and events.

Forest Preserve District of Cook County
(800) 870–3666
www.fpdcc.com

Not to be outdone, Cook County's government administers thousands of acres of forest preserve with trails for hiking, biking, cross-country skiing, and horseback riding. And it runs nature centers and even a water park complete with two waterslides. The water park charges $5 admission, but that's far cheaper than the big-time private water theme parks just north of the city. Search the preserve's Web site for the programs and facilities that meet your interests. You can download maps for biking, skiing, or hiking, learn more about wildlife in the parks, or apply for a permit for your large family picnic. Or just head out to the woods for a nature walk.

SLEDDING

After a hearty Chicago snow, grab your sled, saucer, cardboard box, serving tray, or shovel and hit the slopes. Chicago has a few of them, believe it or not. The hills below are arranged from north to south. When you hear the sounds of screaming kids, you'll know you're close.

Cricket Hill, west of Montrose Beach at 4500 North
Dan Ryan Woods, 87th Street and Western Avenue
Indian Road Woods, North Central Avenue 0.5 mile south of North Caldwell Avenue
Jensen Slides Area, West Devon Avenue and North Milwaukee Avenue
Sledding Hill at Soldier Field, 1410 South Museum Campus Drive at Lake Shore Drive

SKATING

Watch your fellow Chicagoans twirl, glide, and fall down on the ice, or join them for free at ice rinks operated by the Chicago Park District and City of

Chicago throughout the winter. Admission to all is free, but you'll have to pay $5 to $6 for skate rental if you don't bring your own.

Daley Bicentennial Plaza, Grant Park: 337 East Randolph Street, (312) 742-7648

McKinley Park: 2210 West Pershing Road, (312) 747-5992

Midway Plaisance Park: 1130 Midway Plaisance North (at East 59th Street and South Woodlawn Avenue), (312) 745-2470

Millennium Park McCormick Tribune Ice Rink: at North Michigan Avenue and East Washington Street

Mount Greenwood Park: 3721 West 111th Street, (312) 747-3690

Riis Park: 6100 West Fullerton Avenue, (312) 746-5735

Rowan Park: 11546 South Avenue L, (773) 646-1967

Warren Park: 6601 North Western Avenue, (773) 761-8663

West Lawn Park: 4233 West 65th Street, (773) 284-6078

BEACHES

Chicago Park District
Beaches and Pools Information: (312) 742-5121
www.chicagoparkdistrict.com

Chicago's blessed with a beautiful string of public beaches and parks from south to north, thanks to the vision of some city founders and the hard work and protection of the public lakefront ever since. That said, it's quite the summer bummer to have hauled the family and associated beach paraphernalia east for a hot day in the cool waves only to find the water off-limits due to rough surf or high bacteria levels. Call the number above to check the status of your favorite beach before you head out. Many of the beaches listed below are adjacent to each other. Some have lifeguards, bathrooms, and showers, but others have no facilities or lifeguards and don't allow swimming.

LAKEFRONT BEACHES

12th Street Beach, at 1200 South; (312) 742–5121

31st Street Beach, at 3100 South; (312) 742–5121

57th Street Beach, at 5700 South; (312) 742–5121

63rd Street Beach and Beach House, at 6300 South; (312) 742–5121 for beach, (773) 256–0949 for beach house

Ashe Beach Park, 2701 East 74th Street, at 7400 South; (312) 745–1479

Berger Park, 6205 North Sheridan Road, at 6200 North; (773) 761–0376. This is not an official beach, but it's a nice place to sit on a bench or play at the play lot in view of the lake. Lakefront restaurants renting the park district cultural center buildings have come and gone here throughout the years.

Calumet Beach, at 9600, 9800, and 9900 South

Chase Avenue Park and Beach, at 7250 North; no phone number

Columbia Beach Park, 1040 West Columbia Avenue, at 6750 North; (773) 262–8605

Fargo Avenue Beach Park, 1300 West Fargo Avenue, at 7450 North; (773) 262–8605

Foster Avenue Beach and Beach House, at 5200 North; (312) 742–5121

Hartigan Park and Beach, 1031 West Albion Avenue, at 6600 North; (773) 262–8605

Howard Beach, 7519 North Eastlake Terrace, at 7500 to 7600 North; (773) 262–8605

Jarvis Beach and Park, 1208 West Jarvis Avenue, at 7400 North; (773) 262–8605

Juneway Terrace Beach and Park, 7751 North Eastland Terrace, at 7750 North; (773) 262–8605

Lane Beach and Park, 5915 North Sheridan Road, at 5900 North; (773) 262–8605.

Leone Park and Beach, 1222 West Touhy Avenue, at 7200 North; (773) 262–8605

Loyola Park and Beach, 1230 West Greenleaf Avenue, at 7050 North; (773) 262–8605 for field house

Montrose-Wilson Beach and Beach House, at 4400 to 4600 North; (312) 742–5121

North Avenue Beach and Beach House, 1603 North Lake Shore Drive, 1600 to 1800 North; (312) 742–7529

North Shore Beach Park, 1040 West North Shore Avenue, at 6700 North; (773) 262–8605

Oak Street Beach, at 1000 North; (312) 742–5121

Ohio Street Beach, at 500 North; no phone number

Osterman Beach (aka Ardmore Beach aka Hollywood Beach), at 5800 North; (312) 742–5121.

Pratt Boulevard Beach and Park, 1050 West Pratt Boulevard, at 6800 North; (312) 742–7857

Rainbow Beach and Park, 3111 East 77th Street, at 7700 South; (312)

Rogers Avenue Beach and Park, 7700 North Rogers Avenue, at 7700 North; (773) 262–8605

Sherwin Avenue Park and Beach, at 7350 North; no phone number

South Shore Beach, at 7100 South; (312) 742–5121

745–1479 for field house and recreation center, (312) 742–5121 for beach information

INLAND BEACH

Humboldt Beach, 1400 North Sacramento Avenue (enter at North Sacramento Avenue and West Division Street); (312) 742–7549

Try Before You Join

If you've never visited a particular health club before, call or stop in and ask (before the sales pitch and tour) if you can stay to try out their facilities and that day's classes on your own after you've heard their pitch. Many will say yes, and some will even throw in an extra day's pass for you to come back a second time for free. Of course, they hope you'll like the place enough to join, but that's up to you.

FUN **RUNS**

Many running-apparel shops organize regular fun runs. Many let you store your stuff in their shops while you run, and some include seminars and snacks as part of the deal. Yes, it's all a big conspiracy to tempt you into flashy attire and to make you wear out your running shoes sooner. Contact stores for details about ongoing running events throughout the year.

Fleet Feet Sports
www.fleetfeetchicago.com

Lincoln Square Store, 4555 North Lincoln Avenue (at West Wilson Avenue); (773) 271–3338. Fun runs and walks start from the store Monday (co-ed) and Wednesday (women only) at 6:30 p.m. and Saturday (co-ed) at 8:00 a.m. **Piper's Alley Store,** 210 West North Avenue (at North Wells Street); (312) 587–3338. Fun runs and walks start from the store Monday (co-ed) and Tuesday (women only) at 6:30 p.m.

Running Away
1634 West North Avenue (at North Marshfield Avenue)
(773) 395–2929
www.runningawaychicago.com

On Mondays, Running Away will let you change clothes in their store and leave your stuff at the store while you cavort about Bucktown with other runners from 6:30 to 8:00 p.m. Runners divide into three groups of differing fitness levels, running 3, 4.5, or 7 miles. Essential carb loading often follows at a local restaurant for za and beer.

Universal Sole
3052 North Lincoln Avenue (between West Barry Avenue and West Wellington Avenue)
(773) 868–0893
www.universalsole.com

Six- to 10-mile fun runs start at the shop Monday at 6:15 p.m. and Saturday at 8:30 a.m. Runners form groups of varying levels from beginners to speedsters. They jog together to the lakefront and then divide into groups of different paces and run back to the store.

PICKUP GAMES

Chicago Walkers Club
www.chicagowalkers.com

Need a little nudge to keep to a regular walking plan? The Chicago Walkers Club wants to keep you moving. Meet at the east entrance of Lincoln Park Zoo for their weekly 9:00 to 10:00 a.m. Saturday-morning walk or join one of their occasional special dinners or parties to replace some of those precious calories you lost.

Myopic Books
1564 North Milwaukee Avenue (southeast of the intersection of Milwaukee Avenue with North Damen Avenue and West North Avenue)
(773) 862-4882
www.myopicbookstore.com

Move that rook! Move that pawn! All for the chess club, stand up and yawn! Seriously though, folks, join the Wicker Park Chess Club for some brain-expanding games on Wednesday at 7:00 p.m. at Myopic.

Ultimate Frisbee
www.ultimatechicago.org

The object of this competitive Frisbee sport is to pass the disk from player to player and score end-zone goals football style, but without the tackling. The object of Ultimate Chicago is to get more players for more pickup games and league teams. Games are often co-ed. League play will cost you, but pickup games are free. To find one near you, go to the Web address above and click on the "More Ultimate" and "Pickup Games" links. Groups and ad hoc games and times throughout the city and suburbs are listed.

LIBRARIES:
FREE ACCESS

"A library is not a luxury but one of the necessities of life."
—HENRY WARD BEECHER

I know what you're thinking: Yeah, yeah, everyone knows they can borrow books and music, videos, and DVDs from the library. After all, the first free public library was founded in Greece in 330B.C., in Rome in 39B.C., or in Peterborough, New Hampshire, in 1833 (depending on which librarian you ask). Duh! Okay, smarty pants, bet you didn't know you can get legal advice at the Chicago Public Library, did you? And you can hear famous authors read their work, dedicated librarians read to children, and local politicians debate important social issues. You can also see free dances, movies, and plays or attend classes on a variety of topics from finance to literature. What's more, many universities and private libraries also allow public browsing of their collections. Some private libraries charge a membership fee to check out materials, but those listed in this chapter let you browse for free. Oh, you knew all that too? Glad we're on the same page.

CHICAGO **PUBLIC** LIBRARY

Chicago's public library (312–747–4300, www.chipublib.org) was founded in 1873 in the guts of a former water tank (because it was fireproof) at the southeast corner of LaSalle and Adams Streets. They've collected a lot of books since then. Today the library's collection of 5,121,882-plus books is the fifth largest in the world, according to the American Library Association. It also houses a heckuva lotta magazines and journals, videos, DVDs, and CD recordings. And it offers free computer access and free Wi-Fi for your own laptop. You can search the library system's Web site from home, so you can find the closest branch site that has the book, CD, DVD, or other piece of the collection you want to check out or browse. It lists locations by their specialty, such as collections in a particular language, science-fair materials, books for new adult readers, and large music collections. For a complete list of Chicago Public Library's eighty-seven locations and their telephone numbers, see Appendix C.

Harold Washington Library (aka Main, or Central, Library)
400 South State Street (between West Van Buren Street, South Plymouth Court, and East Congress Parkway)

This is the big daddy of the Chicago Public Library, with 756,000 square feet of space. The library offers tours, which help newcomers get a feel for the place and how to best take advantage of all it has to offer. Here's a list of services and specialty libraries within the building.

Learning Services: sixth floor south
Book Check-in, Check-out: third floor
Business, Science, and Technology Division: fourth floor
Chicago Authors Room: seventh floor
Children's Library: second floor
Cindy Pritzker Auditorium: lower level
Circulation Desk: third floor
Computer Commons: third floor south
Copy Center: fourth floor north
General Information and Services Division: third floor
Government Publications: fifth floor south
Electronic Resource Center: fourth floor
Harold Washington Archives and Collections: ninth floor north
History Division (with Social Sciences): sixth floor
Information Desk: first floor Interlibrary Loan: third floor
Library Card and Voter Registration Applications: third floor
Listening and Viewing Center: eighth floor
Literature and Language Division: seventh floor
Main Exhibit Hall: lower level
Municipal Reference Collection: fifth floor south
Music Practice Rooms: eighth floor
Newspapers and General Periodicals: third floor
Popular Library: first floor south (State Street entrance)
Professional Library: sixth floor
Social Sciences Division (with History): sixth floor
Social Sciences Periodicals: fifth floor
Special Collections and Preservation Division: ninth floor north
Special Collections Exhibit Halls: ninth floor
Talking Book Center: fifth floor north
Video Theater: lower level Visual & Performing Arts Division: eighth floor
Winter Garden: ninth floor

GOVERNMENT **LIBRARIES**

Commission on Chicago Landmarks Library
33 North La Salle Street (at West Calhoun Place), suite 1600
(312) 744–3200
www.cityofchicago.org/landmarks

The commission allows public access to binders of research related to Chicago landmarks.

Cook County Law Library
50 West Washington Street (in Daley Center between Dearborn Street and Clark Street), twenty-ninth floor; (312) 603–5423
2650 South California Avenue (in Criminal Court building at South 26th Street), fourth floor; (773) 869–5038
555 West Harrison Street (at Domestic Violence Court location); (312) 325–9390

The public has access to these open-stack libraries, legal databases on public computers, and a reference department, related to Cook County regulations and Illinois and other state laws.

PRIVATE **LIBRARIES**

Alliance Francaise
810 North Dearborn Street (between West Chestnut Street and West Chicago Avenue)
(312) 337–1070
www.afchicago.com

The Catch Nonmembers do not have borrowing privileges. Membership ranges from $35 per year for youth and teachers to $80 for individuals and $150 for a family of four.

Chicago's center of Francophilia allows anyone to browse its library for free. With 12,000 books and guides, several periodicals, audio magazines, music, videos, DVDs, and films, that's a lot of browsing, mon ami.

Chicago History Museum Research Center and Archives
1601 North Clark Street (at North Avenue)
(312) 642–4600
www.chicagohistory.org

The Chicago Historical Society—now called the Chicago History Museum—was founded in 1856, making it the city's oldest cultural institution. That gave the society a head start forming what is today an extensive collection of documents and artifacts that have served generations of professional and amateur historians. Some of those documents are accessible online through links on the society's Web site.

Donors Forum of Chicago
208 South LaSalle Street (at West Adams Street), suite 735
(312) 578–0175
www.donorsforum.org

You've got big ideas for great good works, but your little not-for-profit self or organization needs some help getting starting or keeping going. Good thing the Donors Forum houses more than 3,000 volumes of publications that explain how, when, where, and why to apply for grants from nice people and organizations who want to give nice people like you some free money. The librarian can help you get started.

Gerber / Hart Library
1127 West Granville Avenue (between North Winthrop Avenue and North Broadway Street)
(773) 381–8030
www.gerberhart.org

The Catch Nonmembers do not have borrowing privileges. Membership is $25 a year for full-time students, seniors, or people with low incomes; $40 otherwise.

This library of 14,000 books and periodicals by, for, and about gay, lesbian, bisexual, and transgendered people also serves as a depository of old and newly generated records of GLBT people and organizations in the Midwest.

Goethe-Institut Chicago
150 North Michigan Avenue (at East Randolph Street), suite 200
(312) 263–0472
www.goethe.de/Chicago

Not to be outdone by the French, the Goethe-Institut Chicago has a library too. It includes multimedia resources in German, including magazines and newspapers, and German TV. Their Internet access is free too.

Instituto Cervantes Chicago

31 West Ohio Street (between North State Street and North Dearborn Street)
(312) 335–1996
http://chicago.cervantes.es

The Catch Nonmembers do not have borrowing privileges. Membership is $25 for students and seniors, $50 general, and $75 per family per year.

Not to be outdone by the Germans and French, Instituto Cervantes has a library too. It houses a variety of media to support the learning, teaching, and enjoyment of Spanish in European and American dialects.

Newberry Library

60 West Walton Street (between North Dearborn Street and North Clark Street)
(312) 943–9090
www.newberry.org

The Newberry Library is one of the world's top research libraries, in an achingly beautiful building. A noncirculating library, it's free for public browsing. To help conserve the Newberry's collection, which includes many rare materials, security is a little tighter than your average reading room. You'll need to check coats, umbrellas, bags, scissors, cameras, and other potential tools of vandalism and thievery in their cloakroom lockers. And you'll need to obtain a reader's card (bring a photo ID and proof of current address on your first visit).

UNIVERSITY LIBRARIES

Many public and private colleges and universities in Chicago allow people who aren't students and aren't faculty or staff members to browse at least part of their collections. Here's a sampling of the major institutions in Chicago, and a few minor ones, with open-door policies, along with the telephone numbers of their libraries.

Catholic Theological Union, 5401 South Cornell Avenue; (773) 753–5321; www.ctu.lib.il.us

Chicago State University, 9501 South Martin Luther King Jr. Drive; (773) 995–2341; www.csu.edu/library

Columbia College Chicago, 624 South Michigan Avenue; (312) 344–7900; www.lib.colum.edu

DePaul University, www.lib.depaul.edu

> **Main Campus:** 2350 North Kenmore Street (between West Fullerton Avenue and West Belden Avenue); (773) 325–7862
>
> **Loop Campus:** 1 East Jackson Boulevard (at South State Street); (312) 362–8433
>
> **Rinn Law Library:** 25 East Jackson Boulevard (between South Wabash Avenue and South State Street), fifth floor; (312) 362–8121; www.law.depaul.edu/library

Lutheran School of Theology at Chicago and McCormick Theological Seminary, 1100 East 55th Street (at South Greenwood Avenue); (773) 256–0739; www.jkmlibrary.org

Meadville-Lombard Theological School (Unitarian Universalist), 5701 South Woodlawn Avenue (at East 57th Street); (773) 256–3000; http://www.meadville.edu/Lib_Catalog.htm

Northeastern Illinois University, 5500 North Saint Louis Avenue (at West Catalpa Avenue); (773) 442–4400; www.neiu.edu/~neiulib/

Roosevelt University, 430 South Michigan Avenue (between East Van Buren Street and East Congress Parkway); (312) 341–3639; www.roosevelt.edu/library

Spertus Institute of Jewish Studies, 618 South Michigan Avenue (between East Harrison Street and East Balbo Drive); (312) 322–1749; www.spertus.edu/asher_cja/about.php

University of Illinois at Chicago, 801 South Morgan Street (at West Polk Street); (312) 996–2716; www.uic.edu/depts/lib

City Colleges of Chicago

> **Harold Washington College,** 30 East Lake Street (between North Wabash Avenue and North State Street); (312) 553–5760; www.hwclibrary.net
>
> **Kennedy-King College,** 6800 South Wentworth Avenue (between West 67th Street and West 69th Street); (773) 602–5449; http://kennedyking.ccc.edu/library
>
> **Malcolm X College,** 1900 West Van Buren Street (between South Wood Street and South Damen Avenue); (312) 850–7244; http://malcolmx.ccc.edu/library

Olive-Harvey College, 10001 South Woodlawn Avenue (at East 103rd Street); (773) 291–6477; http://oliveharvey .ccc.edu/studentservices/ library.shtml

Truman College, 1145 West Wilson Street (at North Clifton Avenue); (773) 907–4865; www.trumancollege.cc/library/

Wright College, 4300 North Narragansett Avenue (between West Montrose Avenue and West Berteau Avenue); (773) 481–8400; http:// wright.ccc.edu/library/

COMPUTERS:
FREE WI-FI

"Getting information off the Internet is like taking a drink from a fire hydrant."
—MITCHELL KAPOR

Getting by without a computer or Internet access is getting harder nowadays. Friends, loved ones, bosses, and business contacts all expect to be able to communicate quickly and efficiently via e-mail from anywhere in the world. Teachers, employers, and clients expect well-researched, typed papers more quickly than they used to, thanks to the assumption that more folks have access to computers and the Internet. Whether you're passing through Chicago and just want to send a message home to Mom, want to get your very own computer and use it to access the Internet, or just want to learn how to work the darn things, technically savvy and generous Chicagoans are ready to help.

INTERNET **FREE** CPL

Most Chicago Public Library locations now offer free Wi-Fi Internet connections. The quality of the service tends to be better some days than others. The signal's strongest the closer you are to the library's wireless router equipment. Wireless service at the Harold Washington Library, for example, is best on the third floor, where the routers are located. But you can sometimes catch signals farther away, if the mysterious forces of Internet signals are blowing in your direction. Chicago Public Library branch locations also have computers that allow free public Internet access, or just time to type a term paper or letter to the editor. You might have to reserve a block of time, so call your local branch to check its policies and access times. Most now charge a bit for pages printed. To find the branch nearest you, call (312) 747–4300 or check their Web site at www.chipublib.org.

PRIVATE **PROVIDERS**

Many local cafes, restaurants, and bars have realized that if they offer free wireless Internet connections, some laptop-bearing patrons will stay longer and maybe eat or drink more while they're there. Or we customers may choose to visit one establishment over another based on whether it offers a hot spot. Many Web sites now provide users free directories of free hot spots in Chicago

WiFi Surfing Safety

Chicago is dotted with a proliferating number of "Wi-Fi hot spots," which means places where, if you have a computer with wireless capability, you can access the Internet without telephone cords or network cables. Often, the locations that host free wireless hot spots, such as cafes, hotels, and most Chicago Public Libraries, advertise their services and post instructions on how to connect. Sometimes, hot spots that don't restrict access aren't advertised, but your computer's wireless card will detect them on its own.

Your next-door neighbor may have wireless Internet access and leave the network unblocked so that nearby households, guests, and passing malicious network hackers may enjoy the service for free too.

Whether you're at home or away, be wary of wireless signals whose owners you don't know. They may belong to information pirates whose computers of evil are outfitted with software designed to capture the information you're sending over the Internet or peek into your computer's hard drive, from as far as 300 feet away. Even good-hearted providers of free wireless Internet signals caution that their shared wireless networks may not be completely secure. Good firewall and virus protection software from a trusted source should protect your computer and information reasonably well. But bad guys continually tweak their software to foil such protections, so make sure you keep your laptop outfitted with the latest protection, and exercise caution sharing financial and personal information over the air. And if you and your neighbors want to share Wi-Fi service, share the password with each other and keep the network protected from outside intruders.

Neighborhood Webs

The Wireless Community Networks (WCN) project, an effort of the Neighborhood Technology Resource Center (NTRC) in North Lawndale, recruits residents to place wireless signal-receiving nodes on their roofs. They receive signals broadcast from directional antennas on top of a building in North Lawndale and then spread the wireless signal love around the community. If you're a lucky resident who might be covered by that signal and would like to learn more, contact the NTRC.

Bronzeville: Charles Hayes Family Investment Center, 4859 South Wabash Avenue; (312) 745–2678

LeClaire Courts: LeClaire Courts Apartments, 4446–4448 South Laporte Avenue; (773) 735–1187

Neighborhood Technology Resource Center (NTRC)
Homan Square Community Center
3517 West Arthington Street (between South Saint Louis Avenue and South Homan Avenue)
(773) 722–5653
www.ntrconline.com

There are additional NTRC computer-training centers that are not part of the wireless-access pilot. They offer a variety of computer classes for youth and adults, many of which are free.

West Town: Northwest Tower Apartments, 1170 West Erie Street, first floor; (312) 633–9057

and elsewhere, and some include user ratings of the Wi-Fi services and the venues that host them. Here are just a couple, both of which are free.

JiWire
www.jiwire.com

JiWire will search more than 100,000 free and paid Wi-Fi hot spots based on your city or zip code. Its Web site also includes tips for safer wireless use at home and abroad. They heavily pitch their wireless security software and services and other ads, but of course you're under no obligation to buy.

WI-FI Finders

A number of businesses, from bars and restaurants to bowling alleys, have figured out that more people will visit their fine establishments and linger longer if they have free Wi-Fi access to surf the Internet or conduct official business. With the number of hot spots proliferating around the city, it's easy to find one near you. Look online for free Wi-Fi hot-spot locator services. They're searchable by state and city. Here are just a few:

http://hotspotr.com/wifi
www.jiwire.com
www.wififreespot.com

LOCAL MEDIA:
THE FREE PRESS

"I resent insinuendos."
—MAYOR RICHARD J. DALEY, TO REPORTERS

"I mean, why?
Why do you have to bring that up?"
—MAYOR RICHARD M. DALEY, TO REPORTERS

There are more free papers in this city than you could possibly read, even if you had nothing else to do but eat, sleep, and metabolize. Most of them provide the same news and more on their Web sites. And a growing number of Web sites without paper trails are devoted to all things Chicago. Some of Chicago's print and electronic freebies contain world-class reporting on local topics. Others are just excuses for ads. Most are somewhere in between, offering unique perspectives on specialized subjects for niche audiences. You can find the papers in their own boxes outdoors, inside libraries, and piled in entryways of cafes, bars, clubs, and stores likely to be visited by their target readers. Here are but a few journalistic ventures that offer free papers, free online content, or both.

Bookslut
www.bookslut.com

A Web magazine and blog dedicated to books that provides reviews, news, event announcements, and commentary. It also hosts some fine spoken-word events around town.

Centerstage Chicago
www.centerstagechicago.com

This online guide provides reviews, tips, and announcements covering entertainment, eating, exercising, and other activities around Chicago.

Chicago Free Press
(773) 868–0005
www.chicagofreepress.com

This weekly covers issues relevant to gay, lesbian, bisexual, and transgendered people in Chicago. Coverage ranges from local to international, serious to fun. Arts and entertainment coverage includes reviews and schedules of the best in Chicago. Good reading whatever your orientation. (See also the *Windy City Times* listing.)

Chicago Journal
(312) 243–2696
www.ChicagoJournal.com

This weekly provides news of the South Loop, Near West, and West Loop neighborhoods, along with education news, features, opinions, and arts coverage. Its paper is dyed a pinkish beige, which always makes me feel like I'm reading a newspaper from a century ago, except with news of condo developments, bird-flu fears, and political corruption instead of the swamp drainage projects, Spanish-flu fears, and political corruption.

Chicago Parent
(708) 386–5555
www.chicagoparent.com

This monthly magazine provides valuable news and information for Chicago parents, including coverage of education, health, and fun. It also relays tips on plenty of upcoming free events and services around Chicago. The publisher also produces *Chicago Special Parent* and *Chicago Baby*.

Chicago Reader
(312) 828–0350
www.chicagoreader.com

This weekly tabloid contains top-notch reporting on such issues as police torture and sleazy political deals; profiles of Chicagoans worth knowing; and a local bent on state, national, and international politics. The *Reader* also

Extra! Extra!

In case you've been living under a rock with no Internet access for the past five years, it's high time someone informed you that most daily newspapers (the old-fashioned kind that cost money and publish Family Circus and Cathy comic strips) are available for free online. They publish nearly all of the same stuff as the paper versions, along with extra Internet content that's easy to search and download for future reference. Check the daily news, sports scores, weather, and arts coverage; fire off angry letters to the editor; look for a job, living space, or garage sale just like Grandma and Grandpa used to do, except faster, freer, and without the ink-smudged hands and paper cuts that made their lives so hard. You can find Chicago's two big-daddy dailies, the *Chicago Tribune* and the *Chicago Sun-Times*, at:
www.chicagotribune.com
www.chicagosuntimes.com

includes reviews and listings of music, movies, plays, readings, kids' events, art, outsider fashion shows, and just about anything else that might amuse you. (Ok, I've written for the *Reader,* so I'm a little biased.) It marks free events with "Free" icons and its "Free Shit" blog digs up cheap bastard goodies ranging from free yoga classes to free dental and acupuncture services. The *Reader* earns its keep by selling ads, including personals matching every sexual orientation, apartments for rent, condos for sale, jobs, bands seeking musicians, escorts and other services, and a variety of household products, some free for the pickup. All of the *Reader*'s content is also available online, and blogs provide updates throughout the week. Free book swap events coincide with its spring and fall books issues.

Chicagoist
www.chicagoist.com

The Chicago outpost of a national web of similar sites provides news, events, restaurant reviews, nightlife tips, and observations about Chicago.

Chicagoland Tails
(773) 262–0399
www.tailsinc.com

This magazine for Chicagoans with pets includes local news and reviews of petcentric happenings; tips on local resources; how-to's for raising healthy, happy pets; photos of the pet society world; and plenty of ads and directories to find just the right free or fee-based pet services for your little critters.

Conscious Choice
(312) 440–4373
www.consciouschoice.com

This monthly magazine will inspire you to live a more environmental, spiritual, sensual, physical, feminist, humanist, pacifist, activist, yogic, colonic, nontoxic, non-demonic life. It also might make you afraid to go outside, drink the water, or eat anything nonorganic, with its local and national reporting of environmental, food-safety, and political issues. But that's probably a good thing. The magazine also includes a lot of fun tips and information and profiles of Chicagoans making our backyard a better place.

Extra
(773) 252–3534
www.extranews.net

It's a newspaper and a bilingual Spanish and English lesson. Spanish and English articles are placed side by side. Coverage includes local news and features, police beats, and the occasional recipe.

Gapers Block
www.gapersblock.com

Gapers posts news, commentary by staff and readers, and tips on happenings around town. It's a great place to find out what's happening over the weekend or reviews of bars and other night spots.

The Heckler
(773) 407–2314
www.theheckler.com

Don't be alarmed by headlines like "Cubs Cancel Next Year." This fun freebie is mostly satirical. Look for it in your favorite sports bar or restaurant or in honor boxes near the occasional el stop or around sports venues.

Hoy
(312) 527–8400
www.hoyinternet.com

Owned by Chicago's own Tribune Publishing, *Hoy* is the only national Spanish-language daily newspaper in the United States. And it's completely gratis. Coverage includes local and world events and issues, particularly those of interest to Spanish speakers, along with the usual sports, weather, and celebrity news.

Hyde Park Herald
Lakefront Outlook
(773) 643–8533
http://hpherald.com

Since 1882, the *Hyde Park Herald* has reported news of both the big and extremely local kind, covering Hyde Park and surrounding neighborhoods. *Lakefront Outlook,* its sister publication, just won a George Polk Award for giving Third-Ward alderwoman Dorothy Tillman the kind of extensive, award-winning coverage no politician wants.

N'Digo
(312) 822–0202
www.ndigo.com

N'Digo is a free weekly covering hard news and thoughtful commentary of African-American issues, along with community paper recipes and horoscope fare.

New City
(312) 243–8786
www.newcity.com

This weekly covers arts, entertainment, clubs, hipster happenings, and explorations of local political and social issues. Its Chicago Hype Exchange, which tracks the week's biggest winners and losers according to the "capricious contours of celebrity," is a particularly fun read.

The Onion
(312) 751–0503
www.theonion.com

Chinese government officials reportedly got their undies in a bunch a few years ago over a story in the *Onion,* not knowing that most of the national weekly is a spoof of hokey local and haughty international American news coverage. The one section that is straight (that is, true) reporting is the AV (Audio Visual) section. It provides some of the finest interviews and coverage of national artists and their work coming to Chicago, along with schedules of events going on around town.

Red Eye
(312) 222–4970
www.redeyechicago.com

A popular tabloid that reads like *US Weekly* covering local and world events for teenagers, this is the *Chicago Tribune*'s daily attempt to reach the coveted eighteen to thirty-four-year-old urban-hipster demographic. I've tried to read it regularly, but there's only so much over-reported-celebrity reporting and pithy fluff news filler I can stand.

Today's Chicago Woman (TCW)
(312) 951–7600
www.tcwmag.com

Targeted to affluent and wanna-be affluent Chicago-area women, there's not much free in these pages, but it's a good place to check out this season's fashions, which will start showing up in Chicago's alleys and thrift stores next season. The monthly glossy also covers health, beauty, fitness, politics, arts, food, and local events, and it provides cover stories each month profiling high-profile local women.

UR Chicago
(312) 238–9782
www.urchicago.com

Paper is so, like, 2007! With Twittering twenty-one to thirty-somethings as its target demographic, this monthly ditched the pulp version of itself in 2008 to exist only in the virtual world. Its Web site continues *UR*'s heavy focus on the club scene, hipster fashion trends, arts coverage, and young reporters covering some pretty important issues.

Windy City Times
(773) 871–7610
www.windycitytimes.com

Like the *Chicago Free Press* (earlier in this chapter), this weekly covers local to international issues of importance to gay, lesbian, bisexual, and transgender Chicagoans. Stories of Supreme Court nominations, gay marriage, local methamphetamine abuse, aldermanic stances on issues, and arts and entertainment coverage are well written and timely.

Yoga Chicago
(773) 989–6767
www.yogachicago.com

This biweekly is a great resource for finding yoga classes and activities around Chicago, including free ones. Coverage includes how-to articles about yoga and alternative medicine, yoga-related travel essays, and literary musings on the practice.

SCAVENGING:
RECLAMATION CHIC

"My wife is always trying to get rid of me. The other day, she told me to put the garbage out. I said to her I already did. She told me to go watch it."
—RODNEY DANGERFIELD

When the uninitiated see someone rifling through garbage, their reaction is often pity. When I encounter a "Dumpster diver," I'm more likely to think *Dang, he found my favorite spot!* Chicago is lucky to have an extensive system of alleys that keep most Dumpsters off of front sidewalks and yards and—more importantly—that serve as a citywide strip mall of free used stuff. It's easy to find great furniture, books, clothing, housewares, electronics, sporting goods, music, cleaning supplies, and unused toiletries like soap and shampoo. Many people throw good stuff in with the regular, stinky garbage. But just as many people place usable items next to Dumpsters or on top of them, hoping they'll be reclaimed by passersby. It's a common enough practice that you should be able to clothe and furnish your household without having to "dive" in any Dumpsters or even get your hands dirty.

CHICAGO'S **FINEST** ALLEYS

Here's a sample of the many great scavenging grounds in Chicago.

Andersonville
(between Bryn Mawr Avenue, Broadway Avenue, Foster Avenue, and Clark Street)

A mix of expensive homes and higher-rent apartments, Andersonville is good for toys and other baby and kids' items, barely-used sporting goods, decent artwork, paint, books, and furniture. Sunday afternoons through early weekdays are good times to check for the results of weekend clutter-purging projects.

Moving Day!

The most productive scavenging runs are around the end of the month during mild and warm seasons, when the most people move out of apartments. Folks toss the most when they move, for a variety of reasons. Couples are combining households and don't need two ironing boards. Someone is overwhelmed by packing or can't fit everything into the moving truck. The old stereo doesn't go with the new draperies. Piles will start forming the weekend before the first of the month and continue until the weekend after it. In Chicago, May 1 and October 1 are the biggest moving days of the year, which means that around those dates, in the right neighborhoods, you can find alley after alley piled with mountains of high-quality castoffs. If you're seeking "school supplies" like funky student-apartment furniture, casual clothing, books, high-cost hooch, and scholarly and entertainment electronics, hit the neighborhoods around high-tuition college campuses at the end of each semester.

My Favorite Things

Friends often compliment me on my flair for decorating. Aw, shucks. I thank them, then go through my home pointing out the vast majority of items I rescued from the garbage and worked into my high-class pad: the expansive glass coffee-table top, the ficus tree and ponytail palm, the plush velvet pillow covers, the antique hutch with glass cabinet doors that fits perfectly in my kitchen, the coffee-espresso-cappuccino maker, the hand-knotted oriental rug that I and the cleaner liberated from a bit of dried cat puke, and—my favorite—a little Beavis and Butthead statue that talks when activated by a TV remote control.

Curbside Shopping Tips

1. Shy? Bring friends. You'll have a lot of fun, and the few people who otherwise would disdain your scavenging might wonder what they're missing. Come up with a system ahead of time, like drawing straws, for what you'll do if more than one person wants the same treasure.

2. Find the right neighborhood. The higher the disposable income and corresponding transience of a block, the more stuff you'll find there, so look for the high-rent areas. Neighborhoods with a lot of homeowners may not produce as many good castoffs as consistently, but they can be good sources of baby and children's clothing and toys, sporting goods, bicycles, furniture, books, tools, and other things people purge in those weekend garage- or basement-cleaning projects.

3. Find the right buildings. Smaller apartment buildings generally have accessible Dumpsters kept either in the public alley space or right next to it. Most high-rises keep their Dumpsters inside a locked fence or loading dock, where they're inaccessible. If building managers clearly don't want you getting to their Dumpsters (or if they lock them), don't bother. It's not worth trespassing when you can find plenty in public spaces.

4. Know when the shops are open for business. Check a favorite alley regularly, and you'll notice that garbage trucks tend to arrive the same day each week. The best times to hit your favorite alleys are anytime between weekends (when people purge goods from cleaning or moving) and when the garbage trucks will carry away the goodies with the trash. The end of the month and end of school semesters make for particularly good pickings.

Hyde Park
(between 51st Street, South Cottage Grove Avenue, 59th Street, and the lake)

This area is home to the University of Chicago and some very expensive homes and condos. You will have plenty of scavenging competition here from residents of Hyde Park, especially starving U of C students, and from savvy residents of nearby low-income neighborhoods. Ends of semesters, especially in the spring, are the best times to procure leftovers from students.

5. Keep your eyes open. The more often you pass through alleys, the more likely you are to encounter that perfect something that would go oh so nicely with the other perfect something you found the week before.

6. Bring along some sanitary hand wipes, a damp washcloth in a plastic bag, and waterproof gloves, just in case you see something nifty that's a bit untidy. Plastic garbage bags can keep damp linens or clothing isolated until they can be washed and sanitized. Give upholstered furniture and other items that can't be cleaned the old sniff test. You don't want to go through the trouble of loading and moving something only to discover it smells irreversibly of cat pee.

7. If you do pick through bags in the Dumpster or next to it, watch out for broken glass or other dangerous sharp items.

8. Be nice. If you drive through alleys, drive slowly and quietly. Don't make a mess. Leave stacked or piled items as neat as or neater than you found them.

9. As you "trade up" to better castoffs, donate your old good stuff to nonprofit groups or place them solicitously next to your own Dumpster just after the real trash has been hauled away, ideally when there's little chance of precipitation. It'll keep the reclamation circle going and make another cheap bastard's day. See the sidebar on page 176 about what hazardous wastes (including electronics) NOT to put out with the garbage, and what to do with them.

Lakeview and Lincoln Park
(between Irving Park Road, the lake, North Avenue, and the Chicago River)

One of Chicago's "hottest" rental and condo markets, Lakeview guarantees people moving in and out of apartments almost every month. Great for furniture, small household items, electronics, trendy and classic clothing, CDs, books, and office supplies. The neighborhood around DePaul University is notable for the stuff students toss when they move each spring and for the consistently impressive move-out and weekend-cleaning castoffs of renters and homeowners the rest of the year.

Rogers Park Loyola Area
(between Devon Avenue, Ridge Boulevard, Touhy Avenue, and the lake)

Home to Loyola University, this lovely neighborhood by the lake yields fun student decor, apparel, and textbooks at the end of the spring semester. Homeowners there have given me some nice presents year-round too.

Responsible Refuse

Please don't leave items such as computer monitors and other electronics, batteries, fluorescent lights, paint, and hazardous cleaning products in the alley. If no one claims them, they're likely to wind up in a landfill, where lead, mercury, and other heavy metals and nasty chemicals will leach out and pollute our soil, air, and water. Old medicine, motor oil, and insecticides are other products that should be recycled or discarded with care. You can discard old meds in bins located at Chicago Police Department sites. And you can discard batteries for recycling at Chicago Public Library branches and Walgreen's stores. For more information and to locate a recycling or disposal facility near you, contact Chicago's Department of the Environment at (312) 744–7672, www.cityofchicago.org/Environment. The city also operates a Household Chemicals & Computer Recycling Facility at 1105 North Branch Street (at Division Street, 2 blocks east of the Kennedy Expressway), where you can drop off stuff that should stay out of our waste stream. Their dedicated workers divert electronics that work or can be rehabilitated to not-for-profit programs that can use them. To thank you for your diligence, the facility also offers a materials exchange room, where residents can pick up unwanted-but-usable products such as paint, oil, and wood stains. Check hours of operation, rules for what to drop off and what's not allowed, and fun facts about the facility on the city's Web portal: http://egov.city ofchicago.org. Or call 311 and ask to be transferred to the facility.

CHEAP **BASTARDS** IN **(CYBER)** SPACE

A lot of people hate to see waste as much as you do, and they use the Internet to find new homes for possessions they no longer want. Givers list mundane essentials like furniture and clothing or unique offerings like player pianos and cast-iron tubs. The number of online trading posts of givers and receivers is growing. Here are a couple of tried and true sites for great finds.

Chicago Freecycle Network
www.freecycle.org

The Catch In the spirit of giving, you must first post something to give away before you can access ads of other givers.

This local site of a national phenomenon is like Dumpstering meets a free version of eBay. People post things they don't need and find things they do. Members (free) exchange messages and decide where and when to exchange their worldly possessions.

Suburban Bounty

Once or twice a year, usually sometime in the spring, many suburbs hold community cleanup weeks when residents can place a bunch of large items out with the trash without having to pay extra for the privilege. That makes for fine used-furniture pickings for anyone with the means to haul them away. But it might not be the best idea to show up in a large scavenger truck. While some people are happy to see their unwanted items put to good use and have fun scavenging from their neighbors, too, others are put off by strangers diverting their castoffs from landfills. So drive and load quietly out of respect to the neighborhood, and if someone objects to your presence, leave the loot and move on. There's plenty more just around the corner. Tight budgets and other factors can change municipal cleanup plans, so check village Web sites for announcements or call for specific dates as times of annual cleanups approach.

Like Buying Air

I have countless other possessions that I would never think of buying new because I've found so many of them nearly new in alleys over the years. Here are a few of them.

- Vacuum cleaners discarded by people who don't know that the machines still work if they just change the bags, empty the dirt collection cups, or change the belts.
- Last year's fashions from the likes of Gap, J.Crew, Banana Republic, Hollister, and American Eagle.
- Ironing boards and irons.
- Ficus trees and other houseplants that usually just need a good watering to resurrect. (Check for signs of common plant diseases, most of which can be cured with a little water mixed with dish soap sprayed on the leaves, and keep outside or far from other plants until cleared up.)
- Planting pots and window boxes.
- Cross-country skis and other exercise equipment people used once or twice and then left to gather dust before being abandoned.
- Futon frames.
- Kitchen and dining-room table and chair sets.
- Three-ring binders, envelopes, and other office supplies.
- Telephones.
- Clock radios, boom boxes, and stereo components.
- Dishes, pots, pans, and utensils.
- Posters, paintings, and other art.
- Sheets, pillowcases, and blankets.
- Upholstered sofas and chairs that look and smell clean.
- Unused cleaning chemicals, buckets, gently used brooms and mops with replaceable mop heads.

craigslist

http://chicago.craigslist.org/
Go to the "for sale" section and click on "free."

Posts describe the item or items being offered and sometimes include photos. Interested parties reply to the posts, givers and takers exchange messages and finally coordinate the times and places for home pickups. Or posters just describe items and provide locations of stuff they left in alleys. Make sure you see a photo or confirm the item in question is something you'd really want. Some posters assume they're doing the world a favor by offering up dirty, ripped upholstery with missing legs.

SUBURBS **WITH** CLEANUP **WEEKS**

Glencoe: (847) 835–4114; www.goglencoe.com; usually the first two Wednesdays of May.
Elmwood Park: (708) 452–7300; www.elmwoodpark.org; usually in late April or early May.
Highland Park: (847) 432–0800; http://www.cityhpil.com; usually in late April or early May.
Lake Bluff: (847) 234–0774; www.lakebluff.org; usually the first (west side of town) and second (east side of town) Wednesdays in May and October.
Lincolnshire: (847) 883–8600; http://www.village.lincolnshire.il.us; usually in April.
Mokena: (708) 479–3927; www.mokena.org; usually in late April or early May.
Richton Park: (708) 481–8950; www.richtonpark.org; usually during May or June.
Western Springs: (708) 246–1800; www.wsprings.com; usually the last Saturday in April.
Winnetka: (847) 501–6000; www.villageofwinnetka.org; usually the last week of April or first week of May.

SHOPPING:
IF YOU MUST

"I take Him shopping with me. I say,
'Ok, Jesus, help me find a bargain.'"
—TAMMY FAYE (BAKKER) MESSNER

Sometimes you can't wait for the alleys to provide. You need a suit for a sudden job interview. You don't want your parents to know you've been living without furniture. The new baby is about to arrive and, charming as it sounds to tuck her into a dresser drawer each night just like in those stories from the Old World, a crib must be safer. Or—admit it—you just feel like shopping. What's a thrifty consumer to do? Why, buy used, of course. Chicago hosts such a bounty of thrift stores, resale and consignment shops, and open-air markets that you can go for years without buying much new and still feed your soul while keeping yourself and your surroundings looking spiffy. For the price of one new item you can buy an entire wardrobe, collection, or room's decor without blowing your budget or smug sense of reduce-reuse environmental superiority.

THRIFT **STORES**

To be fair, I have a pretty high standard for what counts as reasonably priced apparel or upholstery: Costs more to clean it than it did to buy it. The sample of shops listed here fit that bill and, therefore, my definition of true thrift stores. Yes, many thrift stores are still as dusty and disorganized as their reputations, with merchandise that looked just as bad when it was new. But don't judge Chicago's thrifts by those you've known in other cities. While most local shops stock the requisite rainbow leg warmers, sad clown paintings, and plaid couches for fans of ironic vintage, the city has a steady supply of donors to keep the thrift stores listed here also stocked with high-end and trendy fashions and household goods from this very decade.

Salvation Army
6434 West 63rd Street (at South Nagle Avenue); (773) 586–0178
3055 West 63rd Street (east of South Albany Avenue); (773) 476–8718
5112 South Ashland Avenue (at West 51st Street); (773) 737–3335
2024 South Western Avenue (at West Cullerton Street); (773) 254–1127
509 North Union Avenue (at West Grand Avenue); (312) 738–4360
5713 West Chicago Avenue (between North Waller Avenue and North Massasoit Avenue); (773) 287–9774
2270 North Clybourn Avenue (between West Fullerton Avenue and West Webster Avenue); (773) 477–1300

2941 North Central Avenue (between West Wellington Avenue and West George Street); (773) 283–1315
2151 West Devon Avenue (at North Leavitt Street); (773) 764–0364
3301 West Montrose Avenue (at North Spaulding Avenue); (773) 342–2068
3837 West Fullerton Avenue (at North Avers Avenue); (773) 276–1955
4141 West North Avenue (between North Kedvale Avenue and North Keeler Avenue); (773) 342–2068
4315 North Broadway Street (at North Sheridan Road); (773) 348–1401

We were hungry and you fed us; strangers and you welcomed us; naked and you clothed us in vintage punk for our Saturday nights, nearly new suits for our Monday morning job interviews, and cabana wear all year-round. God bless you, Sally! You also clothe our kids and give us furniture, books, records, and cool retro curios too. For that we'll overlook the occasional oddly high price and junky stuff no one will ever buy that takes up store space but spares the landfill. Many Salvation Army stores that sell furniture will deliver purchases for an extra fee.

Unique Thrift Store

4441 West Diversey Avenue (at North Kenneth Avenue); (773) 227–2282
4445 North Sheridan Road (at West Agatite Avenue); (773) 275–8623
3748 North Elston Avenue (at North Kimball Avenue); (773) 279–08507530
North Western Avenue (at Howard Street); (773) 338–6898
6560 West Fullerton Avenue (near North Normandy Avenue); (773) 622–6654
3000 South Halsted Street (at West 30th Street); (312) 842–0942
9341 South Ashland Avenue (between West 93rd Street and West 94th Street); (773) 239–3127
3542 South Archer Avenue (between West 35th Street and West 36th Street); (773) 247–2599
5040 South Kedzie Avenue (at West 115th Street); (773) 434–4886

Like many thrift stores, Unique will price some crappy plastic thing several times its worth and an obvious antique at a fraction of its value. Imagine your pride in sharing that little chuckle with some appraiser who gushes over your smart find on the *Antiques Road Show*. Same goes for apparel, so don't be deterred if a dirty, ripped leather coat from an unattractive decade seems unreasonably expensive at $20. Chances are, there's an uber-performance, techno-fabric ski jacket in your size nearby, complete with lift ticket from some exclusive resort, for $5 to $10. Besides clothing, Unique also has a good selection of furniture, music and books, electronics, housewares, and toys. Half-price Mondays are an even better deal if you don't mind big crowds, long lines, and having to wait your turn for a shopping cart.

Village Discount Outlet
Phone number for all stores: (866) LIKE–VDO (545–3836)
www.villagediscountoutlet.com
4898 North Clark Street (at West Ainslie Street)
3301 West Lawrence Avenue (at North Spaulding Avenue)
4635 North Elston Avenue (at North Kildare Avenue)

No Fitting Room? No Problem!

For some mysterious reason, many thrift stores don't have fitting rooms. And for another mysterious reason, size 12 or 36 in one brand isn't the same as size 12 or 36 in another brand. These are but small obstacles between savvy cheap bastards and their bargains. Here are some tips for making it more likely your haute couture finds are the right fit.

- Depending on where you wear your waistband, place the waistband of a pair of pants at your (ahem) back seam or at your lower spine. When the pants are pulled flat around to the front of your body, the waistband should at least reach your belly button, or just above or below it. Make sure the pants' wider and narrower curves (or lack thereof) match your own.
- Hold up shirts or sweaters to your neckline and make sure their bodies and sleeves are wide enough and long enough. (Duh.)
- Better yet, if your modesty allows, wear form-fitting clothing, either on its own or under looser outer layers that you can remove when you're ready to try on potential purchases at the shop. Slip into the new items to see how they fit.

4027 North Kedzie Avenue (at West Irving Park Road)
2043 West Roscoe Street (at North Seeley Avenue)
2032 North Milwaukee Avenue (north of West Armitage Avenue)
7443 South Racine Avenue (south of West 74th Place)
6419 South Kedzie Avenue (at West 64th Street)
2514 West 47th Street (at South Maplewood Avenue)
4020 West 26th Street (at South Komensky Avenue)

With several stores throughout the region, finding a Village Discount Outlet is about as easy as finding a Jewel or Dominick's. The large retail spaces are crammed with clothing, linens, toys, furniture and other household goods, CDs, videos, books, electronics, musical instruments, antiques, and knick-knacks even the staff can't identify. A sign near the front of each store shows which color tags are half price for the day. Most of the clothing is organized by gender, age, and color. But employees, many of them new to the vague boundaries of American fashion, sometimes place women's attire they find masculine (like sensible shoes and dark pantsuits) in the men's

Removing Prices

You found the perfect set of matching china and an antique bronze jewelry box priced less than dollar-store plastic. Before you spend hours cursing as you try to scrub off the prices scrawled in marker or stuck with gooey adhesive stickers on every !%#*! item, try these hints from matronly thrift store clerks.

- To remove marker ink from hard surfaces, use rubbing alcohol soaked into a cotton ball or rag. Rinse away ink and alcohol under running water and then wash as usual. When marker marks have soaked into little cracks in a dish's glaze, lay an alcohol-soaked cotton ball or rag on top of the offending mark and let it soak in a little longer.
- Spray remaining adhesive from stickers with oily furniture polish or rub with baby or cooking oil.
- To remove stapled tags from apparel or linens with less risk of damage, use a staple remover as if you were removing it from paper. Gently rub out the former holes with your thumb. Stitch up any tiny holes you find right away, a la the advice of that cheap bastard founding father Benjamin Franklin.

section and men's attire they find effeminate in the women's section. Same goes for women's clothing that must seem too frisky or form-fitting (including sizes 12 and 14) for sensible matriarchs and is therefore relegated to the girls shirts and sweaters area. It's worth looking around, though. Beneath the hallowed fluorescent lights of my local Village, I regularly find treasures from the likes of Burberry, Ann Taylor, The North Face, REI, Banana Republic, Merrell, Rockport, Pfaltzgraff (matching dish set for six!), Krups, and Cannon.

RESALE **AND** CONSIGNMENT **SHOPS**

Some resale and consignment shops charge high-as-new prices for merchandise that, in my opinion, ain't all that. But if you're intimidated by the dust and bustle of many thrift stores, or you require fitting rooms or a chummier atmosphere, they're a good place to start your thrift store training. Here are a few stores with overall prices that are slightly higher than my preference but with enough good deals to place them among my favorites.

The Ark Thrift Shop
1302 North Milwaukee Avenue (north of West Division Street); (773) 862–5011.
3345 North Lincoln Avenue (between West School Street and West Roscoe Street); (773) 248–1117

Where does plastic-protected furniture go when its owner dies? A lot of it must go to The Ark, judging from the amount of near-mint-condition 1960s- and 1970s-vintage furniture I regularly see here among older and newer decor. Chances are you'll find a nice martini set to go with it. Some of The Ark's goods are way overpriced, and a lot of the cheaper stuff is pretty worn and dingy, but there are always cool bargains to be found. Check out the bargain basement for even cheaper household and office items and sporting goods. I wouldn't recommend a special trip for the clothing, but as long as you're here, you may as well check it out for yourself on the second floor. Delivery service is available in case you find some gonzo California-king bedroom set and don't have another way to haul it home.

Brown Elephant Resale Shop

3651 North Halsted Street (north of West Addison Street); (773) 549–5943
5404 North Clark Street (at West Balmoral Avenue); (773) 271–9382

Brown Elephant shops raise money for the Howard Brown Health Center, which serves anyone but is devoted to the health-care and mental-health needs of the gay, lesbian, bisexual, and transgender community. Besides serving a swell cause, this is one of the few thrift stores where I can always find sassy size 11 women's heels. I buy them for a wedding or special event, wear them once, remember how uncomfortable heels are, hold onto them for six months or so, then donate them back to my local Brown Elephant until the next time I forget why I don't wear heels and buy another pair. This has been going on for years, kind of like a shoe time-share. At least the shoes are only a few bucks a pop. Brown Elephant has fabulous formal and casual couture, furniture and household accessories, and books and music, both classy and kitschy.

Crossroads Trading Company

1519 North Milwaukee Avenue (at North Honore Street); (773) 227–5300
2711 North Clark Street (at West Schubert Avenue); (773) 296–1000
http://crossroadstrading.com

This high-end consignment shop offers the latest trendy and designer clothing and accessories, all from fashionistas with the good sense to sell their separates rather than discard them. You can find big splurges such as a Coach bag at $150, but there are more earthly bargains to be found here too.

Disgraceland

3338 North Clark Street (at West Buckingham Place)
(773) 281–5875

A friend of mine theorizes that employees of stores like Gap and J.Crew help keep Disgraceland stocked with last season's fashions because they must sell their old clothes to pay for the latest apparel they're forced to buy and wear each new season as part of their jobs. Whether she's right or it's just voluntary slaves who feel compelled to trade in last season's wardrobe to help fund their addiction to buying the latest, Disgraceland is a great source for timely, barely worn apparel.

FLEAS **NOT** INCLUDED

Well, maybe sometimes there are fleas at flea markets, but most of the time, you'll just find good, cheap stuff you want, like clothing and the occasional antique, stuff you don't that's amusing nonetheless, and a smattering of knockoffs that's good for a "you gotta be kidding" glance at the questionable vendor in question. The key to finding the best merchandise is showing up early. (Skip the free wine tasting, no-cover band, and tamale feast the night before.) While Chicago's world of outdoor swap isn't what it used to be back when crowds would form organically at vacant lots, there are a few places that are still a swapping good time.

Swap-o-Rama Flea Markets
(708) 344–7300
4350 West 129th Street (east of West Inland Drive), Alsip; outdoors Wednesday 7:00 a.m. to 2:00 p.m.
4100 South Ashland Avenue (between ramp and West 42nd Street); outdoors Thursday 7:00 a.m. to 4:00 p.m.
4600 West Lake Street (near intersection of North 46th Avenue), Melrose Park; outdoors Friday 8:00 a.m. to 3:00 p.m.

This chain proudly declares itself "The first name in flea markets." Well, alright then. All of the indoor and outdoor markets of its three Chicago-area locations are open Saturday and Sunday from 7:00 a.m. to 4:00 p.m. They're also open one weekday for special outdoor-only deals. That's when professional scavengers bring their best finds to sell. Here are their locations and extra-special weekdays they're open.

Wolff's Flea Market Rosemont
Allstate Arena
6920 North Mannheim Road (between Interstate 90 and West Lunt Avenue)
Rosemont
(847) 524–9590
www.wolffs.com
Outdoor market open 7:00 a.m. to 3:00 p.m. Sunday only April through October, weather permitting.

The Catch Admission is $1 for adults, 50 cents for people age sixty-two and older and for kids age six to twelve years old. It's free for children younger than age six.

This arena of heavy metal concerts and monster truck races becomes a parking lot vortex of vending every Sunday that the weather holds up from

---

History of Haggling

Maxwell Street Market
South Desplaines Street and West Roosevelt Road
Sunday from 7:00 a.m. to 3:00 p.m.

Why, you ask, is Maxwell Street Market not on Maxwell Street? To answer this question, we need to go all the way back to the last half of the nineteenth century. With the influx of German, Irish, and Italian immigrants, followed by Jewish immigrants, a bustling open-air market developed on Maxwell Street. Newcomers sold food, clothing, tools, and other useful goods from pushcarts. Over the years, most members of those ethnic groups moved out of the neighborhood and were replaced by African-American and Spanish-speaking residents and merchants. Every Sunday, shoppers from all over the city still came to haggle for clothing (especially tube socks), tapes, records, books, electronics, furniture, musical instruments, tools, religious icons, tires, hubcaps, and all manner of used, new, stolen, or legitimately scavenged essentials of life. Visitors consumed fresh Mexican orchata and tamales or Maxwell-style hot dogs or Polish sausage as they enjoyed outdoor concerts by soon-to-be-famous blues musicians honing their chops and passing the hat. The sons of the African-American owner of a kosher deli exchanged a few words of Yiddish with the old Jewish men who stopped by to eat corned beef and play chess. A good time was had by all until 1994, when the city government shut down the party to make way for expansion by the University of Illinois at Chicago. The city established the New Maxwell Street Market at South Canal Street and West Roosevelt Road, about half a mile east of the old market. They moved it again to its current location in 2008. Though only a third the size of the old market, and lacking much of the old anarchistic charm, the new market is a great place to find new and used bargains, fresh produce, and hard-to-find ingredients to Mexican recipes and other cuisine from around the world. There are even blues concerts in good weather.

---

spring through fall. Someone must make a killing just on the admission, which is cheap if you come home with a bargain. There are many to be had at this largest of Chicago-area flea markets, especially if you show up early to rub asses with the masses. How early? The area officially opens at 7:00 a.m., but the cheap bastards who ain't messing around show up as early as 6:00 a.m. I wish them well. Stalls of new and used, including antiques, are complemented by indoor restrooms, ATMs, and food stands.

DOLLAR **STORES**

Let's start our dollar store discussion with a recent headline: "Family Dollar Stores Announce Recall of Spinning Star Christmas Tree Topper." Apparently, the tree topper tended to melt or smoke near the on-off switch, which wasn't a very good combination with crispy under-watered pine. The lesson? For goddsake, never ever buy anything electrical from a dollar store, especially if it also spins! I'd just as soon buy good used over bad new, but dollar stores are a good place to find, say, five hundred plastic Easter eggs for a craft project, a hundred pack of pencils whose leads you just hope to heaven aren't real lead, and the plastic globe pencil sharpener that has graced my desk for years. Okay, so I have found a few useful new items for a buck a pop. My favorite shops are the mom-and-pops that are packed with character as well as religious icons, incantations, and fabric flowers.

> ## Oh Yeah—and Cheap Paint
> One of the easiest ways to perk up a dingy room is with a fresh coat of paint. Before you pay full price for that liquid latex, ask your local hardware store if they have any paint on hand that was returned or rejected because customers didn't like the hue. The hues might be just right for you, and even if the store doesn't already advertise such mistakes, the manager will likely be happy to make a deal. Or keep your eyes open when you're scanning the alleys. You'll find a lot of sealed cans with a little off-white left over. Combine them and you've got a full gallon. If you're a bit of an eco-freak like me, you'll look for paint that's low in volatile organic compounds.

PETS:
CANINE, FELINE,
BOTTOM LINE

*"Money will buy you a fine dog, but only
love can make it wag its tail."*
—RICHARD FRIEDMAN

Pets give their people a lot of free love and ask little in return. But you should not adopt a pet if you're not sure you're able to provide the food, exercise, socialization, attention, and medical care any living creature deserves. Chicago's animal-loving community wants to help you meet those responsibilities a little more affordably. For starters, the cheapest way to acquire a pet is to avoid the puppy mills and instead adopt from a rescue organization or check "free to a good home" postings in pet shops and on Web sites. From vet screenings to good, healthy exercise, Chicago has a lot of great ways to keep your critter happy, healthy, and safe.

GET A **PET**

Most animal shelters require a donation to adopt pets. Those fees are often negotiable, but keep in mind that they help offset the costs of spaying, neutering, vaccinations, and other health and medical care provided to animals until suitable homes can be found. They usually also include free collars, leashes, pet carriers, and registration tags. Some pets even are implanted with microchips that contain information that can be scanned in case they get lost. In other words, the pet is free. You're paying for basic services and equipment. Shelters usually interview people wanting to adopt, then watch as they interact with prospective pets. They may also require documentation like leases and

---

Surfing for Pets

Chicago's major newspapers list pets for free adoption in their paper and online editions, and so do free online services. Here are a few.

http://chicago.craigslist.org/pet/, craigslist, provider of free listings of free and for-sale stuff in cities all over the world, has a site where Chicago users list pets for free adoption.

http://chicago.oodle.com/sale/pet/, another Web site offering lots of stuff for sale or free, including Chicago-area critters needing good homes.

www.petfinder.com is a national clearinghouse for shelters and rescue organizations, including some in the Chicago area.

---

condo association policies to ensure that you're allowed to keep that pet in your home. This is all to find compatible matches between pets and people and to avoid the sad but common problem of pets being returned to shelters again. Here are some Chicago-area shelters and their adoption fees.

Animal Welfare League, 10305 Southwest Highway, Chicago Ridge (at 103rd Street); (708) 636–8586; www.animalwelfareleague.com. Fee: $98 for dogs and $54 for two cats.

Chicago Animal Care and Control, 2741 South Western Avenue (south of West 28th Street); (312) 747–1406; www.cityofchicago.org/AnimalCare Control. Fee: $65 for dogs and cats.

Chicago Anti-Cruelty Society, 510 North LaSalle Street (between West Grand Avenue and West Illinois Street); (312) 644–8338; www.anticruelty .org. Fee: $55 for all animals, old and young.

Tree House Animal Foundation, 1212 West Carmen Avenue (at North Broadway Street); (773) 784–5488, ext. 235; 1629 North Ashland Avenue (north of West North Avenue); (773) 227–5535; www.treehouseanimals.org. Fee: $75 per cat.

FREE **FIX:** SPAY **AND** NEUTER

Chicago Animal Care and Control
(312) 747–1406

If you live in a zip code the city has designated as being beset by too many unwanted animals, your dog or cat may be eligible for free spay or neuter surgery. The zip codes are: 60608, 60609, 60617, 60618, 60619, 60620, 60621, 60622, 60623, 60628, 60629, 60632, 60636, 60639, 60643, 60647,

---

Finding Fido
If you ever lose your pet, or if you've found a pet and want to find its owner, contact the Missing Pet Center. It's a free online service that lists only lost and found pets in the Chicagoland area. Check it out at www.missingpetcenter.com.

The Gift of Life

Dogs can help save lives just like people can by donating blood. A growing number of veterinarians and vet hospitals welcome donations from healthy canines who have the universal blood type of the canine world. In return, those doggie donors receive such perks as free health screenings, preventative heartworm medication, and free blood if they ever need it. Dogs must meet certain age and weight limits (no sense in tapping a Chihuahua). You can't tell your dog's blood type by breed, but vets who accept donations will gratefully type it for you, as well as let you know whether your dog has any diseases that prevent donation.

Unfortunately, vets generally don't accept donations from cats. Unlike dogs, cats must be sedated to donate blood, and cats who sneak outside unattended for even short periods pose a higher risk of blood-borne feline diseases. But in the hands of a gentle vet, most laid-back dogs don't seem to mind donating blood any more than laid-back people do. In fact, experienced doggie donors often come to like the attention of petting, cooing vet techs. And they like the occasional free biscuit afterwards just like human donors like their free cookies and orange juice. Ask your vet if he or she has a blood donation program. Here's a Chicago emergency pet hospital that does.

Chicago Veterinary Emergency Services
3123 North Clybourn Avenue (at North Oakley Avenue)
(773) 281–7110
www.chicagoveterinaryemergency.com

Doggie universal-type blood donors must be between two and seven years old and weigh at least forty pounds. In return, a donor receives a free general health screen and heartworm test, a year of heartworm prevention meds, and free blood if ever needed for a transfusion.

and 60651. To schedule your pet to do the right thing, call Chicago Animal Care and Control, Chicago Anti-Cruelty Society, or the Animal Welfare League. (See contact information listed above.) Chicago Animal Care and Control also brings its Animobile to neighborhood parks for spay and neuter services on-site. Call for its current schedule.

Lurie Family Spay/Neuter Clinic
3516 West 26th Street (between South St. Louis Avenue and South Drake Avenue)
(773) 521–7729
www.pawschicago.org

This clinic run by the organization PAWS Chicago offers free spay or neuter surgery to the pets of people who receive public assistance or who reside in certain zip codes. Call or check the site to see if yours is listed. Call to schedule an appointment.

DOGGONE **FUN**

The Catch City pet parks now require permits for dogs using them. They cost $5 per year, show that your dog has had all of the necessary vaccinations, and are available at participating vets. Violators face fines of $500. To find a participating vet, call the Chicago Park District at (312) 742–PLAY.

Every dog deserves plenty of leash-free outdoor romp time. Chicago dog lovers are doing their best to make more places for such free frolicking. They and cooperative park districts have established dog parks in neighborhoods throughout the city. Many of these spaces are fenced-in asphalt areas that allow safe running and easy poop cleanup, along with water fountains for extra hydration and regular facility cleaning. Most include benches where people can sit and chat while dogs run, butt sniff, and wrestle. All post commonsense rules for the behavior of dogs and their people. Some parks have complimentary dog doo bags on hand. (Of course, being a good Chicago pet owner, you'll already be in the habit of having plastic bags ready whenever you're out on the town with your polite poopy, now, won't you?) Here are some of Chicago's finest dog parks.

LEASH-FREE PARKS
Churchill Field Park, 1825 North Damen Avenue (at West Churchill Street)
Coliseum Park, 1466 South Wabash Avenue (at East 14th Place)
Hamlin Park, 3035 North Hoyne Avenue (between West Barry Street and West Wellington Avenue)

Margate Park, 4921 North Marine Drive (between West Lawrence Avenue and West Argyle Street)

Noethling (Grace) Park, 2645 North Sheffield Avenue (between West Schubert Avenue and West Wrightwood Avenue)

Walsh Playground Park, 1722 North Ashland Avenue (at West Wabansia Avenue)

Wicker Park, 1425 North Damen Avenue (at West Schiller Street)

LEASH-FREE BEACHES

Belmont Harbor Dog Beach (at Belmont Avenue). What developed on its own as a sand spit has become a fenced-in beach for dogs to romp in the water and with each other. Some dog owners complain that fuel leaked into the water from boats in the marina irritates their dogs' skin. Others say it's fine, but you might want to hose the little guy down anyway after a visit.

Montrose Beach (at Wilson Avenue). Dog owners can legally let them off the leash at the northwestern end. It's not fenced in, so keep an eye on escape artists, and keep them away from the humans-only southern part of the beach.

SECTION 3:

Exploring Chicago

TOURS:
THE FREEDOM TRAIL

"It is hopeless for the occasional visitor to try to keep up with Chicago—she outgrows his prophecies faster than he can make them. She is always a novelty; for she is never the Chicago you saw when you passed through the last time."
—MARK TWAIN, *LIFE ON THE MISSISSIPPI*

Chicago's got a lot to show off, and some free tours to show it, including guided and do-it-yourself walking tours, occasionally free architecture tours, and even a free Downtown tour train. There are even perfect strangers waiting to show you around, just to be nice. Chicago offers free tours based on architecture, history, culture, and neighborhood pride. Since Chicago's nice and flat, you can walk all the farther before your feet protest. You can download do-it-yourself tours, or find a free guide to show you around. Whether you're just passing through town or live here, take an ambling tour and learn something new.

FREE **TOURS**

Chicago Cultural Center
78 East Washington Street (at North Michigan Avenue)
Wheelchair access at 77 East Randolph Street
(312) 744–6630/ TTY: (312) 744–2947
www.chicagoculturalcenter.org
Hours: Monday through Thursday, 8:00 a.m. to 7:00 p.m.; Friday, 8:00 a.m. to 6:00 p.m.; Saturday, 9:00 a.m. to 6:00 p.m.; Sunday, 10:00 a.m. to 6:00 p.m.; closed holidays.

Round up a group of at least ten adults, and you can reserve a free tour of the Chicago Cultural Center. Prearranged tour slots are available starting any weekday at 10:00 a.m. Tours leave from the information desk in the Randolph Street lobby.

Chicago Fed Money Museum
230 South LaSalle Street (at West Jackson Boulevard)
(312) 322–2400
http://www.chicagofed.org/education/money_museum.cfm

This museum tucked inside the Chicago Federal Reserve Bank is free and open year-round from 9:00 a.m. to 4:00 p.m. Monday through Friday, except on bank holidays and when the Fed is closed for security reasons (ah, the life of a banker). Guided tours begin at 1:00 p.m. or by appointment. The tours include a short video about the Chicago Fed's operations, the Federal Reserve, and U.S. monetary policy. You must show a photo ID before entering.

Chicago Greeters
(312) 744–8000
www.chicagogreeter.com

Cities are so much more fun when you have a pal to show you around—and you do. The Chicago Greeter Program provides friendly local volunteers eager to show visitors around their favorite neighborhoods for a free two- to four-hour walking and public transit tour. Parties of six or fewer can register seven business days in advance online or via telephone Monday through Friday from 9:00 a.m. to 5:00 p.m.

Chicago Landmarks Self-Guided Tours
www.cityofchicago.org/landmarks

The Commission on Chicago Landmarks has developed a nifty Web site set of self-guided tours you can research and download based on such themes as historical period, ethnicity, architectural style, music, art, labor, railroads, districts, and religions. Read up, do a dry run, and impress your friends when they come to town.

CTA El Trains
If you're a tourist, don't be afraid of those hulking el tracks and their spark-throwing CTA trains rumbling above your head through the Loop. Climb the stairs, get a little help buying a ticket from the sometimes friendly, sometimes grumpy CTA station staff (see prices and other information starting on page 217), and you've got a ride with one of the best views of the city, particularly on the Brown, Green, Purple, and Orange lines, which stay aboveground for the whole trip. Maps are available at most stations.

Great Chicago Places and Spaces Festival
ArchiCenter
224 South Michigan Avenue (south of East Adams Street)
(312) 922–3432
www.architecture.org

Each May the City of Great Architecture shows it off with a weekend festival of discussions and guided tours. You may have to pay a nominal fee to sign up in advance, but you can show up the day of the event to register for free. Show up early since tours book quickly.

Hostelling International Chicago

24 East Congress Parkway (west of South Wabash Avenue)
(312) 360–0300
www.hichicago.org

This clean, fun, all-ages hostel for budget-smart singles and families offers free walking tours of the Loop for its guests at least twice a week. See the listing in the Real Estate chapter for prices and details on accommodations.

Millennium Park

201 East Randolph Street (at Michigan Avenue)
(312) 742–1168
www.millenniumpark.org
Hours: daily, 6:00 a.m. to 11:00 p.m.

Despite its free admission, the $475 million price tag for Millennium Park's construction makes it far from free for public and private coffers, a sore point for many Chicagoans who believe that money could have been better used. Whatever your opinion, you may as well get your money's worth by seeing what you've paid for. Download a free self-guided audio tour from the park's Web site to your MP3 player. You'll hear the park's architects, artists, and others explain how and why it was built.

National Register of Historic Places
Travel Itinerary
www.cr.nps.gov/nr/travel/chicago/index.htm

The National Register provides locations and histories of a couple dozen Chicago buildings that have achieved protected status as national historic landmarks and therefore can't be torn down for cement-block condo buildings. If only more Chicago gems enjoyed the same federal big-daddy protection.

Riverwalk Gateway
Under the Michigan Avenue Bridge on the south side of the Chicago River, this 336-foot-long series of twenty-eight murals tells the history of the river. Artist Ellen Lanyon created the painted and fired ceramic tile.

A Better World for Walking

Walking is usually a wonderful way to get around Chicago, or anywhere else for that matter. It's great exercise that provides the slower pace to notice and interact with more of the world around you. But at times, walking in the city can be an infuriating experience. Try crossing the street with a green light in a crosswalk during rush hour in the Loop, and you'll know what I mean. In the contest between a pedestrian with the right of way and a motorist with an attitude, the motorist is just—well, bigger and better protected. Now, worthy walkers, you have an advocate! The Active Transportation Alliance plans to achieve for Chicago pedestrianism and public transit what it has achieved for bicycling, which is a heckuva lot. Check the Alliance's Web site for resources, news, and events.

Active Transportation Alliance (formerly the Chicagoland Bicycle Federation)

9 West Hubbard Street, suite 402

(312) 427–3325

www.activetrans.org

BICYCLING:
FREE WHEELING

"Every time I see an adult on a bicycle, I no longer despair for the future of the human race."
—H. G. WELLS

Bicycling is to transportation what scavenging is to acquisition: Ain't nothing better than free. Lucky for us, Chicago is one of the most bike-friendly big cities in America, thanks to pancake-flat topography and a dedicated community of bicycle transportation advocates. The city and many suburbs are crisscrossed with hundreds of miles of on-street bike lanes and off-street trails. Extensive bicycle maps show which streets and trails are the most bike-able and recommend which to avoid. Cycling often will get you to your destination almost as quickly as driving and parking or waiting and taking public transit; and in the most congested areas of the city, it's often faster than car, bus, or train. Sure, Chicago gets bitterly cold for weeks in the winter and oppressively hot for weeks in the summer. Even then, you'll see cyclists—and not just the crazy death-wish kind—whizzing around the busiest streets, looking happier and healthier than average. If you feel timid, stick to empty side streets and uncrowded trails until you build more confidence, and attend classes and easy rides sponsored by the organizations and clubs listed here. They'll put you in touch with plenty of free and cheap resources and friendly people happy to teach you how to safely play in traffic too.

BICYCLING **ORGANIZATIONS** AND CLUBS

Active Transportation Alliance (formerly Chicagoland Bicycle Federation)
9 West Hubbard Street, suite 402
(312) 427–3325
www.activetrans.org

Founded in 1985 as the Chicagoland Bicycle Federation, this organization's years of hard work are largely responsible for the miles of bicycle lanes and trails across the region, not to mention biker-friendly legislation, government funding, educational programs, and continuing research. CBF recently changed its name to Active Transportation Alliance and its mission to formally promoting walking and public transit, too. Active Trans offers a variety of bike-related classes (many, but not all, for a fee) and lectures (mostly free). It also hosts annual free educational events like Bike to Work Week, where you can hear tips such as how to fold business attire so you can quick change into your unwrinkled swanko suit at your destination. The organization's extensive and frequently updated Web site has everything a novice or expert urban cyclist needs to start pedaling around Chicagoland: how-to tips, bike-related laws and news, upcoming events, and lists of bike clubs and shops that sell both new and used bikes and equipment. They also offer the most detailed bicycling map available of Chicago and surrounding suburbs. The Chicagoland Bicycle Map costs $6.95, or it's free with an annual membership starting at $15.00.

Beverly Bike Club
www.beverlybikeclub.org

This bike club centered in the Beverly neighborhood organizes group bicycle rides, classes, and events throughout the year.

Bike Winter
www.bikewinter.org

This loosely organized, unofficial non-club of cycling pals schedules classes and events that encourage winter bicycle riding and posts similar events on their Web site. Most are free. Some are practical, such as bike winterization workshops and winter clothing fashion shows, and some are just for fun, like bicycle poetry nights held at bars and restaurants and all-ages, all-abilities "snow rides" that convene any day that 2 inches (or more) of new snow falls in Chicago.

Chicago Critical Mass (CCM)
www.chicagocriticalmass.org

The Chicago incarnation of this worldwide phenomenon has no formal leaders and no set political agenda other than to assert the rights of bicyclists to the streets for which they've paid taxes too. Ride participants start gathering at Daley Plaza around 5:30 p.m. the last Friday of every month. In summer months, more than 1,000 riders have amassed. In the coldest months, it's down to a hardy few dozen. Every month, would-be ride leaders pass out proposed route maps that highlight certain Chicago neighborhoods or sights based on fun or serious themes. Votes of applause decide which ride proposal wins. Final destinations are places such as the beach, a bar, a cheap restaurant, or someone's house. Cheap bastards abound, so even if some folks, say, order a meal, there are always others who never spend a penny. Chicago Police often tag along, mostly to help direct baffled motorists, but Critical Mass neither endorses nor rejects their presence. Check the Web site for other bike-related events and links. This is a great place to meet kindred bikers, and it's quite the dating scene. Rides are slow, social, and fun but usually crowded. In fact, many cyclists think the last Friday rides have gotten too big and that smaller rides dispersed throughout Chicagoland would be more fun and effective in promoting citywide cycling. Check out the Web site for information about other Critical Mass rides rolling the first Friday of most months. Here are a few First Friday rides:

Evanston: Meet at 6:30 p.m. at Fountain Square (Davis Street, Sherman Avenue, and Orrington Avenue). The ride starts promptly at 7:00 p.m.

Wicker Park: Meet at 6:00 p.m. in the Polish Triangle (North Milwaukee Avenue, North Ashland Avenue, and West Division Street). The ride starts at 6:30 p.m.

Oak Park: Meet at 6:30 p.m. at Scoville Park (at Lake Street and Oak Park Avenue). The ride starts at 7:00 p.m.

Pilsen: Meet at 6:00 p.m. at Tenochtitlan Plaza (West 18th Street, South Loomis Street, and South Blue Island Avenue). The ride starts at 6:30 p.m.

Chicago Cycling Club

P.O. Box 1178
Chicago 60690-1178
Ride Line: (773) 509–8093
www.chicagocyclingclub.org

The club hosts rides three or four times a week April through October. Most, but not all, rides leave from the clock tower in Lincoln Park. It's located by the bicycle path just south of the golf course near Waveland Avenue at about 3700 North. Most rides are free and don't require advance registration or club membership. Social rides, great for any skill level, are less than 40 miles long, slower (about 10 to 14 miles per hour) to accommodate chatting, and include rest stops at fun points of interest. Tour rides are a bit longer, faster, and usually have few or no stops. Training rides are the fastest (more than 16 miles per hour) and designed for skilled riders who want the extra cardio-push of camaraderie and competition.

Chicago Department of Transportation's Chicago Bike Program
30 North LaSalle Street, suite 500
(312) 742–2453
www.chicagobikes.org

CDOT plans and installs those nifty bike lanes, trails, signs, and racks within city limits. The city agency works closely with the Active Transportation Alliance and other advocacy groups to channel public money and intelligence into building a better bicycling infrastructure throughout the metropolitan area. Their Web site (you'll be redirected to a long Web address within the City of Chicago's "egov" realm) includes a lot of useful cycling tips and a summary of cycling-related city traffic laws. They offer free educational materials, including the booklets *Safe Bicycling in Chicago,* and *Kids on Bikes in Chicago.* CDOT publishes the Chicago Bike Map, which covers only Chicago proper but is free. Request your copy from the e-mail address above. The Web site also offers online and printable maps of the city and some of its neighborhoods.

Chicago Major Taylor Cycling Club
P.O. Box 4812
Chicago, IL. 60680
www.mtc3.org

Major Taylor was an African-American cyclist who, during the Jim Crow 1900s, gained fame as the world's fastest athlete and as an all-around swell guy. This South Side bike club named in his honor posts free group rides and other events for adults and families on the Web site listed above. Rides range from leisurely 10-mile social rides to fast-paced century rides. Many trips are between 25 and 50 miles and include stops for lunches or snacks. It's a great way to improve your cycling, make new friends, and tour old neighborhoods and new trails throughout the South Side and northwestern Indiana.

Cycling Sisters
www.cyclingsisters.org

This organization hosts classes, social and educational rides, and other events for women only. Its Web site lists upcoming hands-on bike handling and repair classes. Contact the organization for more information and to reserve a space.

The Recyclery Collective

735 Reba Place (at Sherman Avenue), in basement
Evanston
(847) 424–1419
www.therecyclery.org

This Evanston community of cyclists restores donated and discarded bicycles and shares resources and knowledge to help make cycling possible for more Chicago-area residents. You can show up for an open-shop event and pay a suggested sliding-scale donation of $10 to use their tools and hang out with other bikers. Or you can volunteer to help fix bikes and learn valuable mechanical skills along the way. Novices to experienced mechanics are all welcome. The Recyclery also hosts occasional Saturday morning used bike sales in parking lots around Evanston. Check the organization's calendar for upcoming sales and show up early to line up.

West Town Bikes

2418 West North Avenue (at North Western Avenue; enter in back from alley)
(312) 213–4184
www.westtownbikes.org

This workshop space provides low-income youth (ages twelve to nineteen) living in the West Town, Humboldt Park, and Logan Square neighborhoods with all the tools and used bike parts they need to build their own sweet sets of wheels. After building complete bikes, they get to keep their masterpieces, along with new helmets, locks, and other accessories, all for free. Instructors teach kids how to find the best bus and train routes and how to bring their bikes with them on said buses and trains. West Town Bikes also hosts ongoing workshops for adults of any income levels, ranging from how to ride to basic and advanced repair. Suggested donations for adult classes are generally $10 to $15.

Windy City Cycling Club

www.windycitycyclingclub.com

This club of primarily lesbian and gay riders organizes bike rides, classes, social events, and bicycling advocacy work. A variety of ride lengths and speeds accommodate leisurely through competitive riders. Check the club's online calendar for upcoming events.

BIKE **BOOKS,** BOOKLETS, **AND** MAPS

Chicago Bicycle Map
published by the Chicago Department of Transportation's Chicago Bike Program
30 North LaSalle Street, suite 500
(312) 742–2453
www.chicagobikes.org
cdotbikes@cityofchicago.org

Although this map highlights recommended routes in Chicago only, it's free and includes several handy tips for riding in the city.

Chicagoland Bicycle Map
published by the Active Transportation Alliance
9 West Hubbard Street, suite 402
(312) 427–3325
www.activetrans.org

This map, the most extensive available, provides recommended bike routes throughout Chicago and surrounding suburbs. Dozens of volunteers submit information about what routes to add or remove in the next edition. Routes include off-street trails, on-street bike lanes, and streets rated from recommended to "use with caution." It's $6.95, or free with an annual membership of at least $15.00.

Urban Biker's Tricks and Tips
by Dave Glowacz
published by WordSpace Press
Available on-site or by order from any real or virtual bookstore or library, or from www.mrbike.com

This book costs $14.95 (free to borrow from the library) but can answer pretty much any question you might have about biking in the big city, and a lot of questions you'd never know to ask. Topics include how to find and fix the right bike and accessories, how to dress for a variety of weather, how to mount a bike in a skirt, how to ride in street traffic, and how to get your bike on and off a local train or bus.

The Right Bike

If you don't already own a comfortable and reliable bicycle, you may get lucky and find a great one in an alley. But chances are you'll need to spend some money (up to $200) for all the accoutrements of the perfect urban commuter. Keep in mind that you don't need to acquire everything at once, and your bike will repay you in money saved on bus and train fares or gas. I prefer a good used bicycle to an expensive or even cheap new one. Shiny new bikes invite theft, and many discount store bikes have heavy frames and low-quality parts that soon break and can't be replaced. Do a little research before you buy, and plan to find or buy some parts and accessories too. The organizations and bike shops listed in this chapter can help. Here are a few things I can't live without.

- **Frame.** Make sure it's the right size. When you're straddling the bike and flat-footed, the top tube should be around 1 inch below your crotch, and you shouldn't have to strain to reach the handlebars while you're sitting fairly upright in the saddle. Also strive for lighter weight; no rust; and eyelets (holes) that make it easier to attach accessories such as a rack, water bottle cage, and lock holder.
- **Brakes!** At the risk of ticking off the "brakes weigh too much" track bike cult, please have, use, and maintain good brakes on your bike. Unless you're in a velodrome trying to break a world cycling record, you can afford the extra few ounces for basic, commonsense safety.
- **Handlebars.** I find upright handlebars more comfortable than racing "drop" handlebars, and I find they allow me to more easily glance over my shoulder to check traffic when I'm changing lanes. Many other riders swear by drop bars, though, so experiment with both to decide which you prefer.
- **Comfy seat.** There are a lot of good cheap ones to choose from that can make riding a lot easier on your tush. Again, preferences in seat styles vary, so let your heinie test at least a few.
- **Aluminum wheel rims.** Brake pads still grip these when they're wet, unlike on steel.

- **Tires.** Smoother, thinner tires make it easier to ride faster with less effort than on knobby wide tires. Make sure they're not too smooth. You need a little traction for wet days and the occasional ice patch. And you may want to invest in an extra-thick, flat-resistant rear tire if you get a lot of flats. It will slow you down a little but better resist delays from punctured tubes.
- **Helmet.** Get a new one. Used helmets may have damage you can't see. Make sure it has the Snell or ANSI symbol inside. If your helmet is ever in a crash, dropped from a distance or left in an excessively hot environment, such as a car in the summer, replace it. And please wear it every time you ride to protect that precious, cheap-thinking noggin.
- **Locks.** These are usually worth buying new or gently used. Strength and reliability are key, as a thief can easily cut a cheap thin cable. I prefer a sturdy U-lock and small locking wheel hubs and a locking seat post (available from Kryptonite). Other savvy bikers I know swear by a U-lock and sturdy cables for stringing through wheels.
- **Lights.** Front lights should be white, and rear lights should be red, just like on cars. Blinking, bright LED lights offer long life on small, lightweight batteries.
- **Rear basket, rack, or trailer.** The rack will allow you to attach bicycle bags, panniers, an old milk crate, or some other sturdy-but-light container to haul loads like books and groceries. Or you can tie packages directly to the rack using bungee cords, compression straps, rope, or old bike tubes. A trailer will allow you to haul even larger loads. If you're hauling kids, they'll need a kid trailer, which you can use for groceries too. If you're just hauling stuff, a variety of trailers serve multiple needs, from carrying camping equipment over forest trails to schlepping groceries back from the store.
- **Wheel fenders.** These keep water, mud, and stones from flinging up on your clothes and in your face.

USED-BIKE **SHOPS**

Many shops that sell primarily new bikes also keep a few high-quality used bicycles and parts on hand. And most will gladly repair and supply replacement parts and accessories for the used bike you got elsewhere. There aren't nearly as many shops that specialize in used bikes, but here are a few that offer extensive selections at cheaper-than-new prices.

Chicago Police Department Public Auction
West Side Technical Institute
2800 South Western Avenue (between West 28th Street and West 31st Street)
Police auction hotline: (312) 743–1298

One Saturday each month, the Chicago Police sell property, including bikes, that was stolen or lost but is unclaimed. Sales start at 10:00 a.m. Prices range from $5 to the high triple digits. You can check out the merchandise early during designated viewing times. Call the hotline for the latest info.

Hegewisch Cycle & Hobby Shop
13403 South Brandon Avenue (1340 South and 3200 East)
(773) 646–2584

This shop generally has around 200 used bicycles on hand, about 40 of which are repaired and ready to ride. All makes and models are priced from $19.95 to $49.95. There's a wide selection of new parts too. No helmets are available, but new locks and other accessories are for sale.

Irv's Bike Shop
1725 South Racine Avenue (1725 South and 1200 West)
(312) 226–6330

Irv's usually has about thirty used bikes for sale along with their new ones. Used bikes range from $75 to $250. The place also sells new helmets, locks, and other accessories.

The Recyclery Collective
735 Reba Place (at Sherman Avenue), in basement
Evanston
(847) 424–1419
www.therecyclery.org

This Evanston community of cyclists donates a lot of the bikes its members restore. But they also host occasional Saturday morning used-bike sales in parking lots around Evanston. Check the organization's calendar for upcoming sales and show up early to grab your spot in line.

West Town Bikes

This club hosts a free build-your-own bike program for low-income youth from the Humboldt Park, West Town, and Logan Square neighborhoods. See the entry earlier in this chapter for more information.

Working Bikes Cooperative (WBC)

2434 South Western Avenue (at West 24th Place)
(312) 421–5048
workingbikes.org
workingbikes@yahoo.com

This shop has the most extensive selection of used bikes in the city, ranging in price from $40 to $90. Some of what WBC considers roadworthy is pretty rickety by my standards. But you can find bikes in great shape too. The co-op reclaims donated and discarded bikes, sells them, and uses the proceeds to send refurbished bikes to developing countries. You can help by stopping by any Tuesday between 5:00 and 9:00 p.m. to help repair bikes. No experience is necessary, and you'll gain a lot of experience and know-how in the process.

The Usual Suspects

Also check yard sales, thrift stores, resale shops, and classified ads in local papers and on the Internet for used bikes. You'd be surprised how many people sell their classic or expensive bikes for much less than they're worth because they're moving soon, purging unused stuff from the basement or garage, or can't figure out how to change a flat tire. And, of course, monitor the alleys. You'll find lots of good bikes whose only sin was getting a flat or needing a derailleur adjustment. Don't buy bikes from strangers off the street. They're likely to be stolen.

TRANSIT:
BY LAND AND WATER

"I take all the time I need, and I don't worry where I'm gonna sleep. 'Cause all the maps of the world are bound to take me where I wanna be."
—FROM "APPLE TREE" BY ANA EGGE

How much you spend getting around Chicago can vary widely depending on your needs and resourcefulness. According to the American Automobile Association, it costs some $8,100 per year to own and operate a new vehicle. That counts such things as car payments, insurance, maintenance and repairs, fuel, tires, and parking and other fees. It doesn't count less-tangible costs, like pollution and lack of exercise. For many people, family and job needs or physical disabilities make driving a necessity. But every day, thousands of Chicagoans and suburbanites opt for the many cheaper ways to get around the region. So do savvy tourists who want to spend less time and money on parking and more time and money seeing the sights. Check out your options listed in this chapter and experiment with alternatives—and combinations of alternatives—until you find the best modes to your common destinations. Then balance your wallet, watch, creativity, and conscience to help you decide how best to travel on the cheap.

BUS **AND** TRAIN **CHICAGO**

Considering paltry government funding and the huge population and geography it serves, the Chicago region's collection of public transit modes is remarkably efficient and interconnected. City buses and trains connect to suburban buses and trains. Unlike in many cities, our city train lines connect to both major airports. And Amtrak and Greyhound stand by to carry passengers anywhere in the country too. Most trains run on time most of the time, and Chicago buses are becoming timelier too. But parts of the system are flawed. Some neighborhoods that need public transportation the most have seen the most illogical service cutbacks in recent years. Or they are still waiting for train line extensions and new bus routes that were promised years ago. Other neighborhoods receive adequate service until their leg of the Chicago Transit Authority's ancient el line takes its turn at renovation, leaving el riders out of luck and on the bus for months. To find out whether you're one of the many lucky commuters who dwell in a world of public transit health or if you're one of the unlucky folks in a pocket of transit dysfunction, start by calling the Regional Transportation Authority or checking your route on its Web site. It will deliver the news.

Chicago Transit Authority (CTA)

567 West Lake Street (at North Clinton Street)
(888) 968–7282 (customer service)
www.transitchicago.com

The Chicago Transit Authority oversees trains and buses that run throughout Chicago proper, extending to suburban transit connections in inner-ring suburbs. Its 148 bus routes crisscross the city and provide connections between city and suburban trains and buses as well as Amtrak and Greyhound stations. You can track the estimated arrival times and trip times of a growing number of CTA buses on your computer or mobile phone, thanks to the CTA Bus Tracker. It's at www.ctabustracker.com. The CTA also runs eight train lines whose names were changed in 1993 to colors: the Red Line, Orange Line, Yellow Line, Green Line, Blue Line, Purple Line, Brown Line, and the new Pink Line. The CTA's train lines are colloquially called the "el" or "L," which is short for "elevated," the name the system earned at its inception in 1892 because much of the train line ran—and still runs—on tracks built a couple of house stories above the ground. Even when trains duck underground for parts of their journeys, acting as subways, Chicagoans still tend to refer to those trains as "the el." The best way to learn your way around the system is to procure an RTA system map, which shows all city and suburban routes, or a CTA map, available at many CTA train stations or at RTA headquarters.

The type of CTA pass that's cheapest for you depends on how long you plan to be in town and how often you plan to use buses and trains. If you'll commute every day, an unlimited monthly pass may be just the ticket. Ask at your workplace if your employer offers a tax-deferred transit program, which will save you a little more money off of your monthly pass.

If you plan to use the train only occasionally, a pay-as-you-go Chicago Card (reloadable only with cash at CTA train stations and some retail sites) or Chicago Card Plus (reloadable with cash or online with a credit card) is a better option. You can order one online or through the mail using a form available at CTA train stations and on buses. Or you can pick up a card at RTA or CTA headquarters and at some currency exchanges. The card, which contains a little radio chip that allows users to quickly tap it on payment readers, costs a one-time fee of $5 (free for first-time users who register their cards). For every $20 you load onto the card, you get a $2 bonus. You can register the Chicago Card Plus to your name so it can be deactivated and your funds replaced if it's ever stolen. Or you can maintain your anonymity by buying and loading the Chicago Card with cash.

If you're only passing through and need just one ride, you can still pay cash on buses or buy a floppy plastic transit card you can load with as much money as you want at CTA train stations, but the CTA now charges a little extra (in the form of no transfers or bonuses) for those tenders to discourage their daily use.

CTA allows bicycles on the front racks of all of its buses any time. Passengers can take bikes onto CTA trains only during non-rush-hour periods when trains have space for them.

Here's a list of the CTA's current fare lineup.

Full-Price Fares:
- Cash: $2.25 per ride
- Transit Card used on bus: $2.00 per initial ride
- Transit Card used on train: $2.25 per initial ride
- Chicago Card or Chicago Card Plus: $2.00 per initial bus ride, $2.25 per initial train ride
- Chicago Card or Chicago Card Plus Bonus: 10 percent for every $20 value you add to the card

Free Navy Pier Trolley

The City of Chicago no longer offers free trolleys connecting tourist hot spots. But Navy Pier still offers a free trolley service between the pier and State Street along Grand Avenue and Illinois Street.

- Transfers between train stations or buses:
    - Not allowed for cash-paying customers
    - Full-fare Transit Card, Chicago Card, and Chicago Card Plus transfers are 25 cents for up to two additional rides within two hours after the first ride.
- One-Day Unlimited Ride Pass: $5.75
- Three-Day Unlimited Ride Visitor Pass: $14.00
- Seven-Day Unlimited Ride Pass: $23.00 (CTA only) / $28.00 (CTA and PACE)
- Thirty-Day Unlimited Ride Pass: $86.00

Reduced-Price Fares:

(Available to children between ages seven and eleven, grade-school through high-school students with CTA Student Riding Permits, and seniors and riders with disabilities)

- Cash: $1.00 per ride
- Transit Card: 85 cents per ride
- Transfers between train stations or buses:
    - Not allowed for cash-paying customers
    - Reduced-fare Transit Card transfers are 15 cents for up to two additional rides within two hours after the first ride.
- Thirty-Day Unlimited Ride Pass: $35.00
- Reduced-fare transit card 2 packs: $15.30
- Seniors sixty-five and older with a valid RTA Reduced-Fare Riding Permit or RTA Ride Free Smart. Card ride free (for now). Only seniors living in Cook, DuPage, Kane, Lake, McHenry, or Will counties are eligible. Go to retachicago.com/seniorsridefree or call the RTA to obtain your pass.
- People with disabilities enrolled in the Illinois Circuit Breaker program as also having low income (below $22,218 or $33,740, depending on household size), ride free. Go to www.illinois.gov/transit or call (800) 252–8966 / TTY: (888) 206–1327 to learn more or apply.

Paratransit services throughout Chicago and suburbs are managed by PACE. See entry on page 220.

Chicago Water Taxi

400 North Michigan Avenue
(312) 337–1446
www.chicagowatertaxi.com

This river commuting service is operated by Wendella Sightseeing Boats and operates, depending on weather conditions, from sometime in March or April through mid- to late autumn. The service tugs as far south as Chinatown and as far north as Michigan Avenue. Single-ride fares are $2 for single, one-way trips. Single-ride fares including the Chinatown stop are $4. Seniors, people with disabilities, and Medicare card holders pay half price. All-day, unlimited passes are $4 on weekdays, not including the Chinatown stop. All-day passes including Chinatown, weekends, and holidays are $6. Ten-ride tickets are $16, and monthly unlimited passes are $42. Here's a list of pickup points:

- Chinatown: Ping Tom Memorial Park at the Pagoda (head west to the river between 18th Street and 19th Street).
- Michigan Avenue: At base of Wrigley Building, north side of river, west of Michigan Avenue (at East Kinzie Street).
- LaSalle Street and Clark Street: Fulton's Market, 1 block east of Merchandise Mart, between LaSalle, Clark, and the river
- Madison Street: At Madison Street and Riverside Plaza, directly across the river from the Civic Opera House. Exit at Riverside Plaza to transfer to Metra and Union Stations.

River Taxis

Whether you're a tourist or just trying to get to and from work, a trip along the Chicago River might be the quickest and cheapest way to your destination. It usually will be the most peaceful and enjoyable way around the Downtown. Here are two services that link Chicago's Union Station, home of Metra and Amtrak train terminals, with Downtown tourist spots along the river and lake.

Metra
www.metrarail.com

Metra commuter train tracks fan out from five major Downtown stations to 230 neighborhood stops covering 495 miles of tracks in Chicago and its suburbs and exurbs in Cook, DuPage, Lake, Will, McHenry, and Kane Counties. Trains generally run efficiently and on time. Parking near stations can be a challenge, but bus connections and bike racks at stations provide alternatives to the park-and-ride plan. Fares vary by distance, using a zone system. Use Metra's Fare Check in its Web site to calculate your costs. You can buy single tickets, multi-ride punch cards, or unlimited weekend passes at Metra station ticket booths or by mail. If the train station isn't open, you can pay on the train. During hours stations are open, paying on the train will cost an extra two bucks. On weekends and holidays, youth age twelve to seventeen ride for half fare. Kids younger than age twelve ride free when accompanied by a fare-paying adult. Fares that are about half the full price are available for seniors and disabled riders with RTA Reduced Fare Riding Permit ID cards. U.S. military personnel in uniform also pay about half the normal fare.

Metra allows bicycles on its trains during limited non-rush-hour periods. Call ahead to check allowable times and additional instructions.

PACE Suburban Bus Service
Customer Services
550 West Algonquin Road, Arlington Heights, IL 60005
(847) 364–7223
www.pacebus.com

Pace buses carry more than thirty-five million passengers throughout Chicago's suburbs and into parts of Chicago to connect with other bus and train systems. Buses generally run every twenty to thirty minutes, with many of its 240 routes ending in mid-evening. PACE also runs express rides to many Chicago-area attractions. PACE allows bicycles on the front racks of all of its buses any time.

- Regular full fare: $1.75 per ride, plus 25 cents for up to two additional transfers within two hours to other PACE and CTA buses and trains.
- Children younger than age seven: free.
- Children between ages seven and eleven: $1.50 per ride.
- Pace/CTA 30-day pass: $86 full fare, $35 reduced fare.

- Pace/CTA 7-day pass: $28.
- Premium fare routes (the trips that take passengers express to destinations such as Six Flags, U.S. Cellular Field, Wrigley Field, or Soldier Field): $4 full fare and $2 reduced fare.

PACE offers several unlimited multiday passes and discounted fare programs. Compare your options at www.pacebus.com/paceonlinestore. Reduced fares are available for students, seniors, and people with disabilities.

PACE oversees paratransit services throughout Chicago and the suburbs.

- Dial-A-Ride: Fares vary based on community policy.
- Chicago ADA Paratransit Service in City of Chicago: $2.25 per ride, $22.50 for books of ten fare tickets. Monthly pass for $150.00.
- ADA Paratransit Service in Cook and DuPage Counties: $3.00 per ride, $30.00 for books of ten fare tickets.
- ADA Paratransit Service in Lake, McHenry, Kane, and Will Counties: $2.50 per ride, $25.00 for books of ten fare tickets.
- Taxi Access Program and Mobility Direct: $1.75.

Regional Transportation Authority (RTA)
Customer Service Center
175 West Jackson Boulevard (at South Wells Street), suite 250
(312) 913–3110
Travel Information: (312) 836–7000, (773) 836–7000 and (847) 836–7000
(All area codes route calls to same information center.)
TTY: (312) 836–4949
www.rtachicago.com
Open weekdays 8:30 a.m. to 5:00 p.m.

The Regional Transportation Authority oversees and coordinates the main public transit systems of Chicago and the suburbs, including the Chicago Transportation Authority, PACE, and Metra (see their entries below). Check out RTA's cool trip finder on its Web site. Type in your departing and arrival addresses and planned travel dates and times. The RTA overmind will ponder a few seconds and then provide you with two or three options you can print and take along. You can also call RTA operators for the same information, which can be nice when you're lost and confused while out and about. The RTA also publishes maps that show all city and suburban bus and train routes. You can pick one up at RTA's customer service office, listed above, or check out the online versions on the RTA Web site.

Shoreline Sightseeing Water Taxis

474 North Last Shore Drive
(312) 222–9328
www.shorelinesightseeing.com/taxis.php

Shoreline's water taxi commuter fares are $2.00 for a one-way ride ($1.50 round trip), operating only between its Sears Tower/Union Station stop and its Michigan Avenue Bridge stop. A ten-ride pass is $15.00. Cheaper commuter fare pricing is in effect only during commuting rush hours of 7:00 to 9:30 a.m. and 4:00 to 6:30 p.m. At other times, and between other docks, Shoreline charges higher fares, from $2 for a child on the shortest trip to as much as $13 for an adult on the longest trip. Buy tickets at kiosks at Shoreline docks. Call Shoreline, check the Web site above or stop by a Shoreline kiosk to calculate your costs. Here are Shoreline's destinations:

- 200 South Wacker Drive: Dock is on east side of river, near Sears Tower and across from Union Station (between West Adams Street and West Jackson Boulevard).
- 401 North Michigan Avenue: Dock is on north side of river and east side of Michigan Avenue bridge, south of Tribune Tower.
- Navy Pier: Service between Navy Pier and the Museum Campus runs along Lake Michigan and docks at "Dock Street," at the southwest corner of Navy Pier. Service between Navy Pier and the Sears Tower runs along the Chicago River and departs from the Ogden Slip dock southwest of the circle drive at the entrance of Navy Pier.
- Museum Campus: Dock is on at northeast corner of John G. Shedd Aquarium. Transfer at Navy Pier for rides to destinations along the Chicago River.

Working for Better Transit

Founded in 1985 as the Chicagoland Bicycle Federation, the newly renamed Active Transportation Alliance has formally expanded its mission to improving public transit and walking too. Look for public transit–related news, events and advocacy campaigns on the organization's Web site, www.activetrans.org. And if you've got good ideas or energy to volunteer, Active Trans will welcome your contribution.

South Shore Line
Northern Indiana Commuter Transportation District
Customer Service Department
33 East U.S. Highway 12, Chesterton, Indiana
(219) 926-5744
www.nictd.com

Since 1903 the South Shore Line trains have brought Chicagoans to Indiana's charming towns and sand dunes along the eastern shores of Lake Michigan. You can travel from the South Shore's first Chicago stop at the Randolph Street Station it shares with Metra for a two-and-a-half-hour trip east to the airport in South Bend, Indiana, where you can fly away or just view the statue of vintage-TV talking-horse Mr. Ed. The historic electric trains also get thousands of people to and from work every day. Fares vary by trip length.

GET OUTTA TOWN: PUBLIC TRANSIT TO GREYHOUND, AMTRAK, AND AIRPORTS

Amtrak
Union Station
225 South Canal Street (surrounded by Canal Street, Adams Street, Clinton Street, and Jackson Boulevard)
(312) 655-2101 (Passenger Services)
www.amtrak.com

Historic and stunning Union Station is the same building where many suburban Metra and national Amtrak trains begin and end their journeys. Several CTA buses circle or pass by the building, including numbers 1, 7, X28, 124, 125, 126, 151, 156, and 157. Two CTA train stops are within easy walking distance of Union Station, but you can get to them by bus too. The Quincy stop of the CTA's Brown Line is a few blocks east at Quincy between Adams Street and Jackson Boulevard (catch a bus heading west on Adams Street or east on Jackson Boulevard to connect between the stop and Union Station).

The Clinton stop of the CTA's Blue Line is a few blocks south of the west side of Union Station. CTA buses 7 and 60 run between Union Station and the Clinton stop.

Greyhound
www.greyhound.com
Downtown Station, 630 West Harrison Street (at South Jefferson Street); (312) 408–5800
95th Street Station, 14 West 95th Street (at Dan Ryan Expressway); (312) 408–5999
Cumberland Avenue Station, 5800 North Cumberland Avenue (at Kennedy Expressway); (773) 693–2474

Greyhound runs bus service from sea to sea, north into Canada, and south into Mexico. The Downtown station is just west of the Loop district. The nearest CTA station is the Blue Line stop at Clinton and Harrison Streets a couple of blocks northeast. CTA bus numbers 7, 60, 125, 156, and 157 also stop at the station. Numbers 7 and 60 will take you to and from Amtrak and Metra lines at nearby Union Station.

If you live on (or are visiting) the South Side or anywhere near the Red Line, Greyhound's 95th Street Station might be more convenient for you, as it's part of the CTA station building at the last stop on the CTA's Red Line. Several CTA and PACE buses stop at the station there, including CTA numbers 34, 95E, 95W, 103, 106, 111, 112, 108, 119, 352, 359, and 381.

Greyhound's Cumberland Avenue Station is in the CTA station building at the Cumberland stop of the CTA's Blue Line train. CTA buses stopping at the station include numbers 69, 81W, 240, 241, 290, and 331.

Midway Airport
5700 South Cicero Avenue
(773) 838–0600
www.ohare.com/midway/home.asp

This hardworking smaller airport of mostly national and regional airlines is on Chicago's southwest side. It's easy to get to Midway on public transit too. Midway is the last southwest stop of the Orange Line. The walk to the inside of the terminal from the train stop is fairly long, but most of the hike is enclosed. The Orange Line doesn't run between 12:55 and 4:00 a.m. Monday through Friday or between 12:31 and 4:30 a.m. Saturday and Sunday. Several CTA and PACE buses also stop at Midway, including numbers 47, 54B, 55A, 55N, 59, 62, 62H, 63, 63W, X55, 379, 382, 383, 384, 385, 390, and 831.

O'Hare International Airport
10000 West O'Hare
(773) 686–2200 or (800) 832–6352
www.ohare.com

The airport that likes to call itself the World's Busiest is Chicago's national and international hub to the world, located outside the northwest side of the city proper but connected to it in grand political style by a strip of land running along the Kennedy Expressway and CTA Blue Line train tracks. Depending on the direction you're heading from into O'Hare, taking public transit there can be easier and faster than driving or taking a cab. The easiest way to arrive is to take the Blue Line to its last northwest stop, which is inside O'Hare Airport. Service is less frequent late at night but runs twenty-four hours.

DRIVE **CHICAGO** (IF **YOU** MUST)

Hey, petroleum consumption happens to the best of us. If none of the above work for you and you need access to a trusty car, the companies below are happy to oblige.

Auto Driveaway Company
11235 South Cottage Grove Avenue (at East 112th Street, 2 blocks west of Metra Electric Kensington station); call for more public transit instructions.
(773) 568–5700 / (800) 346–2277
www.autodriveaway.com
mruiz@autodriveaway.com

It's the cheap bastard's answer to the rental car. For a variety of reasons, people across the country pay Auto Driveaway to deliver their private vehicles from one town to another. With some sixty-four offices around the United States and Canada, there's a good chance they'll have a car that comes pretty close to your desired starting and ending points if you can be a little patient and flexible. Start by calling them five to ten days before you want to leave or check the Web site above for listings of cars awaiting pickup and delivery all over North America. You have to post a deposit of $350 that you'll get back when you deliver the car intact, but you get free use of the car, a free first tank of gas, and sometimes a small gas allowance. You must be at least twenty-three years old and provide an official copy of your moving violation report (MVR) from the Department of Motor Vehicles, which Auto Driveaway can help you procure for $12.

FreeCar Media
11990 San Vicente Boulevard, suite 350
Los Angeles, CA 90049
(310) 566–4000
www.freecarmedia.com

FreeCar Media lets you use, for a period ranging from a few months to a couple of years, one of their cars, which is wrapped bumper to bumper in an advertisement. The target demographic sees the ad and is tempted to buy the aforementioned advertised product. Advertisers are happy, FreeCar Media gets more money, and the cycle continues. What a country! You pay for fuel and insurance coverage from the provider of their choice, but otherwise, use of the car is free. Unlike a lot of similar services advertised on the Web, this one costs nothing to apply. Start by filling out an extensive questionnaire on their Web site that profiles you and your habits, then wait to see if you're one of the lucky few chosen. You, the vehicle, and the ad will be carefully matched. On the off chance they offer you a vehicle hawking hemorrhoid cream or feminine hygiene products, you can turn down a car and wait for another one. They'll also pay up to $400 per month if you let them wrap your own car with one of their ads.

I-GO Car Sharing
2125 West North Avenue
(773) 278–4446
www.igocars.org

This not-for-profit car-sharing service is a smart way to use only as much car as you need. Fleets of I-GO vehicles, from small, efficient cars to minivans and SUVs for hauling larger loads, are located in a growing number of locations convenient to a growing number of members. Apply online for a first-year membership of $50. If you're approved, you'll pay future annual fees of $25. You'll get an I-GO smart card that works as a key to the vehicles. RTA now offers I-GO cards that work as CTA and PACE passes too. Additional monthly or as-you-go fees vary based on how much you use, or plan to use, an I-GO vehicle. Here's a rundown of membership plans, all of which include gas, premium insurance, low-emission vehicles, reserved parking, and twenty-four-hour assistance.

- GO Standard: From $6 per hour, does not include miles, which cost an additional 40 cents per mile.
- GO Standard Plus: From $8 per hour, including miles traveled up to 150 miles during the first twenty-four hours of reservation. After twenty-four hours, each hour includes 25 free miles up to 150 miles per day.
- GO Budget: $15 per month, six-month commitment required. Includes three free hours per month and 150 free miles per day. Extra hours and miles are billed at Go Standard Plus rates. Unused hours do not carry over.
- Go Anytime: $30 per month, six-month commitment required. Charges an additional $6 per hour with no restrictions, includes up to 150 miles during the first twenty-four hours of reservation. After twenty-four hours, each hour includes 25 free miles up to 150 miles per day. No free hours are included.

ZipCar
160 North Wabash Avenue
(312) 589-6300
www.zipcar.com
info@zipcar.com

Zipcars live in a growing number of Chicago neighborhoods, especially those with crowded streets and happily carless masses who could use a variety of occasional wheels, from Mini Coopers to big-boy trucks. The company charges a one-time application fee of $25 to cover a background check that takes anywhere from a few days to a week. After that, members pay annual fees of $50 and additional fees based on their car-use preferences. Members reserve cars online or over the phone and use personal electronic cards to unlock and turn on their chosen vehicles. Rental includes gas, insurance, and 180 free miles per day (from 45 cents per mile after that). Here are two plans to choose from:

Occasional Driving: No monthly fees, hourly rates from $9.25 (weekends $9.75), daily rates from $68 (weekends $73).

Extra Value: Monthly fees from $50 to $250 based on use, hourly rates from $8.33 (weekends $8.78), daily rates from $61.20 (weekends $65.70).

GARDENS AND GARDENING:
DIRT CHEAP

"Your first job is to prepare the soil. The best tool for this is your neighbor's motorized garden tiller. If your neighbor does not own a garden tiller, suggest that he buy one."
—DAVE BARRY

Chicago's official city motto is *"Urbs en Horto,"* or "City in a Garden." Many parts of the city, and surrounding suburbs, live up to that name. Gracing public parks and conservatories, street medians, backyards, rooftops, and formerly abandoned lots, the loving expressions of green-thumbed hired workers and volunteer residents feed souls and bodies alike. There's still a lot of gray space to green up in Chicago, though, and government agencies and private organizations are happy to help you add to the effort without making you drop a bushel of cash at your local gardening or home improvement store. They can help you and your neighbors secure space, know-how, and materials to establish or improve community gardens on vacant lots, or just make your thumbs greener through classes and expert advice, all for free.

PUBLIC **GARDENS**

Crystal Garden
Navy Pier (east end of Family Pavilion, Mezzanine Level)
700 East Grand Avenue (312) 595–5436; (800) 595–5436
www.navypier.com

While the garden is often crowded with tourists, it's a welcome escape from the bustle of Navy Pier. The one-acre space inside a six-story glass atrium houses towering palm trees and a changing lineup of seasonal flowers and plants. "Leap-frog" water snake fountains delight children when the water jumps from hidden spigots and then quickly disappears.

Eden Place Nature Center
43rd Place and Stewart Avenue
(773) 624–8686
www.fullerpark.com/EDEN PLACE.html

Come learn about the plants and animals of woodlands, wetlands and prairies at this nature preserve and demonstration center. Eden Place includes multimedia and live presentations for families and school groups.

Garfield Park Conservatory
300 North Central Park Avenue (at West Lake Street)
(312) 746–5100
www.garfieldconservatory.org
Hours: Open year-round, Thursday through Tuesday, 9:00 a.m. to 5:00 p.m.;
Wednesday, 9:00 a.m. to 8:00 p.m.

With gardens occupying four and a half acres, the Garfield Park Conservatory is one of the largest and most beautiful conservatories in the world.
Designed by landscape architect Jens Jensen to mimic midwestern haystacks
of the era, the 7,500-square-foot glass structure was constructed between
1905 and 1907. Jensen's vision created large rooms hosting distinctly different natural landscapes, which now include the soaring trees of the tropical
Palm House, the Show House full of seasonal flowers and flowering trees, the
unique Aroid and Desert Houses, a Children's Garden, and a Sweet House.

Grant Park Rose Gardens
Michigan Avenue and Madison Street (directly north and south of Buckingham Fountain)

On either side of Buckingham Fountain, Grant Park's formal gardens are
landscaped with roses, lush greenery, and their own smaller fountains.

Jackson Park (see Osaka Garden)
Millennium Park Lurie Garden
201 East Randolph Street (at Michigan Avenue)
(312) 742–1168
www.millenniumpark.org
 Hours: daily, 6:00 a.m. to 11:00 p.m.

This 2.5-acre garden on the east end of Millennium Park includes a 15-foot-
tall hedge that encloses the garden on two sides to help protect the garden's
perennial plants from the elements. A long wooden boardwalk separates the
garden into two sections, one for shade trees, the other for perennials. The
garden also hosts free family workshops and classes on gardening.

Lincoln Park Conservatory and Gardens
2391 North Stockton Drive (east of West Fullerton Parkway outside the northwest corner of Lincoln Park Zoo)
(312) 742–7736
www.chicagoparkdistrict.com
Hours: Open year-round, 9:00 a.m. to 5:00 p.m.

What started as a cemetery for victims of cholera and smallpox on the northern boundary of Chicago (the bodies were later exhumed and relocated) began its transformation in the 1860s into what we now know as Lincoln Park (named after President Abraham Lincoln). The Lincoln Park Conservatory was constructed between 1890 and 1895. Designed by Joseph Lyman Silsbee and M. E. Bell, the conservatory still has some of its original plants, and large wheels attached to chains attached to gears in the roof are still used to open ceiling vents. Inside this three-acre house are fish ponds, fountains, stately palms, and hundreds of other species of plants, including ficus, banana trees, bromeliads, orchids, and seasonal flowers. Outside, formal and informal gardens make the perfect spot for strolling, relaxing, or playing during warm weather.

North Park Village Nature Center

5801 North Pulaski Road (Peterson Park entrance between West Thorndale Avenue and West Victoria Street)
(312) 744–5472 / TTY/TTD: (312) 744–3586
www.chicagoparkdistrict.com
Hours: 10:00 a.m. to 4:00 p.m. every day except Thanksgiving, December 24, 25, and 31, and January 1.

North Park Village Nature Center is an educational facility that's part of a forty-six-acre nature preserve. Walk trails through prairie, savannah, woodlands, and wetlands and learn about the animals and plants that reside in each type of environment. North Park's educational center houses bones, pelts, shells, and other natural objects kids can touch, along with tanks and cages of small animals in mini habitats. The center hosts nature walks, maple tree tappings, classes, camps, and other events for children and adults. Many, but not all, are free.

Osaka Garden

5800 South Lake Shore Drive (at north end of Wooded Island in Jackson Park)
(773) 256–0903
www.chicagoparkdistrict.com

This traditional Japanese garden began as the home of a Ho-o-den temple, the Japanese government's pavilion at the 1893 World's Columbian Exposition in Jackson Park. The temple structures were destroyed by a series of fires set by hostile Chicagoans during the years of World War II fighting between the United States and Japan. Over the years the garden became a neglected and dangerous place for people, but a nice resting spot for migratory birds. Efforts to restore the garden began in 1973, when the City of Chicago and Osaka, Japan, became sister cities, and the Park District and volunteer organizations continue working to maintain and improve the garden. Features include quiet lagoons, the arching Moon Bridge, Turtle Island, the Kasuga Lantern remaining from the 1893 exposition, and paths designed to invite peaceful reflection as they curve among rocks and boulders, trees, and other plants.

GARDENING **RESOURCES**

Getting a garden started can be a daunting task, but help is available. Many of the government and nonprofit organizations, conservatories, and schools listed in this chapter work with each other and with state and national entities to provide educational and material resources to the gardens and gardeners of Chicago.

Heavy Metal (The Bad Kind)

Years of pollution from leaded paints, leaded gasoline exhaust and other industrial evils have left high levels of lead in urban soils around the world. Chicago's soil is no exception. High lead levels can make the most beautiful-looking vegetable bounty an IQ-lowering, body-poisoning harvest of doom. So before you turn your backyard or a vacant lot into an urban farm (or even if you're already growing food there), have your soil tested for lead contamination. You'll find more information about lead, other lead testing labs, and what to do if your land is full of the stuff (planters and raised beds are one solution), at GreenNet's Web site, listed in this chapter. A local lab will test a sample of your soil for less than $10. It's well worth the investment. Contact:

Stat Analysis Corporation
2242 West Harrison Street, Suite 200
(312) 733–0551
www.statanalysis.com

Angelic Organics Learning Center
6400 South Kimbark Avenue (in church at East 64th Street)
(773) 288-5462
www.csalearningcenter.org

Midwest organic grower Angelic Organics provides classes and helps organize community gardens and other initiatives for better urban food from this center in Woodlawn. Classes include all aspects of urban farming, from growing vegetables in gardens and on rooftops to keeping chickens and bees.

The Catch Most clases cost around $30, but you can recoup those costs in free food.

Chicago Center for Green Technology
445 North Sacramento Boulevard
(312) 746-9192
www.chicagoofchicago.org/Environment/GreenTech

You can learn a lot about eco-friendly living just by touring Chicago Center for Green Technology's building and grounds. The center also offers a variety of free classes and tips on its Web site related to greening up your home and garden.

Cook County Extension Service of the University of Illinois
www.urbanext.uiuc.edu/hort

The extension service's urban horticulture Web address above is packed with

---

Horse *$#*!
When the Chicago Police Department's equestrians in uniform are off duty from delighting kids around tourist areas or controlling crowds at Downtown protests and other big events, they're hard at work metabolizing high-potency manure to fertilize Chicago's soil. It's free for the asking from the Chicago Police Department Mounted Unit stables, at 7509 South Shore Drive (at 71st Street). Enter the double gates to the grounds of the South Shore Cultural Center and turn right into the courtyard. Knock at the stables door, and the person in charge will help you. The best times to visit are Mondays through Fridays between 8:00 a.m. and 3:00 p.m. Or call ahead to (312) 747–5425.

information that covers just about every question you might have for your home or community garden, including articles, printable brochures, and information about other groups, events, classes, and resources available in Chicago. The extension service's Master Gardener Program offers scholarships based on need. The service works with schools and organizations throughout Chicago, particularly the Garfield Park Conservatory, listed below. The extension service also wants to make Chicago's soil richer. To learn how, check out the Chicago Home Composting Web site it sponsors, at www.chicago homecomposting.org.

Demonstration Garden

Just outside the conservatory, see a city-lot-size organic garden in action. Theme areas show urban agricultural techniques, beekeeping, and composting. Wander on your own or let a master gardener answer your questions as you go. Free classes revolve around the garden and the seasons, including pruning techniques, extending your growing seasons, and keeping the salad bowl full from spring through fall. The conservatory also hosts the Chicago Home Composting Program, offering classes to become a master composter. Yum! Check out the program's Web site at www.chicagohomecomposting.org.

Garfield Park Conservatory Programs and Classes

300 North Central Park Avenue (at West Lake Street)
(312) 746–5100
www.garfieldconservatory.org

Christmas Mulch

Every year in early January, the City of Chicago and Chicago Park District encourage residents to drop off their Christmas trees to be recycled into mulch. Anyone who drops off a once-live holiday pine to a designated park for chipping will receive a free bag of mulch, a live blue spruce sapling, and a year's supply of blue city recycling bags. If you don't have a tree to offer, show up with a bag of clean recyclables to exchange for the free mulch and spruce. Check the City of Chicago's Web site in December for details. It's at www.cityofchicago.org/ environment. Go to the Department of the Environment page.

University of Illinois Extension Master Gardener Office and Plant Clinic at Garfield Park Conservatory

Call the clinic or bring your plants or questions to the clinic in the conservatory's lobby. Trained master gardeners are on-hand to help on Saturday from 12:00. to 4:00 p.m.

Greencorps Chicago

(312) 744–8691
www.cityofchicago.org/environment (Go to the Greencorps link.)
environment@cityofchicago.org

The Catch *Greencorps ensures those applying for more-comprehensive (and expensive) assistance demonstrate the commitment and volunteer base to develop and maintain successful garden spaces, so not every group will qualify.*

This program of the City of Chicago Department of the Environment oversees a number of programs for community and school-based landscaping and gardening efforts. Four times a year, Greencorps Chicago gives community organizations throughout the city free bulbs, seeds, annuals, vegetables, and perennial plants. Greencorps provides qualified groups with training, on-site expertise and professional landscaping assistance and, in some cases, more than $2,000 worth of plant materials, soil, mulch, trellises, and benches. It also hires about twenty-five people per year for its six-month landscaping job-training program.

GreenNet

300 North Central Park (inside Garfield Park Conservatory)
(773) 251–7515
www.greennetchicago.org

GreenNet, Chicago's Greening Network, is a coalition of organizations and agencies organized to share information about making Chicago a greener place. From individual classes for backyard gardeners to helping community gardens find grants for plants, GreenNet has got you covered. Check out their Web site for educational resources and connections to community gardeners. And watch for the annual Green & Growing Fair, an early spring festival of gardening-related activities at Garfield Park Conservatory.

Kilbourn Park Organic Greenhouse and Garden

3501 North Kilbourn Avenue (at West Cornelia Avenue)
(773) 685–3351

The organic garden and greenhouse in Kilbourn Park offer community gardening, classes, and demonstration projects for children and adults.

Openlands

25 East Washington Street
(312) 863–6250
www.openlands.org

This organization devoted to reclaiming and maintaining open, natural spaces in northeastern Illinois wants to help you green up your urban garden, whether that's your backyard, roof, or community garden down the street. Check out their Web site for oodles of free tips and resources and contact the organization for help getting your community garden started.

ART GALLERIES:
SHOW ME THE MONET!

"I do not want art for a few any more than education for a few or freedom for a few."
—WILLIAM MORRIS

Don't be embarrassed if you didn't know until this moment that art galleries don't charge admission. Many of us street-smart Chicago cheap bastards made that erroneous assumption when we too were new to the city's art scene. Art galleries may look and feel just like art museums, but they're really stores. A store doesn't charge you to come in and look around, does it? Most galleries' public viewing hours are more limited than those of stores, and smaller venues may close for weeks at a time between installations. But when galleries are open, they want you there, viewing their wares. Don't worry about being pressured to buy, though. Someone may keep at least a casual eye on shoppers to make sure no one makes off with a $5,000 sculpture. But otherwise, you'll generally be left alone to quietly reflect on the art on display. Chicago's the lucky home of scores of fabulous galleries covering a variety of tastes and artistic ideas. Several are clustered in the art districts of Bronzeville, Pilsen, River North, River West, and Wicker Park, but you'll find lone art outposts tucked into neighborhoods all over the city and suburbs.

BRONZEVILLE

Bronzeville's art and cultural renaissance is growing increasingly organized. Take a free trolley tour on the third Fridays of most months to receptions at participating galleries in the Bronzeville area, including many listed here. Toast the art and artists with beverages and light snacks.

Gallery Guichard
3521 South Martin Luther King Jr. Drive (at East 35th Street)
(773) 373–8000
www.galleryguichard.com

This space in the greater Bronzeville area of Chicago features artists of the African diaspora working in ceramics, blown glass, painting, as well as photography.

Wine Goggles

Opening receptions of new art installations at galleries usually serve free wine to attendees. It may be served in Dixie cups, but that free fermented nectar of the gods helps make even the most obtuse art make perfect sense. Some receptions throw in free food, too, but noshes are hit or miss, so don't show up in a remote gallery district on an empty stomach expecting free appetizers to keep the free wine from going straight to your head. Many galleries host opening receptions on Friday evenings and coordinate their openings so patrons can walk from gallery to gallery (and from free wine to free wine). But you can find opening receptions on weekend afternoons and other nights of the week too. The *Chicago Reader* publishes comprehensive lists of gallery openings each week. If you like what you see at a gallery, sign up for its mailing list to receive e-mail messages or artsy postcards announcing future events.

South Side Community Art Center

3831 South Michigan Avenue (at East Pershing Road)
(773) 373–1026
www.southsidecommunityartcenter.com

Hours: Wednesday through Friday, noon to 5:00 p.m.; Saturday, 9:00 a.m. to 5:00 p.m.; Sunday, 1:00 to 5:00 p.m. Closed Monday and Tuesday.

Since 1940, the South Side Community Art Center has hosted a variety of visual and performing arts, and its collection of fine art includes works by the likes of Charles White, Elizabeth Catlett, and William Carter. In addition to gallery exhibitions and art classes, the Bronzeville gallery hosts spoken word, dance, and music events, many of which are free.

SteeleLife Gallery

4655 South Martin Luther King Drive (between East 46th Place and East 47th Place)
(773) 538–4773

Photographer Bryant Johnson runs this gallery of contemporary art in a variety of media by African-American artists.

CHICAGO **ARTS** DISTRICT **(PILSEN)**

Second Fridays of most months are when this gallery district comes to life. Most serve beverages and sometimes snacks with the culture.

expgallery

726 West 18th Street (between South Halsted Street and South Union Avenue)
(847) 217-7520
www.expgallery.com

This gallery run by an artist and professor features emerging artists in a variety of media and hosts monthly arts discussions and workshops.

Fountainhead Loft

1932 South Halsted Street (at West 19th Place)

This historic building hosts several galleries by emerging and emerged artists. Galleries include:
 4Art Inc.: (312) 850-1816, www.4artinc.com
 Alex Fedirko Studio: www.alexfedirko.com
 Angela Komperda Studio
 Brian Mancl: (312) 208-4555, www.brianmancl.net
 Bryan Sperry Studio: (312) 850-1017, www.bryansperry.com
 Design Lab Workshop: www.designlabworkshop.com
 Get Knifed Gallery: (312) 217-5747, www.GetKnifed.com
 Neo-Fauve Gallery: (312) 421-8552
 Robert Marshall: (312) 208-6610, www.snapjawstudio.com
 Studio 101 within(Reason) Gallery: (773) 562-7464, www.artwithin-reason.com

Larry Roberts Studio

1838 South Halsted Street (at West 18th Street)
(312) 243-3052
www.larryrobertsstudio.com

This artist of abstract contemporary paintings opens his studio for second-Friday showings, displaying his art on the second Friday of each month.

Parts Unknown Gallery

645 West 18th Street (at South Desplaines Street)
(312) 492–9058
www.partsunknown.org

Parts Unknown shows work in a variety of media by emerging artists.

Vespine Gallery

1907 South Halsted Street (at West 19th Street), first floor
(312) 962–5850
www.vespine.org

This artist-run gallery showcases the work of emerging artists.

OTHER **SOUTH** SIDE

Beverly Arts Center

2407 West 111th Street (at Western Avenue)
(773) 445–3838
www.beverlyartcenter.org

The Beverly Arts Center packs a lot of visual art, music, dance, comedy, film, and theater into its space in the Beverly, Morgan Park area. Like the neighborhood, the independent, not-for-profit center is heavily Irish but adds other cultures to the mix too. Many events and classes are pretty pricey by the high standards of this book, but some are free.

eta Creative Arts Foundation

7558 South South Chicago Avenue (near South Kimbark Avenue)
(773) 752-3955
www.etacreativearts.org

This South Shore institution has been preserving and promoting "the African American aesthetic" in Chicago for nearly forty years. It offers free author readings and book signings the third Thursday of most months starting at 6:00 p.m. The eta also hosts theater, music, and dance performances, an art gallery and studio, and classes for adults and children. Most charge a fee, but volunteer ushers can see performances for free. The center welcomes long-term volunteers for ushering, clerical help and other tasks.

Hyde Park Art Center

5020 South Cornell Avenue (between East 50th Street and East 50th Place)
www.hydeparkart.org
(773) 324–5520
Hours: Monday through Thursday, 9:00 a.m. to 8:00 p.m., Friday and Saturday, 9:00 a.m. to 5:00 p.m., Sunday, noon to 5:00 p.m.

This community studio, school, and gallery offers a variety of events and classes for adults and children, some of which are free.

MICHIGAN AVENUE, STATE STREET, RIVER EAST, SOUTH LOOP

Notable galleries dot Michigan Avenue's "Magnificent Mile" and other Downtown shopping and business areas.

Chicago Cultural Center

78 East Washington Street (at North Michigan Avenue)
Wheelchair access at 77 East Randolph Street
(312) 744–6630/ TTY: (312) 744–2947
www.chicagoculturalcenter.org
Hours: Monday through Thursday, 8:00 a.m. to 7:00 p.m.; Friday, 8:00 a.m. to 6:00 p.m.; Saturday, 9:00 a.m. to 6:00 p.m.; Sunday, 10:00 a.m. to 6:00 p.m.; closed holidays.

The Chicago Cultural Center hosts Project Onward, a small store and studio with work by artists with developmental disabilities and other special needs. For more information, check out www.projectonward.com.

Donald Young Gallery

224 South Michigan Avenue (across from Art Institute between East Adams Street and East Jackson Boulevard), suite 266
(312) 322–3600
www.donaldyoung.com

Shows contemporary sculptures by new and established artists.

Hildt Galleries

617 North State Street (at East Ontario Street)
(312) 255–0005
www.hildtgalleries.com

Nineteenth- and early twentieth-century European and American oil paintings and watercolors are on display here.

Joel Oppenheimer

410 North Michigan Avenue (in the Wrigley Building at East Kinzie Street)
(312) 642–5300
www.audubonart.com

Specializes in natural history–based art, particularly the work of John James Audubon.

Kamp Gallery

140 East Walton Place (at North Michigan Avenue)
(312) 664–0090
www.kampgallery.com

European and American paintings from the nineteenth and early twentieth centuries, including impressionist, post-impressionist, modern, and contemporary works, are showcased here.

Ogilvie / Pertl Gallery

435 East Illinois Street (in River East Art Center between North Peshtigo
Court and North McClurg Court), suite 151
(312) 321–0750
www.opgallery.com

Exhibits include a variety of styles and media by new and established artists.

Richard Gray Gallery

875 North Michigan Avenue (in John Hancock Center between East Delaware
Place and East Chestnut Street), suite 2503
(312) 642–8877
www.richardgraygallery.com

Shows work of modern and contemporary master artists such as David Hockney, Henri Matisse, Pablo Picasso, and Andy Warhol.

Rosenthal Fine Art

3 East Huron Street (at North State Street), second floor
(312) 475–0700
www.rosenthalfineart.com

Features twentieth-century American and European art, including modernism, abstract expressionism, post-war, and contemporary styles.

Valerie Carberry Gallery

875 North Michigan Avenue (in John Hancock Center between East Delaware Place and East Chestnut Street), suite 2510
(312) 397–9990
www.valeriecarberry.com

This gallery in the Hancock Center specializes in modern and postwar American art in a variety of media.

RIVER **NORTH**

Addington Gallery

704 North Wells Street (at West Huron Street)
(312) 664–3406
www.addingtongallery.com

Specializes in contemporary art in a variety of media.

Aldo Castillo Gallery

675 North Franklin Street (between West Huron Street and West Erie Street)
(312) 337–2536
www.artaldo.com

Aldo Castillo specializes in Latin-American art.

Andrew Bae Gallery

300 West Superior Street (at North Franklin Street)
(312) 335–8601
www.andrewbaegallery.com

This gallery houses Asian art, particularly from Korea and Japan.

Ann Nathan Gallery

212 West Superior Street (at North Wells Street)
(312) 664–6622
www.annnathangallery.com

Includes painting, sculpture, and functional art by famous and emerging artists. Also features African art and artifacts.

ArchiTech

730 North Franklin Street (at West Superior Street), suite 200
(312) 475–1290
www.architechgallery.com

Here you'll find architectural art, including contemporary and retro drawings and designs by architects, designers, and artists such as Frank Lloyd Wright, Daniel Burnham, and Elizabeth Ockwell.

Belloc Lowndes Fine Art

226 West Superior Street (between North Wells Street and North Franklin Street)
(312) 266–2222
www.belloclowndes.com

Shows paintings, sculptures, and works on paper.

Byron Roche Gallery

750 North Franklin Street (between West Chicago Avenue and West Superior Street), suite 201
(312) 654–0144
www.byronroche.com

This gallery features contemporary art in all media, focusing especially on painting. Included are abstract and landscape pieces and works incorporating metallic paints.

Carl Hammer Gallery

740 North Wells Street (at West Superior Street)
(312) 266–8512
www.hammergallery.com

Features contemporary art and American folk and outsider art.

Cassiopeia
433 North Wells Street (at West Hubbard Street)
(312) 464–1111
www.cassiopeiaonline.com

Cassiopeia specializes in historic African art and objects, including textiles, ceramics, metal, and wooden masks and sculpture. Also displayed are works of other cultures.

Catherine Edelman Gallery
300 West Superior Street (at North Franklin Street), lower level (312) 266–2350
www.edelmangallery.com

Shows photography and mixed-media art that incorporates photographs.

Galeria Gala
708 North Wells Street (at West Huron Street)
(312) 640–0517
www.galeriagala.com

Focuses on Spanish artists working in surrealism, realism, geometric abstractionism, and impressionism.

Gruen Galleries
226 West Superior Street (at North Wells Street)
(312) 337–6262
www.gruengalleries.com

Houses contemporary paintings and sculptures mostly by European and American artists.

Habatat Galleries
222 West Superior Street (at North Wells Street)
(312) 440–0288
www.habatatchicago.com

Features contemporary glass sculpture by the likes of Dale Chihuly and Kathy Ruttenberg.

I space
230 West Superior Street (at North Wells Street), second floor
(312) 587–9976
www.ispace.uiuc.edu

The gallery space is run by the College of Fine and Applied Arts at the University of Illinois in Urbana-Champaign. Exhibitions are complemented by performances, classes, lectures, and demonstrations.

Judy A Saslow Gallery

300 West Superior Street (at North Franklin Street)
(312) 943-0530
www.jsaslowgallery.com

This space features contemporary outsider, intuitive, and folk art from around the world.

Kass Meridian

325 West Huron Street (at North Orleans Street), suite 315
(312) 266-5999
www.kassmeridian.com

Contemporary and modern prints, paintings, and sculptures on display here include works by such artists as Lichtenstein, Miro, and Warhol.

Marx-Saunders Gallery Limited

230 West Superior Street (at North Wells Street)
(312) 573-1400
www.marxsaunders.com

Exhibits glass sculpture from around the world.

Maya Polsky Gallery

215 West Superior Street (at North Wells Street)
(312) 440-0055
www.mayapolskygallery.com

Art displayed here includes works by local artists such as the late Ed Paschke, as well as other American and international artists.

Melanee Cooper Gallery

740 North Franklin Street (at West Superior Street)
(312) 202-9305
www.melaneecoopergallery.com

The gallery's collection of contemporary art pays special attention to surfaces and textures.

Mongerson Galleries

704 North Wells Street (at West Huron Street)
(312) 943–2354
www.mongersongalleries.com

Features nineteenth- and twentieth-century American and western art.

Nicole Gallery

230 West Huron Street (at North Wells Street)
(312) 787–7716
www.nicolegallery.com

Nicole Gallery displays a collection of contemporary Caribbean (particularly Haitian), African, and African-American arts. It includes one of America's largest collections of Shona sculpture from Zimbabwe.

Perimeter Gallery

210 West Superior Street (at North Wells Street)
(312) 266–9473
www.perimetergallery.com

Perimeter houses contemporary sculptures, paintings, works on paper, and ceramic and fiber arts. It features young and established artists.

Portals Ltd.

742 North Wells Street (at West Superior Street)
(312) 642–1066
www.portalsgallery.com

Features magical realism art of contemporary international artists, as well as antiques and decorative arts.

Primitive

130 North Jefferson Street (at West Randolph Street)
(312) 575–9600
www.beprimitive.com

The gallery collects artifacts, textiles, rugs, furniture, and jewelry from around the world.

Printworks

311 West Superior Street (at North Franklin Street), suite 105

(312) 664–9407
www.printworkschicago.com

The gallery shows contemporary prints, drawings, artists' books, and photographs. Printworks features both established and emerging artists.

Richard Norton Gallery
612 Merchandise Mart Plaza
(312) 644–8855
www.richardnortongallery.com

Offers American and European impressionist and modern drawings, sculpture, and paintings from the nineteenth and early twentieth centuries.

Robert Henry Adams Fine Art
715 North Franklin Street (between West Superior Street and West Huron Street)
(312) 642–8700
www.adamsfineart.com

This gallery houses modern American painting, drawing, and sculpture from 1910 to 1970. Special focus is placed on social realism, regionalism, abstract expressionism, modernism, impressionism, and African-American art.

Roy Boyd Gallery
739 North Wells Street (at West Superior Street)
(312) 642–1606
www.royboydgallery.com

Features contemporary paintings and sculpture.

Russell Bowman Art Advisory
311 West Superior Street (at North Franklin Street), suite 115
(312) 751–9500
www.bowmanart.com

The gallery houses modern and contemporary art.

Schneider Gallery
230 West Superior Street (at North Wells Street)
(312) 988–4033
www.schneidergallerychicago.com

Features contemporary photographs from here and abroad.

Stephen Daiter Gallery (suite 404) / Daiter Contemporary (suite 408)

311 West Superior Street (between North Franklin Street and North Orleans Street)
(312) 787–3350
www.stephendaitergallery.com

Stephen Daiter Gallery features fine and vintage black-and-white photography, specializing in documentary and experimental photography of the twentieth century. Rare photos include those from Bauhaus and the Chicago School of Design.

Vale Craft Gallery

230 West Superior Street (at North Wells Street)
(312) 337–3525
www.valecraftgallery.com

Sells contemporary American craft and sculpture, including objects in fiber, glass, metal, clay, wood, textiles, and mixed media.

Zolla/Lieberman Gallery

325 West Huron Street (at North Orleans Street)
(312) 944–1990
www.zollaliebermangallery.com

This gallery features contemporary artwork in all media from established and new artists.

Zygman Voss Gallery

222 West Superior Street (at North Wells Street), suite 1E
(312) 787–3300
www.zygmanvossgallery.com

Features master artists from the seventeenth through twentieth centuries, including Renoir, Rembrandt, Picasso, Dali, Lautrec, Cassatt, and Chagall. The gallery also shows contemporary works.

RIVER **WEST,** WEST **LOOP**

Carrie Secrist Gallery
835 West Washington Boulevard (at North Green Street)
(312) 491–0917
www.secristgallery.com

Shows contemporary works in all media by new and established artists.

Douglas Dawson Gallery
400 North Morgan Street (at West Kinzie Street)
(312) 226–7975
www.douglasdawson.com

Specializes in ancient and historic art and artifacts from throughout the world. Collection includes textiles, sculpture, furniture, and ceramics.

G.R. N'Namdi Gallery
110 North Peoria Street (at West Washington Boulevard)
(312) 563–9240
www.grnnamdi.com

Specializes in abstract art from around the world.

Intuit: The Center for Intuitive and Outsider Art
756 North Milwaukee Avenue (southeast of North Ogden Avenue)
(312) 243–9088
www.art.org

This not-for-profit organization features the work of self-taught "outsider" artists who show little influence from the mainstream art establishment. Intuit houses a large collection of work by late Chicagoan Henry Darger, best known for his obsessive and controversial epic of the Vivian girls, young girls who, often naked, fight to save their world from destruction by forces of evil.

Linda Warren Gallery
1052 West Fulton Market (at North Carpenter Street)
(312) 432–9500
www.lindawarrengallery.com

The space shows art in all styles and media by new and established artists.

Navta Schulz Gallery
1039 West Lake Street (at North Carpenter Street)
(312) 421–5506
www.navtaschulzgallery.com

The gallery features paintings, prints, drawings, and sculptures from new and established artists.

Packer Schopf Gallery
942 West Lake Street (at North Sangamon Street)
(312) 226–8984
www.aronpacker.com

Packer Schopf shows contemporary art in all media.

Rhona Hoffman Gallery
118 North Peoria Street (between West Randolph Street and West Washington Boulevard)
(312) 455–1990
http://rhoffmangallery.com

Rhona Hoffman shows contemporary art in all media by new and established artists.

Rowland Contemporary
1118 West Fulton Market (between North May Street and North Aberdeen Street)
(312) 421–6275
www.rowlandcontemporary.com

Contemporary art by new and seasoned artists working in all media is on display here.

Spencer Weisz Galleries Limited
843 West Chicago Avenue (West of North Green Street)
(312) 527–9420
www.antiqueposter.com

Sells original European vintage posters, especially late nineteenth- and early twentieth-century stone lithography from such folks as Toulouse Lautrec and Jules Cheret.

Thomas McCormick Gallery

835 West Washington Boulevard (at South Green Street)
(312) 226–6800
www.thomasmccormick.com

Modern and contemporary paintings, works on paper, and sculpture.

Walsh Gallery

118 North Peoria Street (between West Randolph Street and West Washington Boulevard)
(312) 829–3312
www.walshgallery.com

Focuses particularly on contemporary art from throughout the Asian continent and from the Asian diaspora.

FAR WEST SIDE, HISTORIC SEARS ROEBUCK & CO. BUILDING

Marc Rubin Gallery

3333 West Arthington Street (between South Spaulding Avenue and South Homan Avenue), third floor
(773) 404–2233
www.chicagoroomgallerycafe.com

This gallery takes up half the 35,000-square-foot space of the sprawling former Sears building not far from Garfield Park Conservatory. (Murphy Hill Gallery, listed below, takes up the other half.) Its fine art covers a variety of media and styles, including painting, sculpture, stained glass, Venetian glass, and photography. The gallery also serves as a venue for performing arts, including tapings of *No Restrictions,* a new comedy show produced by Earl Winfrey, Oprah's local cable-accessible cousin.

Murphy Hill Gallery

3333 West Arthington Street (between South Spaulding Avenue and South Homan Avenue), third floor

www.murphyhillgallery.com
(773) 324–5781

Every six weeks or so, this gallery and store exhibits a different theme of contemporary art, drawing from a variety of topics such as architecture, gender, cultural diversity, and nature. The venue presents many group shows as expositions of a variety of media, including sculpture, film, video, painting, photography, and performance art. Occupying half of the 35,000-square-foot third floor of this former Sears building (see Marc Rubin Gallery, above) Murphy Hill has plenty of space for such variety.

BUCKTOWN, **WICKER** PARK, **LOGAN** SQUARE, **OTHER** NORTH **SIDE**

Chicago Art Source
1871 North Clybourn Avenue (at West Wisconsin Street)
(773) 248–3100
www.chicagoartsource.com

This gallery covers a variety of styles from abstract to traditional, including works on paper, canvas, photography, sculpture, digital imaging, and posters.

Chicago Hot Glass Gallery
1250 North Central Park Avenue (between West Potomac Avenue and West Division Street)
(773) 394–3252
www.chicagohotglass.com

Associated with Chicago Hot Glass, a studio that specializes in and teaches glassblowing techniques. It displays work of emerging and established local and international artists.

Contemporary Art Workshop
542 West Grant Place (between North Cleveland Avenue and North Geneva Terrace)
(773) 472–4004
www.contemporaryartworkshop.org

Logan Square Artists Unite!

The Neighborhood Artists in Logan Square (http://nailslogansquare .com) collective is a forum for Logan Square artists to share ideas and techniques, constructively critique each others' work, and organize exhibitions and art sales by members. N.A.I.L.S. meets monthly at New Wave Coffee (2557 North Milwaukee Avenue, www.newwavecoffee .com) and occasionally other venues. Check the Web site calendar for updates. To join in (you must live in Logan Square), send an e-mail to nails.logansquare@gmail.com. The group shares correspondence and announcements through the Arte Logan Square Yahoo! group.

Supports and features local emerging artists working in a variety of media.

Havana Gallery Limited
1139 West Webster Avenue (at North Clifton Avenue)
(773) 549–2492
www.havanagallery.com

Sells contemporary work of artists living in Cuba.

Madron LLC
1000 West North Avenue (at North Sheffield Avenue), third floor
(312) 640–1302
www.madronllc.com

Madron specializes in American art from 1890 through 1940 but also includes modern and contemporary works.

Mess Hall
6932 North Glenwood Avenue (at West Morse Avenue)
(773) 465–4033
www.messhall.org

The Mess Hall is a cultural center, gallery, potluck party, performance venue, lecture space, sewing parlor, spoken-word cafe, clothing exchange, and meeting place for the confluence of all ideas lefty. Its members screen videos too.

Moka Gallery

2112 West Belmont Avenue (West of North Hoyne Avenue)
(773) 975–2280
www.mokagallery.com

Moka features works in a variety of styles by emerging and established artists from around the world.

Platt Fine Art

561 West Diversey Parkway (at North Cambridge Avenue), suite 213
(773) 281–2500
www.plattfineart.com

The gallery features nineteenth- and twentieth-century American prints, paintings, and works on paper, especially impressionist, post-impressionist, modernist, Works Progress Administration, social realism, and abstract work.

Thomas Masters Gallery

245 West North Avenue (at North Wieland Street)
(312) 440–2322
www.thomasmastersgallery.com

Displays contemporary art in a variety of media.

MUSEUMS:
FREE TO SEE

"I went to the museum where they had all the heads and arms from the statues that are in the other museums."
—STEPHEN WRIGHT

Chicago's museums range from world-famous to obscure, from conventional to bizarre, and from cheap to pricey. Show up unprepared at certain museums on the wrong day, and you could end up spending your dinner money; bring the family, and you could blow the week's grocery budget. Not to worry. You can see the treasures of most Chicago museums for free if you know when, where, and how to go. Some institutions are always free, some are free only on certain days or during certain hours, and some charge suggested donations. Others are free anytime with a weeklong pass Chicago residents can check out from the Chicago Public Library. So arm yourself with the facts (check hours and other essentials that change before you go), and soon you'll be marveling at the wealth of knowledge, beauty, and kitsch on display in any of our fine institutions.

ALWAYS FREE

CenterSpace Gallery at Gallery 37
Gallery 37 Center for the Arts, fifth floor
66 East Randolph Street (between Wabash Avenue and Michigan Avenue)
(312) 744–8925
www.gallery37.org
Hours: Monday through Saturday, 10:00 a.m. to 5:00 p.m.

CenterSpace brings young artists, arts educators, professional artists, and arts organizations together. Come see some of the results of that collaboration. The gallery includes work from teenaged and professional adult artists alike.

Chicago ArchiCenter
224 South Michigan Avenue (at East Jackson Boulevard)
(312) 922–3432
www.architecture.org/cac.html
Hours: Tuesday through Sunday, 9:30 a.m. to 4:00 p.m.

The Chicago Architecture Foundation offers rotating exhibits, lectures, and events related to Chicago's architecture and neighborhoods inside the historic Santa Fe Building. Learn how Chicago's world-class and hardworking building designs came to be, and see and hear proposals for improving Chicago's built environment with new ideas for design of everything from buildings to recycling bins.

Chicago Cultural Center

78 East Washington Street (at North Michigan Avenue)
Wheelchair access at 77 East Randolph Street
(312) 744–6630/ TTY: (312) 744–2947
www.chicagoculturalcenter.org
Hours: Monday through Thursday, 8:00 a.m. to 7:00 p.m.; Friday, 8:00 a.m. to 6:00 p.m.; Saturday, 9:00 a.m. to 6:00 p.m.; Sunday, 10:00 a.m. to 6:00 p.m.; closed holidays.

The Chicago Cultural Center pops up in a few chapters of this book. There's that much culture packed into its five stories, including dance, music, lectures, literary programs, history, and art, and almost every event is free. The center's historical, cultural, and visual arts exhibits employ a variety of media to tell Chicago's rich and continuing cultural story. The building itself is worth the trip. Completed in 1897 as the city's main library and dubbed "The People's Palace," the beaux-arts-style structure became one of the first free municipal cultural institutions in the United States. Check out the building's newly restored stained- glass domes and chandeliers, some of the earliest and most-extensive commissions by the artist Louis Comfort Tiffany.

Chicago Fed Money Museum

230 South LaSalle Street (at West Jackson Boulevard)
(312) 322–2400
http://www.chicagofed.org/education/money_museum.cfm
Hours: Monday through Friday, 9:00 a.m. to 4:00 p.m., except on bank holidays when the Fed is closed for security reasons. Guided tours begin at 1:00 p.m. or by appointment.

Come ponder where our banking system went so horribly wrong at this museum of money tucked into the Chicago Federal Reserve Bank. The tours include a short video about the Chicago Fed's operations, the Federal Reserve, and U.S. monetary policy. You must show a photo ID before entering.

City Gallery in the Historic Water Tower

806 North Michigan Avenue (at East Chicago Avenue)
(312) 742–0808 / TTY: (312) 744–2947
www.cityofchicago.org/Tourism/ThingsToDo/CityGallery/CityGallery.html
Hours: Monday through Saturday, 10:00 a.m. to 6:30 p.m.; Sunday 10:00
a.m. to 5:00 p.m.

The Water Tower earned its capital letters by being one of the only structures, along with the Chicago Avenue Pumping Station, to survive the Chicago Fire of 1871. Residents used it as a guidepost as they hunted for the
ruins of their former homes. Of course, they're now historic landmarks. The
City Gallery, inside the Water Tower, displays the mostly Chicago-centric
work of Chicago photographers as a project of the Chicago Department of
Cultural Affairs.

DePaul University Art Museum

2350 North Kenmore Avenue (south of Fullerton Avenue)
(773) 325–7506
http://museums.depaul.edu/artwebsite
Hours: Monday through Thursday, 11:00 a.m. to 5:00 p.m.; Friday, 11:00 a.m.
to 7:00 p.m.; Saturday and Sunday, noon to 5:00 p.m.

This 4,000-square-foot facility on DePaul's Lincoln Park campus includes collections the university has acquired during its 100-plus-year history as well
as new works from faculty, staff, and artists outside the university, with a
particular focus on art of and from the Chicago area. Exhibits include historical and contemporary themes.

Gage Gallery

18 South Michigan Avenue (between East Monroe Street and East Madison
Street)
www.roosevelt.edu/gagegallery
Hours: Monday through Friday from 9 a.m. to 5 p.m.

Across the street from "The Bean" in the Gage building, is a tiny art gallery
operated by Roosevelt University. The Gallery's artwork and photography
embodies the school's ideals of social justice.

Intuit: The Center for Intuitive and Outsider Art

756 North Milwaukee Avenue (southeast of North Ogden Avenue)
(312) 243–9088
www.art.org

Hours: Tuesday through Saturday, 11:00 a.m. to 5:00 p.m., Thursday, 11:00 a.m. to 7:30 p.m.

Intuit defines intuitive and outsider art as the work of artists who show little influence and training from the mainstream art establishment, what is also called art brut and folk, self-taught, and visionary art. The center's members work to discover, catalog, preserve, and exhibit such art in its gallery space.

Jane Addams Hull House Museum

800 South Halsted Street (between West Harrison Street and West Roosevelt Road)
(312) 413-5353
www.uic.edu/jaddams/hull
Hours: Tuesday through Friday, 10:00 a.m. to 4:00 p.m.; Sunday, noon to 4:00 p.m. Closed Mondays, Saturdays, and during holidays and many semester breaks when the University of Illinois is closed.

This remaining building of the original Hull House complex celebrates Jane Addams's pioneering work in creating community-based programs and political pressure to address a host of social ills, such as crushing poverty, xenophobia, and child labor. Addams and her colleagues founded the Hull House settlement house in 1889, and she lived and worked in its complex of buildings until her death in 1935. The building housing the museum was one of the few in the neighborhood to survive demolition to make way for the University of Illinois' campus, which is an achievement in itself. It houses some of its original furniture, including Addams's office, and historic photographs, documents, and artwork that evoke the era and educate about the work of Addams and other social and political reformers of her time. Hull House also hosts a variety of educational events, such as lunchtime lectures that include free soup.

Mary and Leigh Block Museum of Art

40 Arts Circle Drive (first enter Campus Drive heading east from Sheridan Road at southeastern end of Northwestern University campus)
Evanston, Illinois (847) 491-4000
www.blockmuseum.northwestern.edu
Hours: Tuesday, 10:00 a.m. to 5:00 p.m.; Wednesday through Friday, 10:00 a.m. to 8:00 p.m.; Saturday and Sunday, noon to 5:00 p.m.

The museum's fine-arts exhibitions cover early through contemporary art, including a permanent collection consisting primarily of works on paper, which includes paintings, cartoons, and photographs.

Museum of Contemporary Photography
Columbia College Chicago
600 South Michigan Avenue (at East Harrison Street)
(312) 663–5554
www.mocp.org
Hours: Monday through Friday, 10:00 a.m. to 5:00 p.m.; Thursday, 10:00 a.m. to 8:00 p.m.; Saturday, noon to 5:00 p.m.

The museum exhibits the work of photographers from around the world, both professional and Columbia College students. Exhibitions include experimental, artistic, and documentary photographic work.

National Museum of Mexican Art
1852 West 19th Street (between South Wolcott Avenue and South Wood Street)
(312) 738–1503
www.nationalmuseumofmexicanart.org
Hours: Tuesday through Sunday, 10:00 a.m. to 5:00 p.m.; closed Mondays and New Year's Day, Martin Luther King's Birthday, Memorial Day, Independence Day, Labor Day, Thanksgiving, and Christmas Day.

The mission of the National Museum of Mexican Art (formerly the Mexican Fine Arts Center Museum) is to preserve and promote Mexican and Mexican-American visual and performance art. This is one of the finest museums in Chicago and one of the largest Latino cultural organizations in the country. Permanent and temporary exhibitions include paintings, objects, and photographs that depict the art, culture, and history of Mexico, from its ancient past to the present, as well as the Mexican and Mexican-American experience in the United States. The museum also hosts many events, classes, and educational programs for all ages, many of which are free.

Renaissance Society
5811 South Ellis Avenue (on University of Chicago campus, near East 58th Street)
Cobb Hall, fourth floor
(773) 702–8670
http://renaissancesociety.org
Hours: Tuesday through Friday, 10:00 a.m. to 5:00 p.m.; Saturday and Sunday, noon to 5:00 p.m.; closed Monday.

Since 1915 the Renaissance Society has produced exhibitions, events, and publications devoted to contemporary art.

The Great Museum Pass

Not so long ago, museums on Chicago Park District property were free at least one day a week year-round. Sure, it was reasonable to charge admission most of the time to fund research and acquiring and protecting collections, but public institutions on the public's property should give said public free glimpses of the goods on a regular basis. Or so the thinking went. That thinking has changed slightly. Museums on park property still offer fifty-two free days per year, but they tend to be clustered during slower seasons. The good news is that you still can visit them for free any time of the year. The Chicago Public Library (www.chipublib.org) still has you covered for ten top Chicago institutions listed here. Any adult resident of Chicago may check out a Kraft Great Kids Museum Passport with a Chicago Public Library card. The pass provides free admission to a single person and up to seven people, with admission rules varying by institution. Sometimes a certain number of those people must be children, and sometimes they are supposed to be "immediate" family. (No museum employee has ever challenged my loose interpretation of who counts as immediate family.) The passports are good for a week and can't be renewed or reserved. Usually the passports cover only general admission, not special exhibits that cost extra. Passes for the more-famous museums are often checked out, so call your nearest library branch first to see if one for your favorite is available.

The Catch As with all library materials, respect those due dates! Fines for overdue passes are $2 per day to a maximum of $20. Lost passes will set you back $60.

You can try other branches next if necessary.

Smart Museum of Art

5550 South Greenwood Avenue (on University of Chicago campus, at East 55th Street)
(773) 702–0200
http://smartmuseum.uchicago.edu
Hours: Tuesday, Wednesday, and Friday, 10:00 a.m. to 4:00 p.m.; Thursday, 10:00 A.M. to 8:00 p.m.; Saturday and Sunday, 11:00 a.m. to 5:00 p.m.; closed Monday and holidays and closes at 4:00 p.m. in summer.

The David and Alfred Smart Museum of Art's collection covers five centuries from Eastern to Western civilizations. Permanent collections include more than ten thousand objects. The museum also provides classes, lectures, and other free educational programming on-site and in Chicago neighborhoods.

Smith Museum of Stained Glass
600 East Grand Avenue (east of Lake Shore Drive)
Lower Level of Festival Hall at Navy Pier
(312) 595–5024
www.navypier.com
Hours: Sunday through Thursday, 10:00 a.m. to 8:00 p.m.; Friday and Saturday, 10:00 a.m. to 10:00 p.m. (Open during Navy Pier's operating hours.)

An oasis from Navy Pier's tourist hubbub (and tourist prices), this museum displays 150 stained-glass windows along an 800-foot-long gallery. The windows showcase the art from 1870 to the present, encompassing Victorian, Prairie, modern, and contemporary styles. View a Louis Comfort Tiffany creation or one from Chicago's own Ed Paschke. Many of the windows were saved from Chicago churches and other buildings. Free tours begin every Friday at 2:00 p.m. at the museum's entrance.

SOMETIMES **FREE**

Adler Planetarium and Astronomy Museum
1300 South Lake Shore Drive (on the east end of the museum campus)
(312) 922–7827
(312) 322–0995 (TTY for hearing-impaired)
www.adlerplanetarium.org
Regular hours: Monday through Friday 10:00 a.m. to 4:00 p.m. and Saturday and Sunday from 10:00 a.m. to 4:30 p.m.; first Friday of every month, 9:30 a.m. to 10:00 p.m. Closed on Thanksgiving and Christmas Day.
Summer Hours (June 15 through Labor Day): Monday through Sunday, 9:30 a.m. to 6:00 p.m.; first Friday of every month, 9:30 a.m. to 10:00 p.m.
LIBRARY PASS: Admits up to four immediate family members; kids younger than age twelve must be accompanied by an adult; pass valid only for general admission, not special exhibits.

Adler is a classic planetarium on Chicago's lakefront, complete with exhibits about neighboring planets and distant galaxies, explorations of astronomy from ancient times to the present, and telescope viewings open to the public for significant astronomical events. The museum includes extensive interactive exhibits for children, and plenty for grown-ups to ponder too.

The Art Institute of Chicago

111 South Michigan Avenue (at Columbus Drive)
(312) 443–3600
www.artic.edu
Hours: Monday through Wednesday and Friday, 10:30 a.m. to 5:00 p.m.; Thursday, 10:30 a.m. to 8:00 p.m.; Saturday and Sunday, 10:00 a.m. to 5:00 p.m.
Note: Children under age twelve are always free.
Free Evenings: Thursday 5:00 to 9:00 p.m. year-round; Thursday and Friday 5:00 to 9:00 p.m. in summer.
LIBRARY PASS: Admits up to four immediate family members; kids under twelve must be accompanied by an adult. Pass is valid for general admission and, when available, up to four same-day tickets to special exhibits. Show your pass and ask about special exhibit tickets at the admission desk.

No, the admission booth cashier is not holding out on you: The Art Institute did away with its famed small-print suggested donation a few years ago. Those admissions are now mandatory, folks, unless you're younger than twelve or know how and when to visit. Get a museum pass or stop by on Thursday or summer Friday evenings to see it for free. This expansive, world-class museum houses the big names of art like Monet, O'Keeffe, and Picasso, along with lesser-known artists and anonymous artifacts from the distant past to the present. Collections span the globe and all its art forms, including African, American, Amerindian, Asian, European, ancient to contemporary, architecture, arms and armor, photography, textiles, prints and drawings, a miniature room, and an interactive children's museum. Lockers and a coat check are available.

Chicago Children's Museum

700 East Grand Avenue (on Navy Pier)
(312) 527–1000
www.chichildrensmuseum.org
Hours: Friday through Wednesday, 10:00 a.m. to 5:00 p.m.; Thursday and first Monday of each month 10:00 a.m. to 8:00 p.m.; open every holiday except Thanksgiving and Christmas Day.

Free days: The first Monday of every month is free (without a library pass), as is every Thursday night from 5:00 to 8:00 p.m.
LIBRARY PASS: Admits up to four immediate family members for general admission only; one adult must accompany every three kids younger than age sixteen.

The museum's three floors of interactive exhibits and climbing apparatuses, with daily performances, workshops, and other events, are the perfect place to let the kids burn off some extra energy while they learn. First Free Mondays, the first Monday of each month, include storytellers and other special literacy programming.

DuSable Museum of African American History
740 East 56th Place (in Washington Park west of South Cottage Grove Avenue)
(773) 947–0600
www.dusablemuseum.org
Hours: Tuesday through Saturday, 10:00 a.m. to 5:00 p.m.; Sunday, noon to 5:00 p.m.; closed on Monday between June 1 and January 2 except for school holidays, the third Saturday and Sunday in February, and on New Year's Day, Easter, July 4th, Labor Day, Thanksgiving, and Christmas.
Free day: Sunday.
LIBRARY PASS: Admits up to four immediate family members for general admission only.

Named after Jean Baptist Pointe DuSable, a Haitian fur trader who was the first permanent settler in what would become Chicago, this is the oldest museum dedicated to the art, culture, and history of African Americans and Africans. The displays include artifacts, art, recordings, photographs, and documents that lead visitors through years of struggle and achievement from slavery to the present. It also includes profiles of prominent African Americans who have enriched Chicago and beyond with their lives and work, and many inventions. The museum also conducts many programs and activities, some of which are free. Check out the Children's Penny Cinema, which usually costs a penny per person.

The Field Museum
Museum Campus
1400 South Lake Shore Drive at Roosevelt Road
(312) 922–9410 or (312) 341–9299 TDD
www.fieldmuseum.org
Regular hours: Monday through Saturday 10:00 a.m. to 5:00 p.m., Sunday

11:00 a.m. to 5:00 p.m. Last admission at 4:00 p.m.; closed Christmas.
LIBRARY PASS: Admits up to four immediate family members for basic admission and Underground Adventure; kids younger than age twelve must be accompanied by an adult.

This classic old museum is home to Sue, the world's largest, most complete Tyrannosaurus rex skeleton; ancient Egypt displays teeming with kids; buttons to push and recordings to hear; gems; masks; rocks; plants; ecosystems; statues; thought-provoking photographs and sounds depicting people from around the world past and present; an ark of taxidermy (including two lions of Tsavo famed and feared for their tastes for human flesh); and plenty of relevant-but-forgotten exhibits great for quiet, leisurely reflection. The palatial building is yet another product of the Columbian Exposition of 1893. It was named after mercantile titan Marshall Field in 1905 after he became the institution's first major benefactor.

John G. Shedd Aquarium

1200 South Lake Shore Drive (in the Museum Campus adjacent to the lake)
(312) 939–2438
www.sheddaquarium.org
Hours Labor Day to Memorial Day: Weekdays from 9:00 a.m. to 5:00 p.m. and weekends from 9:00 a.m. to 6:00 p.m. Closed Christmas Day.
Summer Hours: Daily 9:00 a.m. to 6:00 p.m.
LIBRARY PASS: Admits up to two adults and two children to general admission areas (Wild Reef and Oceanarium exhibits still cost extra.) Kids must be accompanied by an adult.

Chicago's big fancy fish tank houses some 19,000 representatives of the fish, reptiles, amphibians, birds, mammals, and invertebrates that inhabit the waters and beaches of the world. Check the Web site or call to find out the latest schedule of days when general admission is free for everyone.

Museum of Contemporary Art (MCA)

220 East Chicago Avenue (at North St. Clair Street)
(312) 280–2660 / TDD: (312) 397–4006
www.mcachicago.org
Hours: Tuesday, 10:00 a.m. to 8:00 p.m.; Wednesday through Sunday, 10:00 a.m. to 5:00 p.m.; closed Monday, New Year's Day, Thanksgiving, and Christmas.
Restrictions: Groups must include one adult for every three children.
Note: Children younger than age twelve are always admitted for free but must be accompanied by an adult. Members of the military are free.
Free Day: Tuesday.

LIBRARY PASS: Admits up to four people during regular public hours.

The MCA's permanent and temporary exhibits include paintings, sculptures, photography, video, and film created since 1945. Its more than 6,000 objects include works by upcoming and famous artists, such as Max Ernst and Marcel Duchamp. The museum also hosts lectures, performances, and other events, many of which are free.

Museum of Science and Industry
57th Street at Lake Shore Drive
(773) 684–1414
www.msichicago.org
Regular hours: Monday through Saturday, 9:30 a.m. to 4:00 p.m. and Sunday, 11:00 a.m. to 4:00 p.m. Extended hours (summer, local school spring and holiday breaks): Monday through Saturday, 9:30 a.m. to 5:30 p.m. and Sunday, 11:00 a.m. to 5:30 p.m. Closed Christmas Day
LIBRARY PASS: Admits up to four immediate family members for general admission only; kids younger than age twelve must be accompanied by an adult.

The museum offers fourteen acres of interactive exhibits, so make sure to bring good walking shoes and plenty of energy, or focus on a few sections per visit. Travel into a virtual coal mine, tour a human heart or World War II–era German submarine, see robots at work and exploding chemistry demonstrations, watch chickens hatch, ponder your genetic code or the war against AIDS, or take a virtual ride into space. Younger children can bounce off the walls (literally) in a room of interactive fun just for them.

Notebaert Nature Museum
2430 North Cannon Drive (at Fullerton Parkway in Lincoln Park)
(773) 755–5100
www.naturemuseum.org
Hours: Open every day except New Year's Day, Thanksgiving, and Christmas; Monday through Friday, 9:00 a.m. to 4:30 p.m.; Saturday and Sunday, 10:00 a.m. to 5:00 p.m.
Free/suggested donation day: On Thursday, kids are free and suggested donation for adults is $7.
LIBRARY PASS: Admits up to four immediate family members. Children younger than twelve must be accompanied by an adult.

The Notebaert Nature Museum houses—and is surrounded by—exhibits devoted to understanding and appreciating the natural world, with plenty of fun educational stuff for kids and adults. Take nature walks, crawl through models of animal homes, splash in rivers, tour an eco-friendly cottage, and relax in a butterfly habitat. The outdoor habitats surrounding the museum are accessible and free.

MUSEUMS **WITH** SUGGESTED DONATIONS

Chicago History Museum

1601 North Clark Street (at North Avenue)
(312) 642–4600
www.chicagohistory.org
Hours: Monday through Wednesday, Friday, and Saturday, 9:30 a.m. to 4:30 p.m.; Thursday, 9:30 a.m. to 8:00 p.m., and Sunday noon to 5:00 p.m.
Suggested admission: $12 for adults, $10 for seniors sixty-five and older and for students thirteen to twenty-two years old. Children twelve years old and younger are free.
Free day: Monday.
LIBRARY PASS: Admits up to four immediate family members for general admission only.

The Chicago Historical Society (now called the Chicago History Museum) was founded in 1856, making it the city's oldest cultural institution. Since 1932, it has been located in a brick Georgian building that recently underwent

---

Bring Food, Forget the Car

Many museums listed in this chapter are in congested Downtown or campus areas, or on the tourist-teeming Museum Campus. As such, parking is often difficult or can cost more than a ride on public transit. Check your options for bicycling, walking, public transit, or driving (or a combination of those options) to decide your best way to arrive (See RTA public transit trip planner at www.rtachicago.com). Some museums also house cafeterias or restaurants, but being a cheap bastard, you know to bring a sack meal or snacks.

---

extensive renovation. The museum's permanent collections include Chicago's first el car, displays of pioneer life, dioramas, photographs, and a low-rider car. Extensive collections of documents and artifacts in the research room have served generations of professional and amateur historians. Many of them are accessible online through links on the society's Web address—for free, of course.

Loyola University Museum of Art (LUMA)
820 North Michigan Avenue (at East Pearson Street)
(312) 915–7600
www.luc.edu/luma
Hours: Tuesday, 10:00 a.m. to 8:00 p.m.; Wednesday through Sunday, 10:00 a.m. to 5:00 p.m.; closed Monday.
Suggested admission: Tuesdays are free for everyone, and every day is free for children younger than age fourteen, students younger than age twenty-five, military dependents, and Loyola employees (bring an ID to prove your status). Otherwise, the suggested general admission is $6, and senior admission is $5.

The Loyola University Museum of Art is tucked into the school's historic Lewis Towers on its Michigan Avenue campus. It is devoted to the exploration of spiritual concerns through art of all cultures and societies, but it covers other facets of life too. LUMA houses permanent exhibits, including medieval and Renaissance art, and visiting exhibits. Free guided tours start at noon and 2:00 p.m.

Oriental Institute Museum
1155 East 58th Street (at South Woodlawn Avenue)
(773) 702–9520
http://oi.uchicago.edu
Hours: Tuesday and Thursday through Saturday, 10:00 a.m. to 6:00p.m.; Wednesday, 10:00 a.m. to 8:30 p.m.; Sunday, noon to 6:00 p.m.; closed Monday.
Suggested admission: $7 for adults and $4 for children younger than age twelve.

This museum on the University of Chicago campus exhibits art, archaeology photographs, and historical artifacts of the ancient Near East (better known in the United States as the Middle East) and many items from its most recent century. On display are many of the antiquities the Oriental Institute has acquired since 1919 in its archaeological excavations in Egypt, Mesopotamia, Iran, Syria, Anatolia, Israel, and Palestine.

ZOOS AND OTHER MENAGERIES:
BORN FREE

"I think the monkeys at the zoo should have to wear sunglasses so they can't hypnotize you."
—JACK HANDY

Animals are an important part of Chicago's history. It was Mrs. O'Leary's cow, after all, who was wrongly accused of starting the Great Chicago Fire that leveled much of the city in 1871, huge stockyards made Chicago worthy of its title "Hog Butcher to the World," and the owner of the Billy Goat Tavern put a curse on the Cubs baseball team in—wait a minute, maybe this isn't a very good way to start a chapter about the love of animals. Chicago still has a lot of animals within its borders, and I'm not just talking about those who drink too much on Rush Street every weekend. The city is home to two major zoos, a couple of tiny menageries, an aquarium, and seasonal and year-round butterfly habitats. Residents range from farm animals to exotic and rare species from around the world, and you can visit each of them for free.

ALWAYS **FREE**

Eden Place Nature Center
43rd Place and Stewart Avenue
(773) 624–8686
www.fullerpark.com/EDEN PLACE.html

Come learn about the plants and animals of woodlands, wetlands, and prairies at this nature preserve and demonstration center. Eden Place includes multimedia and live presentations for families and school groups.

Remember Snacks

The big zoos listed in this chapter have cafes and restaurants on-site, but they can be pretty pricey, especially if you're feeding your own herd of hungry kids. For an extra-thrifty adventure, bring your own food to keep tummies and your wallet equally full. Yes, you'll sound just like your parents did saying no to children whining for freshly fried junk food, and you'll enjoy saying it just as much as they did.

Indian Boundary Park Zoo

2500 West Lunt Avenue (at North Rockwell Street; zoo is at northwest corner of park)
(773) 764-0338
www.chicagoparkdistrict.com

Taking its name from an old boundary line established in a treaty between the Pottawattomie Indians and the U.S. government in 1816 (honored until 1883, when the United States forced the Pottawattomie out of the area), this gem of the Chicago Park District has hosted a small zoo since the mid-1920s. It was one of only two zoos in Chicago back then, initially housing only an unlucky black bear. Now the open-air zoo hosts a small collection of animals perfect for the attention spans of young children, including a cow, alpaca, goats, and sheep.

Lincoln Park Zoo

North Cannon Drive and Fullerton Parkway (off Fullerton Parkway exit of Lake Shore Drive)
(312) 742-2000
www.lpzoo.com
Hours: Vary by season, from 9:00 a.m. year-round until 5:00 p.m. in winter, until 6:00 p.m. in spring and autumn and on summer weekdays, and until 7:00 p.m. on summer weekends. Buildings and farm close half an hour before grounds close.

The Lincoln Park Zoo has all the attractions of the classic city zoo, such as primates, big cats, wolves, warnings of pending extinctions, and a children's zoo. The indoor wild bird, small mammal, and reptile habitats, and African Journey make for a great mini-vacation to warmer climates when it's cold outside and you need a better habitat than your own chilly home.

SOMETIMES **FREE**

Brookfield Zoo

3300 Golf Road (at First Avenue between Ogden Avenue and 31st Street)
Brookfield (708) 485-0263
www.brookfieldzoo.org

Hours: Open every day of the year. Hours vary by season from 9:30 or 10:00 a.m. to 5:00 or 7:30 p.m. During Holiday Magic in December, zoo remains open until 9:00 p.m. Indoor exhibits close thirty minutes before zoo closes. Free days:

> **Main Zoo:** Tuesdays and Thursdays in January, February, October, November, and December. Saturdays and Sundays are also free during the chilly months of January and February.
>
> **Children's Zoo:** November through February.

LIBRARY PASS: Admits up to four people free. Kids must be accompanied by an adult.

Brookfield Zoo is the largest in the region, with 216 acres of beautiful landscaping and more than 3,000 animals in 21 exhibits. Don't balk at the free days being mostly during cold months. The tropical indoor habitats provide a great escape from Chicago's harsh winters.

John G. Shedd Aquarium

1200 South Lake Shore Drive (in the Museum Campus area of Grant Park)
(312) 939–2438
www.sheddaquarium.org
Hours Labor Day to Memorial Day: Weekdays from 9:00 a.m. to 5:00 p.m. and weekends from 9:00 a.m. to 6:00 p.m. Closed Christmas Day.
Summer Hours: Daily 9:00 a.m. to 6:00 p.m.
LIBRARY PASS: Admits up to two adults and two children to general admission areas (Wild Reef and Oceanarium exhibits still cost extra.) Kids must be accompanied by an adult.

The Shedd Aquarium boasts the world's most diverse aquatic animal collection, with more than 19,000 local and international representatives of fish, amphibian, reptile, bird, mammal, and invertebrate species. There's still a lot to see without paying extra for the Oceanarium or Wild Reef, including the big tank of sharks, turtles, eels, and other fish, where an aquarium employee narrates aquatic facts through a diving-mask microphone as he or she swims among and feeds the animals.

North Park Village Nature Center

5801 North Pulaski Road (Peterson Park entrance between West Thorndale Avenue and West Victoria Street)
(312) 744–5472 / TTY/TTD: (312) 744–3586
www.chicagoparkdistrict.com
Hours: 10:00 a.m. to 4:00 p.m. every day except Thanksgiving, December 24, 25, and 31, and January 1.

All sorts of wildlife are crawling around Chicago. North Park Village Nature Center will help you find it. The center is an educational facility that's part of a forty-six-acre nature preserve. Walk trails through prairie, savannah, woodlands, and wetlands and learn about the animals and plants that reside in each type of environment. North Park's educational center houses bones, pelts, shells, and other natural objects kids can touch, along with tanks and cages of small animals in mini habitats. The center hosts nature walks, maple tree tappings, classes, camps, and other events for children and adults. Many, but not all, are free.

Notebaert Nature Museum

2430 North Cannon Drive (at Fullerton Parkway in Lincoln Park)
(773) 755–5100
www.naturemuseum.org
Hours: Open every day except New Year's Day, Thanksgiving, and Christmas Day, Monday through Friday, 9:00 a.m. to 4:30 p.m.; Saturday and Sunday, 10:00 a.m. to 5:00 p.m.
When free: Always free for children younger than three. Thursdays, children free, suggested donation of $7 per adult.
LIBRARY PASS: Get a pass for free admission for up to four immediate family members by checking out a Museum Pass from the Chicago Public Library (see page 263 for details).

The Notebaert Nature Museum is a year-round haven for some 1,000 butter-flies from 75 species, give or take a few. They flutter among tropical trees, pools of water, and flowers in a 2,700-square-foot greenhouse. Live crit-ters along the museum's Wilderness Walk include reptiles, amphibians, small mammals, and an ant farm. And check out a full-size "extreme green" house in the middle of the museum.

AFTER **SCHOOL** MATTERS **SITES**

(See page 109 for program descriptions)

ACT Charter High School, 4319 West Washington Boulevard, (773) 626–4200

Al Raby School for Community and Environment, 3545 West Fulton Boulevard, (773) 534–6755

Austin Campus

Austin Community Academy High School, 231 North Pine Avenue; (773) 534–6300

Austin Branch Library, 5615 West Race Avenue; (312) 746–5038 or (312) 746–5039

Austin Town Hall, 5610 West Lake Street; (312) 746–5006

Bogan High School, 3939 West 79th Street, (773) 535–2180

Bowen Campus

Bessemer Park, 8930 South Muskegon Avenue; (312) 747–7665

Bowen High School, 2710 East 89th Street; (773) 535–6000

South Chicago Branch Library, 9055 South Houston Avenue; (312) 747–8065, (312) 747–0300

Carver Campus

Altgeld Branch Library, 950 East 132nd Place; (312) 747–5952

Carver Military Academy High School, 13100 South Doty West Avenue; (773) 535–5250

Carver Park, 939 East 132nd Street; (312) 747–6047

Chicago Academy Campus

Chicago Math & Science Academy, 1705 West Lunt Avenue; (773) 761–8960

Clark Campus
Clark High School, 5101 West Harrison Street; (773) 534–6250
Clark Park, 4615 West Jackson Boulevard; (312) 746–5043
Austin Branch Library, 5615 West Race Avenue; (312) 746–5038 or (312) 746–5039

Clemente Campus
Clemente High School, 1147 North Western Avenue; (773) 534–4000
Clemente Park, 2334 West Division Street; (312) 742–7538
Humboldt Park Branch Library, 1605 North Troy Street; (312) 744–2244 or (312) 744–3012

Collins Campus
Collins High School, 1313 South Sacramento Drive; (773) 534–1500
Douglas Park, 1401 South Sacramento Drive; (312) 747–2842
Douglass Branch Library, 3353 West 13th Street; (312) 747–3725 or (312) 747–3261

Crane Campus
Crane Tech Prep Common School, 2245 West Jackson Boulevard; (773) 534–7550
Touhy-Herbert Park, 2106 West Adams Street; (312) 746–5562
Legler Branch Library, 115 South Pulaski Road; (312) 746–7730 or (312) 746–7731

Curie Campus
Curie Metro High School, 4959 South Archer Avenue; (773) 535–2100
Curie Park, 4949 South Archer Avenue; (312) 747–6098
Archer Heights Branch Library, 5055 South Archer Avenue; (312) 747–9241

Dunbar Campus
Dunbar Vocational Career Academy High School, 3000 South King Drive; (773) 534–9000
Lake Meadows Park, 3117 South Rhodes Avenue; (312) 747–6287

Englewood Campus

Englewood Academy High School, 6201 South Stewart Avenue; (773) 535-3600

Sherwood Park, 5705 South Shields Avenue; (312) 747-6688

Kelly Branch Library, 6151 South Normal Avenue; (312) 747-8418 or (312) 747-8504

Farragut Campus

Farragut Career Academy, 2346 South Christiana Avenue; (773) 534-1300

Shedd Park, 36630 West 23rd Street; (312) 747-7685

Fenger Campus

Fenger Academy High School, 11220 South Wallace Street; (773) 535-5430

Ada Park, 11250 South Ada Street; (312) 747-6002

Pullman Branch Library, 11001 South Indiana Avenue; (312) 747-2003

Foreman Campus

Foreman High School, 3235 North LeClaire Avenue; (773) 534-3400 or (773) 534-3403

Kosciuszko Park, 2732 North Avers Avenue; (312) 742-7546

Portage-Cragin Branch Library, 5108 West Belmont Avenue; (312) 744-0152 or (312) 744-2251

Gage Campus

Gage Park High School, 2411 South Rockwell Street; (773) 535-9230

Gage Park, 2411 West 55th Street; (312) 747-6147

Gage Park Branch Library, 2807 West 55th Street; (312) 747-0032

Harlan Campus

Harlan Community Academy, 9652 South Michigan Avenue; (773) 535-5400

Abbott Park, 49 East 95th Street; (312) 747-6001

Woodson Regional Library, 9525 South Halsted Street; (312) 747-6900

Hancock High School, 4034 West 56th Street, (773) 535-2410

Harper High School, 6520 South Wood Street, (773) 535-9150

Hubbard High School, 6200 South Hamlin Avenue, (773) 535–2200
Hyde Park Academy, 6220 South Stony Island Avenue, (773) 535–0633

Juarez Campus
Juarez Community Academy, 2150 South Laflin Street; (773) 534–7030
Harrison Park, 1824 South Wood Street; (312) 746–5491
Lozano Branch Library, 1805 South Loomis Street; (312) 746–4329
Julian High School, 10330 South Elizabeth Street, (773) 535–5170

Kelly Campus
Kelly High School, 4136 South California Avenue; (773) 535–4900 or (773) 535–4901
Kelly Park, 2725 West 41st Street; (312) 747–6197 or (312) 747–6196
Brighton Park Library, 4314 South Archer Avenue; (312) 747–0666 or (312) 747–1554

Kelvyn Park Campus
Kelvyn Park High School, 4343 West Wrightwood Avenue; (773) 534–4200
Kelvyn Park, 4438 West Wrightwood Avenue; (312) 742–7547
North Pulaski Branch Library, 4300 West North Avenue; (312) 744–9573 or (312) 744–6281

Lindblom Campus
Lindblom College Preparatory High School, 6130 South Wolcott Avenue; (773) 535–9300
Lindblom Park, 6054 South Damen Avenue; (312) 747–6443
Sherman Park Branch Library, 5440 South Racine Avenue; (312) 747–0477 or (312) 747–1611
Little Village Lawndale High School, 3120 South Kostner Avenue, (773) 535–4200

Manley Campus
Manley Career Academy, 2935 West Polk Street; (773) 534–6900
Douglas Park, 1401 South Sacramento Drive; (312) 762–2842
Douglass Branch Library, 3353 West 13th Street; (312) 747–3725 or (312) 747–3261

Marshall Metropolitan High School, 3520 West Adams Street, (773) 534–6455

Noble Street Charter High School, 1010 North Noble Street, (773) 862–1449

North Grand High School, 4338 West Wabansia Avenue, (773) 534–8520

Orr Campus

Orr Community Academy High School, 730 North Pulaski Road; (773) 534–6500

Orr Park, 744 North Pulaski Road; (312) 746–5354

Legler Branch Library, 115 South Pulaski Road; (312) 746–7730 or (312) 746–7731

Perspectives Charter School at Calumet Academy High School, 8131 South May Street; (773) 358–6100

Phillips Campus

Phillips Academy, 244 East Pershing Road; (773) 535–1603

Anderson Park, 3748 South Prairie Avenue; (312) 747–6007

Chicago Bee Branch Library, 3647 South State Street; (312) 747–6872

Phoenix Military Academy High School, 145 South Campbell Avenue; (773) 534–7275

Prosser Campus

Prosser Career Academy High School, 2148 North Long Avenue; (773) 534–3200

Blackhawk Park, 2318 North Lavergne Avenue; (312) 746–5014

North Austin Library, 5724 West North Avenue; (312) 746–4233

Ramirez Computer Science Charter High School, 2435 North Western Avenue, (773) 252–6662

Robeson Campus

Robeson High School, 6835 South Normal Avenue; (773) 535–3800

Hamilton Park, 513 West 72nd Street; (312) 747–6174 or (312) 747–1529

Kelly Branch Library, 6151 South Normal Avenue; (312) 747–8418 or (312) 747–8504

Roosevelt Campus

Roosevelt High School, 3436 West Wilson Avenue; (773) 534–5000

Horner Park, 2741 West Montrose Avenue; (312) 478–3499

Mayfair Branch Library, 4400 West Lawrence Avenue; (312) 744–1254 or (312) 744–1265

Schurz Campus

Schurz High School, 3601 North Milwaukee Avenue; (773) 534–3420

Kilbourn Park, 3501 North Kilbourn Park; (312) 742–7624

Portage-Cragin Branch Library, 5108 West Belmont Avenue; (312) 744–0152 or (312) 744–2251

Senn Campus

Senn High School, 5900 North Glenwood Avenue; (773) 534–2365

Rickover Naval Academy, 5900 North Glenwood Avenue, (773) 534–2890

Broadway Armory, 5917 North Broadway Avenue; (312) 742–7502

Edgewater Branch Library, 1210 West Elmdale Avenue; (312) 744–0178 or (312) 744–9884

Simeon Campus

Simeon Career Academy, 8147 South Vincennes Avenue; (773) 535–3200

West Chatham Park, 8233 South Princeton Avenue; (312) 747–6998

South Shore Campus

South Shore Community Academy, 7529 South Constance Avenue; (773) 535–6180

Nash Community Center, 1883 East 71st Street; (312) 747–1883

South Shore Branch Library, 2502 East 73rd Street; (312) 747–5281 or (312) 747–5649

Steinmetz Academic Centre High School, 3030 North Mobile Avenue; (773) 534–3030

Sullivan Campus

Sullivan High School, 6631 North Bosworth Avenue; (773) 534–2000

Loyola Park, 1230 West Greenleaf Avenue; (312) 742–7857

Rogers Park Branch Library, 6907 North Clark Street; (312) 744–0156 or (312) 744–0353

Taft Campus
Taft High School, 6545 West Hurlbut Street; (773) 534–1000
Norwood Park, 5801 North Natoma Avenue; (312) 742–7847
Roden Branch Library, 6083 Northwest Highway; (312) 744–1478 or (312) 744–1154

Tilden Campus
Tilden Career Community Academy High School, 4747 South Union Avenue; (773) 535–1625
Fuller Park, 331 West 45th Street; (312) 747–6144
Sherman Park Branch Library, 5440 South Racine Avenue; (312) 747–0477 or (312) 747–1611
Uplift Community Performance High School, 900 West Wilson Avenue; (773) 534–2875
Vaughn Occupational High School, 4355 North Linder Avenue; (773) 534–3600
George Washington High School, 3535 East 114th Street; (773) 535–5725
Wells Community Academy High School, 936 North Ashland Avenue; (773) 534–7010
Youth Connections High School, 10 West 35th Street; (773) 921–1315

BOYS AND GIRLS CLUBS OF CHICAGO

(See page 109 for program description)

Freestanding Clubs

Daniel A. Cotter Club, 2915 North Leavitt Street; (773) 348–1866

James R. Jordan Club, 2102 West Monroe Street; Club: (312) 226–2323, Child Care: (312) 432–4294

Dr. Martin Luther King Jr. Club and Child Care, 2950 West Washington Boulevard; Club: (773) 638–5464, Child Care: (773) 638–4678

Little Village Club, 2801 South Ridgeway Avenue; Club: (773) 277–1800, Child Care: (773) 762–6100

Logan Square Club, 3228 West Palmer Street; Club: (773) 342–8800, Child Care: (773) 252–4161

Robert R. McCormick Club, 4835 North Sheridan Road; Club: (773) 271–8400, Child Care: (773) 989–0222

Louis L. Valentine Club and Child Care, 3400 South Emerald Avenue; Club: (773) 927–7373, Child Care: (773) 376–2222

General Robert E. Wood Club and Child Care, 2950 West 25th Street; Club: (773) 247–0700, Child Care: (773) 847–5172

School-hosted Clubs (only for students of hosting schools)

Beethoven Club at Beethoven School, 25 West 47th Street; (773) 268–5999

Cather Club at Cather School, 2908 West Washington Boulevard; (773) 533–0416

Chicago Heights Club at Washington Junior High School, 25 West 16th Place, Chicago Heights; (708) 756–1727

Dett Club at Dett School, 2306 West Maypole Avenue; (312) 226–2323

Englewood Club at Englewood Tech Prep Academy, 6201 South Stewart Avenue; (773) 535–0010

Ford Heights Club at Tidye A. Phillips Grammar School, 1401 East 13th Place, Ford Heights; (708) 758–1960

Green Elementary Club at Wendell E. Green Elementary School, 1150 West 96th Street, (312) 235–8000, ext. 5101

Holy Angels Club at Holy Angels School, 750 East 40th Street; (773) 268–4819

Logandale Club at Logandale Middle School, 3212 West George Street; (773) 342–8800

McCutcheon Club at McCutcheon Elementary School, 4865 North Sheridan Road; (773) 271–8400

Paderewski Club at Ingance Paderewski Elementary Learning Academy, 2221 South Lawndale Avenue; (312) 235–8000, ext. 5104

Park Manor Club at Park Manor Elementary School, 7037 South Rhodes Avenue, (773) 235–8000, ext. 5100

Reed Club at Reed School, 6350 South Stewart Avenue; (773) 535–0010

Schiller Club at Frederick Von Schiller Elementary School, 640 West Scott Street; (312) 235–8000, ext. 5102

Schneider Club at Schneider School, 2957 North Hoyne Avenue; (773) 348–1866

Stockton Club at Stockton School, 4420 North Beacon Street; (773) 271–3530

Tilton Club at George W. Tilton Elementary School, 223 North Keeler Avenue; (773) 533–1688

Vernon Johns Club at Vernon Johns Academy, 6936 South Hermitage Avenue; (773) 535–9144

Wilson Club at Wilson School, 422 West 16th Place, Chicago Heights; (708) 747–7150

APPENDIX B:

CLINICS **AND** HEALTH **CENTERS**

The City of Chicago Public Health Department and Cook County
Bureau of Health Services have sliding-scale and free clinics dispersed throughout the city and nearby suburbs. Bring a photo ID when you visit a city or
county health facility. City of Chicago clinics charge on sliding scales based
on your ability to pay. Appointments are available, but unless you're really
hurting, you'll have to schedule six to nine months ahead. Most people drop
by their local clinic and wait two to three hours. Bring a good book. Cook
County clinics require appointments and provide care only to children and
adults whose income is low enough. To find the Cook County clinic nearest you,
call their Primary Care Directory Line at (312) 864–6420. It's a cosmopolitan
computer that speaks English, Spanish, and Polish. Be ready to provide your
zip code and to write down the address.

NORTH SIDE
Lakeview Specialty Clinic, 2861 North Clark Street (at West Surf Street and
North Orchard Street): HIV/STD prevention, testing, and counseling, and
primary care for people with HIV; (312) 744–5507. (Chicago Department of
Public Health)

Northtown-Rogers Park Mental Health Center, 1607 West Howard Street
(between North Marshfield Avenue and North Ashland Avenue); (312) 744–
7617. (Chicago Department of Public Health)

Uptown Health Center, 845 West Wilson Avenue (between North Claren-
don Avenue and North Hazel Street); comprehensive clinic for children and
adults: (312) 744–1938; Uptown (HIV) Early Intervention Services Clinic,
HIV prevention, testing, and counseling, and primary care for people with
HIV; (312) 744–1935. (Chicago Department of Public Health Clinic)

NORTHWEST SIDE
Logan Square Health Center of Cook County, 2840 West Fullerton Avenue
(at North Mozart Street); (773) 395–7400. Primary and preventative care,
specialty outpatient, and diagnostic services for children and adults. (Cook
County Bureau of Health Services)

North River Mental Health Center, 5801 North Pulaski Road (at Peterson Park entrance between West Peterson Avenue and West Bryn Mawr Avenue); (312) 744–1906. (Chicago Department of Public Health)

Northwest Mental Health Center, 2354 North Milwaukee Avenue (at West Medill Avenue south of Fullerton Avenue); (312) 744–0993. (Chicago Department of Public Health)

SOUTH SIDE

Greater Grand / Mid-South Mental Health Center, 4314 South Cottage Grove Avenue (at East 43rd Street); (312) 747–0036. (Chicago Department of Public Health)

John H. Sengstacke Health Center of Cook County, 450 East 51st Street (east of South Dr. Martin Luther King Jr. Drive across from northwest corner of Washington Park); (312) 572–2900. Primary and preventative care and specialty outpatient and diagnostic services for children and adults. (Cook County Bureau of Health Services)

Near South Health Center of Cook County, 3525 South Michigan Avenue (at East 35th Street); (312) 945–4010. Primary and preventative care and specialty outpatient and diagnostic services for children and adults. (Cook County Bureau of Health Services)

Roseland Mental Health Center, 28 East 112th Place (between South State Street and South Michigan Avenue); (312) 747–7320. (Chicago Department of Public Health)

Roseland Neighborhood Health Center, 200 East 115th Street (at South Indiana Avenue); (312) 747–9500. Comprehensive clinic for children and adults. (Chicago Department of Public Health)

Roseland Specialty Clinic, 200 East 115th Street (at South Indiana Avenue); (312) 747–2817. HIV/STD prevention, testing, and counseling. (Chicago Department of Public Health)

South Chicago Clinic, 2938 East 89th Street (at South Exchange Avenue); (312) 747–5285. Provides women's, maternal, and children's health care. (Chicago Department of Public Health)

Woodlawn Health Center of Cook County, 6337 South Woodlawn Avenue (at East 64th Street); (773) 753–5500. Primary and preventative care and specialty outpatient and diagnostic services to children and adults. (Cook County Bureau of Health Services)

Woodlawn Mental Health Center, 6337 South Woodlawn Avenue (at East 64th Street); (312) 747–0059. (Chicago Department of Public Health)

FAR SOUTH SIDE

Auburn-Gresham Mental Health Center, 1140 West 79th Street (at South May Street east of South Racine Avenue); (312) 747-0881. (Chicago Department of Public Health)

Beverly-Morgan Park Mental Health Center, 1987 West 111th Street (at South Hale Avenue); (312) 747-1100. (Chicago Department of Public Health)

SOUTHWEST SIDE

Back of the Yards Mental Health Center, 4313 South Ashland Avenue (at West 43rd Street); (312) 747-3560. (Chicago Department of Public Health)

Cook County/Englewood Health Center, 1135 West 69th Street (at South May Street); (773) 483-5011. Primary and preventative care and specialty outpatient and diagnostic services for children and adults. (Cook County Bureau of Health Services)

Englewood Early Intervention (HIV) Services Clinic, 641 West 63rd Street (at South Lowe Avenue); (312) 747-0667.

Englewood Mental Health Center, 641 West 63rd Street (at South Lowe Avenue); (312) 747-7496. (Chicago Department of Public Health)

Englewood Neighborhood Health Center, 641 West 63rd Street (at South Lowe Avenue); (312) 747-7831. Comprehensive clinic for children and adults.

Englewood STI Specialty Clinic, 641 West 63rd Street (at South Lowe Avenue); (312) 747-8900. HIV/STD prevention, testing, and counseling, and primary care for people with HIV.

Greater Lawn Mental Health Center, 4150 West 55th Street (at South Kedvale Avenue); (312) 747-1020. (Chicago Department of Public Health)

WEST SIDE

Austin Health Center of Cook County, 4800 West Chicago Avenue (at North Cicero Avenue); (773) 826-9600. Primary and preventative care and specialty outpatient and diagnostic services to low-income adults and their children. (Cook County Ambulatory & Community Health Network)

Dr. Jorge Prieto Health Center of Cook County, 2424 South Pulaski Road (at West 24th Place); (773) 521-0750. Primary and preventative care and specialty outpatient and diagnostic services for children and adults. (Cook County Bureau of Health Services)

Fantus Health Center of Cook County, 621 South Winchester Avenue (at West Harrison Street); (312) 864-6221. Primary and preventative care and specialty outpatient and diagnostic services for children and adults. (Cook County Bureau of Health Services)

Lawndale Mental Health Center, 1201 South Campbell Avenue (at West Roosevelt Road); (312) 746-5905. (Chicago Department of Public Health)

Lower West Side Neighborhood Health Center, 1713 South Ashland Avenue (at West 17th Street); (312) 746-5157. Comprehensive clinic for children and adults. (Chicago Department of Public Health)

South Austin Specialty Clinic, 4958 West Madison Street (at South Lavergne Avenue); (312) 746-4871. HIV/STD prevention, testing, and counseling. (Chicago Department of Public Health)

South Lawndale Clinic, 3059 West 26th Street (between South Whipple Street and South Albany Avenue); (312) 747-0066. Provides women's, maternal, and children's health care. (Chicago Department of Public Health)

Specialty Care Center of Cook County, 1901 West Harrison Street (at Stroger Hospital between West Damen Avenue and South Wood Street); (312) 864-7589. Houses specialty clinics for such issues as eye care, pain management, and hypertension.

West Town Neighborhood Health Center, 2418 West Division Street (between North Western Avenue and North Artesian Avenue); Comprehensive clinic for children and adults: (312) 744-0943. West Town Adolescent Specialty Clinic: HIV/STD prevention, testing, and counseling services for youth; (312) 742-4092. (Chicago Department of Public Health)

Westside Health Center of Cook County, 3410 West Van Buren Street (at South Homan Avenue), fifth floor; (773) 265-2800. Primary and preventative care and specialty outpatient and diagnostic services for children and adults. (Cook County Bureau of Health Services)

Cook County Bureau of Health Suburban Health Clinics

Cicero Health Center of Cook County, 5912 West Cermak Road (between South 59th Court and South 59th Avenue), Cicero; (708) 783-9800

Cottage Grove Health Center of Cook County, 1645 Cottage Grove (between 17th Street and East Lincoln Highway), Ford Heights; (708) 753-5800

Oak Forest Specialty Health Center of Cook County, 15900 South Cicero Avenue (at 159th Street), Oak Forest; (708) 633-2555

Robbins Health Center of Cook County, 13450 South Kedzie Avenue (north of West 135th Street), Robbins; (708) 293-8100

Vista Health Center of Cook County, 1585 North Rand Road (south of East Dundee Road), Palatine; (847) 934-7969

CHICAGO **PUBLIC** LIBRARY **REGIONAL** AND **NEIGHBORHOOD** BRANCH **LIBRARIES**

REGIONAL LIBRARIES

Sulzer, 4455 North Lincoln Avenue; (312) 744–7616
Woodson, 9525 South Halsted Street; (312) 747–6900

North District Branches

Albany Park, 5150 North Kimball Avenue; (312) 744–1933
Austin-Irving, 6100 West Irving Park Road; (312) 744–6222
Bezazian, 1226 West Ainslie Street; (312) 744–0019
Bucktown/Wicker Park, 1701 North Milwaukee Avenue; (312) 744–6022
Budlong Woods, 5630 North Lincoln Avenue; (312) 742–9590
Edgebrook, 5331 West Devon Avenue; (312) 744–8313
Edgewater, 1210 West Elmdale Avenue; (312) 744–0718
Galewood-Montclare, 6969 West Grand Avenue; (312) 746–5032
Humboldt Park, 1605 North Troy Street; (312) 744–2244
Independence, 3548 West Irving Park Road; (312) 744–0900
Jefferson Park, 5363 West Lawrence Avenue; (312) 744–1998
John Merlo, 644 West Belmont Avenue; (312) 744–1139
Lincoln Belmont, 1659 West Melrose Street; (312) 744–0166
Lincoln Park, 1150 West Fullerton Avenue; (312) 744–1926
Logan Square, 3030 West Fullerton Avenue; (312) 744–5295
Mayfair, 4400 West Lawrence Avenue; (312) 744–1254
North Austin, 5724 West North Avenue; (312) 746–4233
North Pulaski, 4300 West North Avenue; (312) 744–9573
Northtown, 6435 North California Avenue; (312) 744–2292
Oriole Park, 7454 West Balmoral Avenue; (312) 744–1965
Portage-Cragin, 5108 West Belmont Avenue; (312) 744–0152
Roden, 6083 Northwest Highway; (312) 744–1478
Rogers Park, 6907 North Clark Street; (312) 744–0156
Uptown, 929 West Buena Avenue; (312) 744–8400
West Addison, 7536 West Addison Street; (312) 746–4704
West Belmont, 3104 North Narragansett Avenue; (312) 746–5142

Central District Branches

Archer Heights, 5055 South Archer Avenue; (312) 747–9241
Austin, 5615 West Race Avenue; (312) 746–5038
Back of the Yards, 4650 South Damen Avenue; (312) 747–8367
Blackstone, 4904 South Lake Park Avenue; (312) 747–0511
Brighton Park, 4314 South Archer Avenue; (312) 747–0666
Canaryville, 642 West 43rd Street; (312) 747–0644
Chicago Bee, 3647 South State Street; (312) 747–6872
Chinatown, 2353 South Wentworth Avenue; (312) 747–8013
Douglass, 3353 West 13th Street; (312) 747–3725
Eckhart Park, 1330 West Chicago Avenue; (312) 746–6069
Gage Park, 2807 West 55th Street; (312) 747–0032
Garfield Ridge, 6348 South Archer Avenue; (312) 747–6094
Hall, 4801 South Michigan Avenue; (312) 747–2541
King, 3436 South King Drive; (312) 747–7543
Legler, 115 South Pulaski Road; (312) 746–7730
Mabel Manning, 6 South Hoyne Avenue; (312) 746–6800
Marshall Square, 2724 West Cermak Road; (312) 747–0061
McKinley Park, 1915 West 35th Street; (312) 747–6082
Midwest, 2335 West Chicago Avenue; (312) 744–7788
Near North, 310 West Division Street; (312) 744–0991
Richard J. Daley, 3400 South Halsted Street; (312) 747–8990
Roosevelt, 1101 West Taylor Street; (312) 746–5656
Rudy Lozano, 1805 South Loomis Street; (312) 746–4329
Sherman Park, 5440 South Racine Avenue; (312) 747–0477
Toman, 2708 South Pulaski Road; (312) 745–1660
West Chicago Avenue, 4856 West Chicago Avenue; (312) 743–0260

South District Branches

Altgeld, 950 East 132nd Place; (312) 747–5952
Avalon, 8148 South Stony Island Avenue; (312) 747–5234
Bessie Coleman, 731 East 63rd Street; (312) 747–7760
Beverly, 2121 West 95th Street; (312) 747–9673
Brainerd, 1350 West 89th Street; (312) 747–6291
Chicago Lawn, 6120 South Kedzie Avenue; (312) 747–0639
Clearing, 6423 West 63rd Place; (312) 747–5657
Hegewisch, 3048 East 130th Street; (312) 747–0046

Jeffery Manor, 2401 East 100th Street; (312) 747–6479

Kelly, 6151 South Normal Boulevard; (312) 747–8418

Mount Greenwood, 11010 South Kedzie Avenue; (312) 747–2805

Pullman, 11001 South Indiana Avenue; (312) 747–2033

Scottsdale, 4101 West 79th Street; (312) 747–0193

South Chicago, 9055 South Houston Avenue; (312) 747–8065

South Shore, 2505 East 73rd Street; (312) 747–5281

Thurgood Marshall, 7506 South Racine Avenue; (312) 747–5927

Tuley Park, 501 East 90th Place; (312) 747–7608

Vodak / East Side, 3710 East 106th Street; (312) 747–5500

Walker, 11071 South Hoyne Avenue; (312) 747–1920

West Englewood, 1745 West 63rd Street; (312) 747–3481

West Lawn, 4020 West 63rd Street; (312) 747–7381

West Pullman, 830 West 119th Street; (312) 747–1425

Whitney M. Young, Jr., 7901 South King Drive; (312) 747–0039

Wrightwood-Ashburn, 8530 South Kedzie Avenue; (312) 747–2696

INDEX

ABOUT THE AUTHOR

Born in Chicago but raised in a Central Illinois hamlet, Nadia Oehlsen returned to the big city as a young writer eager to make a name for herself. As a freelancer, she soon developed the essential career skills of touring museums on their free-admission days, finding no-cover concerts at local music venues, ushering to see plays for free, finding free cheese samples, and living in stylish comfort by acquiring other people's trash. She even got around to writing sometimes. As a journalist for general interest and trade publications,  Nadia has churned out a lot of how-to articles over the years, including how to process chemicals, how to fix bicycles, how to remove body parts from crime scenes, and the various methods one may employ to pay for goods and services. She prefers explaining how not to pay. Nadia lives and works in Chicago and da 'burbs.